WITHDRAWN

Making Globalization

Making Globalization

Robert J. Holton

First published 2005 by
PALGRAVE MACMILLAN
Houndmills, Basingstoke, Hampshire RG21 6XS and
175 Fifth Avenue, New York, N.Y. 10010
Companies and representatives throughout the world

PALGRAVE MACMILLAN is the global academic imprint of the Palgrave Macmillan division of St. Martin's Press, LLC and of Palgrave Macmillan Ltd. Macmillan® is a registered trademark in the United States, United Kingdom and other countries. Palgrave is a registered trademark in the European Union and other countries.

ISBN-13: 978–1–4039–4867–0 hardback
ISBN-10: 1–4039–4867–4 hardback
ISBN-13: 978–1–4039–4868–7 paperback
ISBN-10: 1–4039–4868–2 paperback

This book is printed on paper suitable for recycling and made from fully managed and sustained forest sources.

A catalogue record for this book is available from the British Library.

A catalog record for this book is available from the Library of Congress.

Library of Congress Catalog Card Number: 2005048849

10   9   8   7   6   5   4   3
14   13   12   11   10   09   08   07   06

Printed in China

Contents

List of Figures

Preface

This book is a study of globalization written by an author working in Ireland who holds dual British and Australian nationality, having migrated between these three countries in pursuit of academic employment. This represents only one of a range of global trajectories that individuals and families make in the contemporary world, one located within wealthier and more powerful settings. There are many far riskier and often tragic global trajectories for those who seek asylum, or for whom mobility in the search for employment and security is a day-to-day struggle for survival in the face of exploitation and danger. In writing any book on globalization, it is important to be aware of this, and the obligation placed on any social analyst not simply to seek truths about global processes, but also to identify and comment upon the way inequalities within the global arena are understood and acted upon. At the same time it is equally important to register the diversity of aspirations that are evident amongst human actors, and the ways in which these connect with global inequalities and global opportunities.

This book has been written very much from a sense of dissatisfaction with the debates around globalization. These are typically polarized between supporters and opponents, often fatalistic in their sense of an inevitable global fate – whether for better or worse – and quick to resort to highly moralized judgements when a healthy dose of scepticism is called for. I hope this book will be helpful for engaged partisans for and against globalization, but it has been written primarily for those who remain puzzled, sceptical, and equivocal about the issues at stake, and for those keen to understand more about the origins, dynamics, scope, and limits of globalization.

In an enterprise of this kind, many acknowledgements are due to those who have influenced my views and approaches. I am particularly grateful to John Braithwaite and Roland Robertson for their different but distinctive perspectives on the study of globalization, but have also learnt much from a range of other scholars including Kevin O'Rourke, Rosemary Byrne, Sandra Holton, Leslie Sklair, Saskia Sassen, Constance Lever-Tracy, Noel Tracy, Zlatko Skrbis, and Tanya Lyons.

My postgraduate students, especially Aisling McCormack, Martha van der Blij, and Christian Gheorghiu, also assisted greatly in responding to many arguments in the process of formulation with a healthy scepticism, and sometimes incredulity. This helped me back to earth on a number of occasions.

I am also grateful to those who contributed to seminars in which a number of ideas in this study were first formulated, often in quite confused form. I am especially grateful to seminar audiences at the University of Aberdeen; University College, Cork; and Trinity College, Dublin.

Funding for research into the theme of globalization and the nation-state was generously provided by the Institute for International Integration Studies at Trinity College, Dublin. I am also grateful for financial support from the Irish Research Council for the Humanities and the Social Sciences (IRCHSS) that permitted me to include material from an IRCHSS-funded project on The Historical Sociology of Global Networks within this study.

Begun on Castle Cary railway station in England, this book was written in three countries and two hemispheres, and the toing and froing involved was very far from the supposedly quiet and dreamy spires of academe. In all of this I owe a particular debt of thanks to Sandra Holton, both for her intellectual input and for her support and stoicism in the face of many mobilities and disruptions.

1

Introduction

I think globalization is the taking over of society by a few key people in big companies.

It [globalization] can be good and it can be bad . . . it can be good because it can work for people . . . because we all care about things like international solidarity . . . that couldn't happen without globalization.

It's a way of using and abusing a lot of the people who don't have a lot of power in their hands, and a lot of the third world, and a lot of the people who are more humble. I think its very organised, that's why I'm here, because I feel its time that we got organised also to combat it.

I just think it means that the world's shrinking in terms of communication. . . . And really, you know good technology.

I've got nothing against it [globalization], I think it's probably inevitable. . . . But what globalization isn't and shouldn't be is uncontrolled and unregulated.

– Lyons 2001

These five statements by Australians demonstrating outside the World Economic Forum Conference in Melbourne in September 2000 (Lyons 2001) indicate a range of views amongst activists as to the meaning of globalization. These views come from individuals and groups expressly mobilized over the meeting of an elite organization of corporate and government decision-makers. The processes to which they draw attention – economic and political, technological and cultural – remain matters of controversy, clamour, and debate. They lie at the heart of the myriad of aspirations felt and decisions made by individuals, households, communities, and governments. These affect employment and consumption, whether to move or stay put, how to achieve security with freedom and justice, whether to go to war or to resist.

Globalization for many signifies a major root cause of inequality, human misery, and injustice, while for others it is seen as a way of addressing these social ills. The polarization of much debate is important, but it should not drown out those who see globalization as good and bad, those who remain baffled as to what exactly it means, and finally

1

those who are sceptical as to whether it exists at all, except in the minds of social observers. Whether we are dealing with a fateful force for better or worse, or an unnecessary and misleading piece of academic or marketing jargon, requires serious investigation. This book is one contribution to this end. It is, however, a book written from a particular perspective.

The title *Making Globalization* carries with it two equally significant meanings. The first centres on the idea that the social changes that have come to be called globalization are actively made by human actors, rather than fateful forces that are out of control. This is not to say that globalization is simply a wonderful world of opportunity, since inequalities of power are endemic. The picture is rather one both of opportunity and of constraint, and this book attempts to emphasize both aspects in a manner that is neither excessively optimistic nor unduly pessimistic. The perspective from which it is written is one of critical scepticism towards both would-be globalizers and their critics.

This book is above all a critique of fatalism. It rejects the view that globalization happens, driven variously by markets or technology, leaving human actors to adjust as best they can. Rather globalization is seen both as an outcome of and as a context for human activity. We make ourselves, to paraphrase Marx, as much as we are made. Globalization, in its various manifestations, has been made, and by implication can be un-made or re-made. To say this is to identify with a long tradition of thought from Marx and Weber to E.P. Thompson and Pierre Bourdieu, which places human agency at the heart of social change. In this approach, people attempt to actively make and shape their destiny, engaging with evolving structures of power, knowledge, and cultural meaning. Notwithstanding imperfect knowledge of the situations in which they find themselves and the unintended consequences that actions often have, we may say the same of globalization, as E.P. Thompson (1963: 9–10) said of the English working class, namely that globalizing processes are embodied in relationships between people, whose experiences are registered in ideas, institutional forms, and traditions.

In this study, I chart very different kinds of human agency across the fields of culture, politics, and economic life and across time and space; activities within which people have engaged with and participated within the making of globalization, whether as active proponents, through rejection or reform.

The second meaning in the book's title has to do with the terms we use to analyse, make moral judgements, and act within the world. *Making Globalization*, in this second sense, refers to the making of concepts and ways of thinking about the world, many of which now centre on the idea of globalization. Concepts are made, un-made and re-made too. Is globalization a worthwhile way of understanding the world, or is the concept rapidly approaching its use-by date?

In this book, attention is given to both these senses of *Making Globalization*. Its subject matter is both contemporary and historical, since much about globalization that is claimed to be new has longer-term roots stretching back hundreds if not thousands of years. It is concerned with the people, networks, organizations and social processes that have been involved in the making of globalization, whether intentionally or unwittingly. In meeting this aim, many puzzles, problems and unexpected paradoxes emerge. These extend throughout economic, political and cultural life, implicating civil society and religion as much as markets, states, and technology.

Understanding globalization demands an approach that is both multi-disciplinary and multi-cultural: multi-disciplinary in the need to combining insights from a range of intellectual sources, and multi-cultural in the sense that human experience from all parts of the world must be drawn upon. It is only through such multi-disciplinary and multi-cultural perspectives that issues like the changing social organization of time and space, global inequalities and opportunities, or the complex articulation of the global with the national and local can be adequately explored.

In reviewing what others have said and felt about globalization, one is immediately struck by the significant moral and emotional discourses involved; as much if not more than any recourse to a well-researched and substantiated analysis. Globalization evokes a range of reactions from anger to pride, and from enthusiasm to fear. Both the word itself and the realities that it is taken to represent provoke strong opinions and powerful emotions. While many are incensed at global inequality, poverty and deprivation, others take pride in the unprecedented post-war expansion of economic growth, technological dynamism and very recent revolutions in communication. While some people feel global or believe in globalization, for others it is an anathema. These reactions apply across leading world languages, where, as Scholte (2000: 43) has noted, equivalent terms such as 'globalisierung' (German), 'globalización' (Spanish), and 'Quanqiuhua' (Chinese) engender similar effects and controversies.

Moral evaluations of globalization are then typically polarized. Those involved in global non-governmental organizations like Greenpeace International are heroes to some but undemocratic activists to others. Similarly corporate leaders and those who operate the International

Monetary Fund (IMF) and World Bank (WB) are seen as arrogant exploiters of the poor by many, while for others they are taken as engineers of economic advance, essential to a prosperous and stable world. The moral resonances of globalization therefore run the whole gamut from exploitation and sin to human emancipation and saintliness. Anger, pride, and polarized rhetoric are nonetheless shaky foundations upon which to base an understanding of global society. The danger is that moral rhetoric predominates over analysis. Polarization between those who see globalization as either automatically good or necessarily bad also tends, as Amartya Sen (2001: 1–2) points out, to create a kind of passivity of the moral imagination. 'The optimist finds resistance unnecessary while the pessimist finds it to be useless.... The opposite viewpoints unite in resignation (1).' An ethics sensitive to global inequalities and opportunities can be a major casualty.

Contemporary scholarship and globalization

The polarization in contemporary debates around globalization is also often reflected in profound disagreement among scholars. For Vandana Shivu, founder and director of the Research Centre for Science, Technology, and Ecology in New Delhi 'globalization is a project of domination by the North over the South, by corporations over citizens, by patriarchal structures over women, by humans over other species' (Smith 2003: 88–89). For Vernon Smith, joint Nobel Prize winner for Economics in 2002, 'Globalization, profit and exchange should be seen as good words, peaceful words' (ibid.).

Some maintain we are talking about a process designed to benefit the world's rich at the expense of the world's poor – a force that undermines the integrity of local community, erodes social welfare provisions and destroys the sovereignty of the nation-state. Global inequality is seen as unquestionably growing in multiple forms associated with class, gender, and ethnicity, while nation-states remain morally indifferent, multinational enterprises pursue self-interest in an unregulated manner, and global regulatory bodies are seen as captured by corporate interests. This view is sometimes combined with a strong element of fatalism, whereby globalization appears as a Juggernaut beyond human control. *Runaway World*, the title of a book by Anthony Giddens (1999), encapsulates this feeling. Where the purposive role of human agency is recognized, it is typically in the form of elite control and exploitation of global processes. This sense of elite domination and popular marginalization is a powerful and continuing theme within the angry street protests that occurred in Seattle in 1999, and subsequently in many other cities hosting conferences of global economic organizations.

For others, a more positive optimistic global future is emphasized. For many economic liberals, globalization is associated with the wealth-generating effects of free trade and the free movement of capital, the liberating effects of new information technology on human communication and exchange. Much global poverty, as seen in many parts of Africa, is claimed to be the result of local conflict, civil war and corruption, that is *too little* globalization rather than too much. Bring in the market and de-regulation, and an upward trajectory of growth and development will, it is claimed, emerge. Meanwhile many commentators on contemporary technological change emphasize the potential of the Internet both as a source of virtual community and as a means of improving the quality of democracy. For their part, cosmopolitan globalizers draw attention to the emergence of cosmopolitan virtue in global movements and networks that seek to create a more tolerant, just and peaceable world – a new global civil society with the potential to stand above social division and resolve conflict. Among optimists these three approaches may be held in common, though it is more usual to find adherence to one of the three strands and indifference or opposition to the other two.

In threading our way through existing approaches to globalization, it is helpful to think in terms of *three* broad waves of analysis, namely *hyper-globalism*, *scepticism*, and a third option, which might be called *post-scepticism* (for similar typologies see Hay and Marsh 2000, Held and McGrew 2003). This tripartite schema is intended as a preliminary way of understanding the general contours of scholarly debates, rather than a rigid template into which all writers may be neatly fitted. What is at stake in the debates between these three positions is not simply what globalization means, but whether, and in what senses, it is present at all. One way of summing up the set of questions involved is encapsulated in Jan Arte Scholte's question, 'What is global about globalization?' (Scholte 2000: 41ff.).

While it is conventional to begin studies of a particular subject with an initial definition, the considerable doubt about the meaning and very existence of globalization makes this procedure extremely difficult. There are, for example, many misgivings about whether the idea of globalization is any more than a modish piece of jargon. It lacks precision, has been applied to a seemingly endless variety of social phenomena, and invites highly rhetorical responses. Yet for all this scepticism, the word itself shows no sign of diminishing in its visibility and usage. We therefore begin with three waves of thinking about globalization before attempting a working definition.

Much of the initial debate around globalization (and a good deal of popular thinking too) took what may be termed a 'hyper-globalist' position. This was organized around a set of arguments dealing with trends in the world economy, in the institutional arrangements of the nation-state as well as global cultural patterns. Like many pioneering contributions to a new area of debate, much work in this genre was conjectural in method. It was presumed that globalization can be easily defined, has a singular logic that leads in a specific direction, and, for those interested in evaluation, can be seen as progressive or repressive, good or bad. The basis of evidence on which it drew was generally limited.

The major propositions associated with *first*-wave thinking are to do with cross-border processes of change, resulting forms of trans-national inter-dependency, and the consequences of these processes for human welfare, democratic politics and cultural identity. Cross-border economic relationships engendered by free trade, and the increased mobility of capital and labour were believed to be rendering national economies outmoded, and undermining the sovereignty of the nation-state whose lifespan was now threatened by imminent demise (Ohmae 1990, 1996, Reich 1992). This in turn generated arguments that the erosion of the welfare state was underway (Gill 1992, Hoogvelt 1997). Meanwhile global corporate power was creating globalized mass markets that brought low-cost goods to many but, for critics, threatened to undermine local culture and produce global cultural homogenization (Levitt 1983, Sklair 1991). A final plank of much first-wave thinking also stressed the relative historical novelty of globalization. This depended in large measure on hype surrounding new information technology, the Internet, and impending shifts to e-commerce.

Sharp differences of opinion are nonetheless evident among first-wave thinking. They centre, in the main, on distinctions between liberal and critical thought. While economic liberals typically see economic globalization as a positive contribution to economic growth and human welfare, critics see it as a cause of worsening global poverty, and hence as a threat rather than solution to the welfare of most of the world's populations unable to access the potential benefits of markets (compare WB 2003 with Hoogvelt 1997). While liberals see globalization under-writing successful social progress and a healthy democracy, critics see it as undermining democracy through challenges to the sovereignty of the nation-state, and the pursuit of labour market and social policy de-regulation (for further detail of this debate see Held and McGrew 2002 and Chapter 7).

It should also be noted that a number of influential scholars, also interested in cross-border inter-dependencies, chose to work without seeing any need to develop or make use of the concept of globalization. The most notable example is the work of Immanuel Wallerstein and world-system theorists (Chapter 3), who helped to stimulate, as well as work in parallel with, the critical wing of first-wave global thinkers.

The major difficulty with first-wave thinking is not that many of the arguments put forward lack empirical foundation. Cross-border inter-dependencies are clearly growing in significance evident in a diverse range of processes from free trade and capital mobility to the expanding number of global organizations and social movements, and through chain migration processes and diasporic social networks to the development of global consumer brands from McDonalds to Coca-Cola. There is then much evidence that appears consistent with the propositions listed above. The problem is rather that there is also much counter-evidence too, the significance of which is downplayed or ignored among those with a preference for simple unidimensional accounts of social change. Much of the difficulty here is posed by the contested role of the nation-state in a globalizing world. Are nations being rendered thoroughly outmoded by cross-border movements of power, resources, technology and identity? Types of counter-evidence include the robustness of the world of individual nation-states embracing areas such as inter-national diplomacy, or national systems of law and social regulation. Equally, nationalism and various forms of ethnic particularism appear as resurgent features of social life.

For many, nation-states remain the predominant institutions and points of cultural reference within and between which cross-border movements and inter-dependencies take place. Thinking in this vein may think of the world as both a single space of intensified interconnection, and equally as one inhabited by nation-states. Inter-nationalism based on national representation is after all how the UN and the bodies like the World Health Organization (WHO) are constituted, as are major world sporting events such as the Olympic Games or the World Cup organized. Ostensibly 'global' organizations turn out to have a strong national resonance.

These data re-bound on the coherence of globalization as a distinct trans-national social process. They suggest that inter-national phenomena have often been conflated with trans-national phenomena under the common hyperbolic heading of globalization. They also indicate that globalization is nowhere near as easily defined or understood as first-phase thinking assumes. This is not only because the trans-national and the inter-national require analytical separation, but also because of a growing sense that the two may sometimes be linked rather than being seen as two conflicting processes. The UN or the Olympic Games, somehow involve vague senses of cross-national feeling and the projection of a single global world order, even while being inhabited by nationally organized bodies, which is one reason why some nationalists oppose inter-national organization. The same ambivalence applies to those globally active corporations, labelled variously as multi-national or trans-national, which somehow combine a trans-national reach across border and multi-cultural workforces with a legal domicile in a particular country of origin.

Phenomena grouped under the heading of globalization are, then, often very complex and paradoxical. And it cannot be emphasized enough that this is not simply a matter for academic debate, but something that effects the activities and choices facing all individuals, families, communities, nations and peoples, together with public policy-makers, regulators, corporations, and social movements. If social groups and populations are to make intelligent and sustainable choices about their welfare and future then an alternative to the comforting simplicity of enthusiastic over-generalization is required.

Thinking about globalization has then moved on through two further waves. The *second* symbolized by Hirst and Thompson's study *Globalization in Question* (1996) and Rugman's book *The End of Globalization* (2001) is highly sceptical of first-wave thinking. Their claim is that evidence from the key domain of corporations does not support trans-nationalism as a feature of the world economy. Corporations, for example, typically remain embedded in the institutions and culture of the country of origins. Hirst and Thompson (1996) use evidence on the operation of multi-national companies to challenge ideas of an emerging trans-national global order. They argue that theories of hyper-globalization have mistakenly concluded that cross-border activity is intrinsically trans-national. Nations remain alive and well. Even if some functions are lost, others are gained (Mann 1993). National markets, and national policies in domains such as education, training and infrastructural planning remain of considerable importance, also throwing doubt on theories of the imminent decline of the nation-state (see also Weiss 1997).

Another important and related aspect of *second*-wave scepticism is that globalization does not mean the demise of the welfare state in a simplistic way. Rather many relatively open economies (e.g. in

Scandinavia) have higher levels of social spending than is the case in some more closed economies (Rodrik 1996, Therborn 1999b). This argument attacks one of the rhetorical certitudes of the anti-globalization camp. It may be linked with a further point that globalization has not created high levels of convergence in either welfare state systems (Esping-Anderson 1990) or patterns of economic activity, such as the importance of foreign trade within national economies (Berger and Dore 1996).

These arguments are also linked with a historical perspective critical of the assumption in much business literature that globalization is novel and unprecedented. Hirst and Thompson counter with evidence that levels of free trade and capital mobility were higher in the period leading up to the First World War than those achieved for most of the post-1945 period (see also O'Rourke and Williamson 1999).

Other themes in the second wave of debate include the economic effects of free trade on employment and inequality. Here some scepticism has been directed at over-generalized forms of optimism among free-trade globalizers. Research here indicates that free trade may have positive effects on employment and incomes in some contexts and for some groups, while in other contexts it may be less beneficial or unambiguously harmful (Rodrik 1996, 1999, Stiglitz 2002). Martin Khor, director of the Third World Network (2001) notes that many poor countries appear not to have gained at all from free trade, while also arguing that many of the reasons for this have to do either with rich-country protectionism or with the lack of 'infrastructural, human, and enterprise capacity' to develop new exports in the poorest nations (33–35). Other research throws doubt on the idea that economic globalization uniformly creates greater inequality between nations (O'Rourke 2002).

Further second-wave criticisms have been applied to ideas of global cultural homogenization. Both Barber (1996) and Huntington (1996), for example, have countered with theories of polarization. For the former, this pits McWorld (symbolizing the globalized consumerism of McDonalds, MacIntosh computers and Music Television [MTV]) with Jihad (symbolizing for Barber at least, ideas of righteous tribalism and cultural fragmentation). For Huntington, by contrast, the spectre is one of wars between civilizations, seen in his case as the West versus the 'Islamic–Confucian' world. The events of 9/11 certainly lay to rest any global assumption of cultural homogenization around consumerism.

Second-wave thinking therefore has had a good deal of success in scrutinizing and evaluating speculative propositions against more considered accounts better grounded in evidence. It has also begun a process of seeking out clearer and more plausible concepts in an effort to avoid the pitfalls of applying simplistic theories to very complex social changes. This has required a measure of scepticism towards propositions that are regarded as self-evident by many and cherished as articles of faith by some. More sophisticated empirically grounded work has emerged, though it is not clear how far this has connected with the clamour of public debate. All of this is no guarantee that such work is free from error or intrinsically reliable. It is itself liable to criticism and re-evaluation, the main difference being that such debates may occur to a greater degree than before on the basis of conceptual rigour and empirical plausibility.

Thinking about globalization may nonetheless need a more thorough-going overhaul than the sceptical empirically grounded second-wave accounts have provided. One example of the mood of restless dissatis-faction with existing conceptual approaches to globalization may be found in the work of James Rosenau (1996: 249–250). 'Does globalization', he asks, 'refer to a condition, an end-state, or to a process/Is it mostly a state of mind, or does it consist of objective circumstances? What are the arrangements from which globalization is a departure? ...'.

His extensive list of questions goes on to include substantive issues such as whether globalization means homogenization, whether it is unidirectional, and whether it derives from some causal prime mover. Any definition should somehow assist the explanation of specific social processes, but Rosenau, like many others, finds it hard to offer a succinct operational definition for all analytical purposes. His most generic comments nonetheless focus on boundary broadening processes with respect to territory and territorially based identity, as distinct from localizing boundary-heightening process. These affect people, goods, information, norms, and institutions.

A more radical proposal, advanced by Hay and Marsh (2000), is to call for a *third* phase, based on the re-thinking of core concepts and indeed the very definition of globalization. Their own version of this exercise requires thinking of globalization neither as a singular and inexorable process causing change nor as a Juggernaut beyond human control. Rather they see globalization as a trend, the effect of a range of processes such as cross-border interconnection and inter-dependence, but a trend which is reversible by counter-trends. Globalization is the *explanandum*, which means that which is to be explained, not the *explanans*, which means the explanation of change. Globalization, in short, is an effect not a cause.

Theorists of long-run processes of social change are well aware of the pitfalls of confusing *explanans* with *explanandum*. One classic example is the debates over the origins of capitalism and market society (Holton 1985). Here capitalism has often been treated both as the phenomenon to be explained and as the explanation of this phenomenon. This creates the logical absurdity of capitalism being responsible for its own emergence. Hay and Marsh are right to introduce some logical rigour into the globalization debate by distinguishing *explanans* and *explanandum*.

The work of David Held and his associates organized around the idea of 'global transformations' (Held *et al.* 1999, Held and McGrew 2002, 2003) represents another powerful statement of the *third*-wave position. This line of argument is critical of certain aspects of both first- and second-wave approaches. Put simply, their position is twofold. First, much second-wave scepticism about first-wave thinking is correct. Much that is called globalization or trans-nationalism is really still contained within inter-national relations, while counter-trends to glob-alization are ignored. Nation-states do not wither away, nor are the economic consequences of globalization either as dire or as positive as the respective critical and liberal forms of first-wave thinking assume.

Second, however, second-wave thinking is too sceptical. The world of nation-states cannot contain or structure many significant elements of global life, including the ordering of territory. This was dramatically registered in 9/11, when Al Quaida, a trans-national network of ter-rorists, struck successfully at the heartlands of the world's number one super-power, using techniques very different from the geo-political wars of territorial states. The case for using the term 'Globalization' is that it enables us to understand the extent to which many forms of transformation are no longer containable within or fully controllable by inter-national arrangements. These include mobilities of finance and technology creating and re-creating complex spatial divisions of labour, global communications technology, and the operation of global social movements (Held *et al.* 1999). Proponents of the third-wave approach, therefore, takes globalization as trans-nationalism seriously, while being aware of its limits.

Held sees globalization as a fluid set of processes amenable to the impact of human agency and the design and re-shaping of social institutions. The contemporary forms of globalization are not immutable, suggesting that globalization is neither necessarily unjust nor undemocratic. This position links normative issues such as the desirability of a cosmopolitan democratic world order with empirical issues, such as the emergence of what might be called proto-cosmopolitan trends in areas such as the inter-national law of human rights, and the ideals of many global social movements.

Another profound element in third-wave thinking is that we should study the limits of globalization (Scott 1997, Reiger and Liebfried 2003), as much as its seemingly ubiquitous scope. Such limits may be set either by non-global preconditions upon which globalization processes may depend (e.g. national legal, infrastructural and welfare state provision) or by counter-trends and resistance (e.g. nationalism and localism). They may also be identified with historical phases of de-globalization as those occurred between the pre-1914 and the post-1945 periods (James 2001). In addition, laying to rest the demonic myth of Globalization as unstoppable Juggernaut also makes it easier to bring human agency back into the analysis, a theme common to third-wave thinking.

The plea to bring human agency back in is a refreshing move away from abstract conjectures, which draws on multi-disciplinary research assembled by historians, anthropologists, sociologists, and practitioners of cultural studies. Some of this is centred on questions of globalization and cultural identity, pursuing alternatives to the idea of global cultural homogenization (e.g. Hannerz 1992). In addition, studies of economic actors in multi-national corporations (Sklair 2001), traders, warriors, and cosmopolitans across world history (Hopkins 2001), labour (Munck 2000) and social movements (Cohen and Rai 2000), and global advocacy, policy and knowledge networks (Keck and Sikkink 1998, Holton 2002, Stone 2002) have emerged. All these in their different ways focus not on passive victims of globalization, but rather on the active role of human agents in the making of the global world – whether intentionally or unwittingly.

Another feature of third-wave thinking is the idea of multiple, different, or alternative globalizations. This has become a more prominent element in debates over globalization in the last 10 years (e.g. Therborn 1999a, Geyer and Paulmann 2001, Hopkins 2001, special edition on 'Different Globalizations', *Policy, Organisation and Society*, 20(2), 2001). For Therborn, the distinction is between globalizing structures, including markets, finance, culture, and human rights, and what he calls the interactive 'world stage of actors' very often operative within nations through cross-cultural interchanges or experience of global governance. As with all such structure/agency contrasts, however, the danger remains of treating structures as if they are somehow distinct from human interactions, rather than formed, reproduced, and challenged through processes of human agency.

Geyer and Paulmann (2001), by contrast, distinguish between two kinds of global human agency: the one organized, formal, and intent on creating global arrangements; the other a more informal set of polycentric processes that somehow push ahead of the formalized world. Examples given include the distinction between the establishment of formal world scientific congresses and the more diffuse world of scientific opinion. This distinction is a useful reminder that globalization is not simply a matter of activities that bear an explicitly global name or strive for an explicit global outcome, whether centred on the UN, G8 group of leading economic nations, or the World Trade Organisation (WTO). It is equally a matter of polycentric global processes such as markets, cultural exchanges, and cross-border communication via new information technology. We shall return to this point later in discussing the development of global civil society.

The most influential distinction between the types of globalization is the contrast between 'elite globalization' or 'globalization from above' and 'globalization from below'. The former is represented by the activities of multi-national corporations and regulatory bodies like the IMF and WB. The latter is associated with global social movements such as Amnesty International, or Friends of the Earth, and in global citizen and civil society movements.

Once we think in terms of different globalizations it is easier to see that many of those who take part in anti-globalization protests are really opposed to market-oriented economic globalization, or even more specifically to Americanization through economic globalization, rather than necessarily opposed to any kind of globalization (Lyons 2001). While defence of national sovereignty or local community values have been invoked in protest against these forms of economic globalization, what is interesting is how alternative ostensibly global ideas have also been enunciated. These include human rights (including human rights for perceived victims of economic globalization) and ideas of global social justice. They also sometimes involve notions of inter-national civil society as a 'bottom-up' community-centred rather than 'top-down' corporate-centered or IMF–WB-centred version of globalization.

The idea of different globalizations has certainly not gone unchallenged. One argument, advanced by both Castells (1996) and Bauman (1998), is that global society is in the process of a profound re-stratification. Here a mobile cosmopolitan elite is able to enjoy the fruits of globalization, while a peripheralized set of economic victims is doomed to local immobility. For Bauman this means globalization for some, localization for others. The difficulty with this argument is not that the benefits of globalization are very unequally distributed. It is rather that spatial mobility and cosmopolitanism are by no means the privilege of the rich and well-connected. Global migration proceeds on a massive scale (Castles and Miller 1993), while cosmopolitan identity is multifarious and culturally diverse in origin (Gilroy 1993, Cheah and Robbins 1998, Holton 2002). This reflects the widespread availability of global imagining as a cultural resource, and directs our attention to global consciousness as a dimension to be built into any agent-centred account of the making of globalization.

Defining globalization

We have so far proceeded without a systematic definition of global-ization, preferring to note significant trends that might be built into a definition, while also identifying reasons why any stable meaning of the concept is so hard to identify. Definitions may of course serve different purposes at the same time. Moral, political, and commercial functions exist alongside, and may easily be entangled with analytical ones. When Anita Roddick, founder of the Body Shop retail chain, referred to globalization as 'the latest name for the conspiracy of the rich against the poor', she evoked both moral concern about global inequality, and the commercial positioning of her business as economically responsible in its global sourcing policies vis-à-vis poor countries (Roddick 2001). This kind of rhetorical approach is not, however, very helpful in constructing a definition for analytical purposes.

A more sophisticated approach is to be found in Bourdieu's (1998) account of globalization as a 'myth' or 'discourse' used by neo-liberal ideologues to dismantle welfare-states and construct a universe of individualistic consumers. This discursive definition draws attention to the use of the word globalization within ideological understandings of contemporary trends. However, it offers too arbitrary a foreclosure on the multiple ways the term has been used including those that attempt an empirically grounded analysis of processes, institutions and identities.

A suitable third-wave agent-centred definition of globalization – drawing on the themes of interconnection, inter-dependence (Held 1995), and global consciousness (Robertson 1992) – involves the following:

(a) The intensified movement of goods, money, technology, information, people, ideas and cultural practices across political and cultural boundaries. Such movements combine cause and effect. They implicate the interests and activities of merchants and bankers, migrants and religious leaders, media representatives and activists.

(b) The inter-dependence of social processes across the globe, such that all social activity is profoundly interconnected rather than separated off into different national and cultural spaces. Once again inter-dependence arises out of human activity and involves particular agents, whether global entrepreneurs or regulators, medical professionals or lawyers, social movement activists or world musicians. It involves formally organized undertakings as well as those embodied in networks and looser forms of co-operation and conflict.

(c) Consciousness of and identification with the world as a single place, as in forms cosmopolitanism, religion or earth-focused environmentalism. This approach, pioneered by Roland Robertson (1995) embraces global imaginings and is thus also centrally concerned with initiative and undertaking. Cosmopolitanism, moreover, is not an exclusively Western orientation (Cheah and Robbins 1998, Holton 2002) and this alerts us to the multi-cultural roots of global consciousness.

This set of three elements is of course a composite account of ongoing processes, which may or may not be interlinked. Globalization remains in the making, and may indeed be subject to periodic forms of un-making or re-invention. If globalization is an unfinished process, then it is surely premature to speak of the arrival of Global Society. To speak this way is to treat Global Society as if it were an end-state, a global condition that has finally arrived, where the only remaining task is for latecomers to catch up with or be guided towards the blessed state achieved by those 'mature' others, who have already arrived.

The position argued in this book is that globalization is an ongoing set of processes shaped by human agency, and far too complex to be encompassed within a single master process. The definition offered above does not specify whether one specific element is more crucial than any other, or tie globalization too narrowly to a particular context in time and space. Globalization can certainly be defined more narrowly (e.g. as contemporary Western capitalism). This procedure, however, tends to divert attention away from globalizing phenomena outside the West, and global themes other than the familiar focus on economic processes and elite actors.

Structure of the book

The book is structured around a set of themes each of which draws attention to issues of human agency in the making, shaping, and resistance to globalization, pursued within a third-wave perspective.

In Chapter 2 we focus on the question 'When did globalization begin?' If globalization began in the West in association with capitalism, we might perhaps look for its origins in the 1940s with the foundation of the UN, WB, and IMF. However, one could equally go back 100 years to the epoch of free trade and the Gold Standard, 250 years to the Enlightenment and Adam Smith's economic liberalism, or 500 years to the voyage of Christopher Columbus to the Americas. If the Western focus is relaxed, we might however go back even further as McNeill (1990) and Frank (1990), and Frank and Gills (1993) encourage us to do across millennia to empires, long-distance trade and expansive religion. All of these are relevant to cross-border movement, inter-dependence and global thinking, that is as forms of (partial) globalization prior to recent more complete forms of Western globalization.

In Chapter 3, issues of power and social organization touched on in the historical survey are investigated more explicitly. One influential way of thinking about power and globalization is encapsulated in Wallerstein's World-System theory. This approach is based on extensive empirical research (see especially Wallerstein 1979, 1991) as well as conceptual and theoretical ingenuity. It was developed as a way of shifting social science thinking about social change away from a national to a world focus. Whereas world empires once represented the main historical form in which social life was organized across political and cultural boundaries, a new more economically focused capitalist world system has now taken their place. This is a system but not in the sense of an entity that is self-subsistent with respect to an environment. Rather it functions as a highly patterned social organization capable of generating global economic development and social change, as well as global inequality and resistance. This is achieved through processes of capital accumulation and social exchange that create spatial structures of inequality separating a capitalist metropolitan 'core' from 'peripheral' and 'semi-peripheral' regions and countries.

One of the major puzzles with this approach, to be explored further in Chapter 3, is the extent to which the idea of system is the most useful metaphor through which to analyse the making of globalization. For one thing, world system connotes a unitary process dominated by a single logic, and extensive in time and space to the exclusion of all else. For

Wallerstein (1990a,b), even the contours of resistance become incorp-orated into the system. This point of view has been criticized for economic reductionism, whereby the characteristics of culture and politics are simply read off from the economy (Boyne 1990). It may similarly be criticized for an excessively deterministic approach, whereby structures of global power dominate and re-model human agency. Reference to core and periphery also suggests patterns of global power that are centralized around a few metropolitan centres. Political empires may have declined with the rise of a capitalist world system, yet the major actors in this system are still seen as core nation-states, whose military machines and core ideologies predominate. This 'top-down' mode of thinking has little place for the global networks and webs through which individuals, households, social movements, professionals, and other experts have sought to influence, promote, protest, or re-shape global processes. It also failed to adequately anticipate the mass 'anti-global protests' of the last 5 years.

The excessively unitary and deterministic characteristics of world-system theory contrast with the wisely used metaphors of network or web that abound in more recent literature on globalization. These connote a more complex multi-centred loosely coupled approach, one that is more sensitive to human agency. The technological invention of the World Wide Web, symbol of interconnectivity, is only the most obvious instance of these widely used metaphors. Castells (1996, 2001) theory of Network Society manages to encompass the reality of capitalist economic power, the autonomy of new information technology from any overriding social purpose such as capital accumulation, and the reality of systematic resistance to capitalist forms of globalization.

In Chapter 3 we also explore the utility of web and network as ways of understanding globalization, and of understanding the operation of power within global arrangements. What, first of all, are the most signifi-cant kinds of networks? Much popular attention has been given to elite networks such as the World Economic Forum, connected with large corporations, governments, regulatory bodies like the IMF and WB, and economists. To restrict the focus to elites, however, produces a skewed picture of what is a complex multi-dimensional area. One well-researched example of this complexity is that of 'knowledge networks'. These include, as Diane Stone (2002) has pointed out, a range of organizations and looser patterns of association around scientific and professional associ-ations, development agencies, universities, and foundations. By this means a range of ideas, research findings and policy options are circulated, diffused and addressed. In the process, such networks intersect with advocacy and issue-based networks, embracing social movements, and with policy networks, including official as well as unofficial actors. Amongst unofficial networks, the figure of the 'activist' has become a major point of reference and controversy in current accounts of the contemporary global polity. In Chapter 3 a more extensive classification of network types, mechanisms of operation, and impact will be attempted.

Globalization: Space and time

Globalization is clearly a process of profound consequence for both space and time as we shall discuss in Chapter 4. In a spatial sense, it has been argued that the intensified development of cross-border communications in virtually instantaneous time renders geography redundant. New information technologies allow the transmission of text, speech, video, and other data in real time in an instant. De-regulation of global financial, and capital markets means that huge volumes of finance flows remorselessly around the world in search of profitable use, while the data mining of information on consumers and individual citizens is available at multiple points in the global arena, rather than being monopolized by states.

The mobility and fluidity of processes and people within global space is, as Urry (2000) points out, perhaps the defining feature of contemporary society within the imagination as much as the production and distribution of economic resources. The development of instantaneous time alongside globally oriented actors with the power or desire for mobility has clearly compressed space (Harvey 1996). Physical distance is no longer in and of itself a critical obstacle to social exchange except for the world's poorest populations, unable to move far through hunger while simultaneously unable to access the telephone, let alone the Internet, as a result of poverty. In much first-wave thinking about globalization, all this led to the supposition that time had destroyed space.

Yet, as many subsequent researchers have pointed out, there are a number of senses in which geography still matters. Even within a mobile world, a great deal depends on where and how nodules, residues, or resistances form within global space. Sassen (1994) has pointed out that while information technology may permit decentralization of the sites of production, economic and financial power is still concentrated within global cities. The existence of a complex and constantly shifting global division of labour does not mean that fluidity destroys spatial inequalities of wealth and power. Particular spaces, better-termed places, also matter. This is obvious in the politics of culture where the burgeoning of nationalist movements and identity politics is organized around either real or idealized spaces. But it is also to be found within the heart of global economic arrangements.

O' Riain (2000), in an ethnographic study of Irish software development engineers working for a US multi-national, shows how the specific Irish workplace was largely controlled according to the dictates of central office received in instantaneous time via the Internet and conference calls, and enforced via project deadlines. Rather than being dissolved into cyberspace, the highly educated workers involved faced an intensification of time–space relationships. They were both intimately bound together as a workgroup creating co-operative technical networks within a particular local space, and at the same time being subjected to pressures towards individual spatial mobility, which are characteristic of career paths in this sector of the industry. Globalization therefore does not mean an end to place even though the interconnection between places becomes deeper and more intense. The global economy operates rather through networks that link particular places with 'patterns of mobility of people, information and resources' (198).

Naming the world's spaces and places has, however, been made harder by the unevenness of global economic and technological change, as well as the complexities of cultural change. The tripartite distinction between First World, Second World, and Third World is a prominent casualty here. The largest problem here is with the term 'Third World' (Kamrava 1995) developed to encapsulate the African, Asian and Latin American world beyond Europe and North America, and their settler extensions around the globe. The idea of a Third World, homogenous in its lack of economic development and power, and subservient to other worlds, has, however, been profoundly undermined. This is not because the worst global economic inequalities has been corrected – far from it. It is rather because of a striking divergence in the situation of different nation-states lumped together in the Third World category. China, parts of Southeast Asia, and parts of South and Central America have achieved significant levels of growth and development over the last decades. While this has not been without periods of crisis, none have fallen back into the position of the poorest and least powerful, rendering the original idea of a Third World redundant. Increasing reluctance to use the idea of a simple First World–Third World split may be seen as another victory for more recent thinking over what went before.

Even if economic and social geography is not dead, it may nonetheless be necessary to examine other ways of understanding space beyond the conventional political and juridical boundaries between nations and regions. One way of doing this, elaborated further in Chapter 4, is to think in terms of pacified and feral spaces defined in terms of levels of social order, examples of which may be found equally in the West and the world beyond (Friedmann 1994). Different sets of globalizing actors may, within the same global city such as Los Angeles, help to create pacified spaces within which to locate core elements of market-driven economic activity and elite residential housing, and at the same time supply illegal drugs that contribute to feral social disorganization in other parts of the same city.

Notions of time, meanwhile, are equally problematic when one considers the complex multi-dimensionality of globalization. A superficial examination that focused solely on the contemporary information technology revolution might lead one to suppose that there was one global time. Building on the standardized measures of time developed towards the end of the 19th century, modern digitalized communications technology appears to render instantaneous time as the predominant mode of temporal organization. Information travels in small fractions of a second. Yet human consciousness, human bodies, cultural forms, and the natural environment do not. This raises the puzzle of the simultaneous existence of multiple times, and the possibility of collisions between them. In Chapter 4, the discussion involves the identification of a variety of times, and the ways in which human actors within the global arena both make time for their activities and are simultaneously shaped by it.

How then do people live in the era of accelerating globalization? And how do patterns of opportunity and constraint influence global life-chances? If human actors shape globalization as much as being shaped by it, how far is access to innovative and effective activity constrained by structures of power, and what are the mechanisms through which global actors operate? These fundamental questions will be explored in the next three chapters.

The global, the regional, the national, and the local

Many of the questions regarded as settled in the first-wave debates over globalization remain unresolved. One of the most important of these is the question of the viability of nation-states in an epoch of globalization. Do they simply wither away in the face of globalization, or is it possible for national and global institutions and identities to complement and reinforce as much as they conflict with each other? The complex ways in which the global, the regional, the national, and the local intersect, conflict, and sometimes complement each other will be explored in Chapter 5.

The issue of relationships between national, global, and other levels of social life cannot, as we shall see, be resolved conjecturally or be deduced from some general theory of the nation-state. This is partly because nation-states vary in size, power, resources, and institutional coherence. The US or Japan are far larger, more powerful, and have many more resources than Bangladesh or Tanzania. Nor are the relatively stable institutional structures of Western states easy to compare with post-colonial quasi-states (Jackson 1991) of Central Africa based upon somewhat arbitrary colonial boundaries and riven by civil war.

Another complicating issue – arising from the development of the European Union (EU), and to a lesser extent the North American Free Trade Association (NAFTA) – is that of regionalism. Is regionalism to be seen as the erosion of individual states which cede power to regional states, or a way by which nation-states may secure their future by pooling sovereignty and resources? And what of regional states themselves? Are they run simply as inter-national entities, where the national members govern the region, or do they develop trans-national principles, rules of operation, and organizations that increasingly stand above nation-states?

Globalization processes may both rely on aspects of the nation and in some circumstances help to constitute or re-constitute nation-states. Multi-national companies, for example, often prefer to locate production in stable national societies with stable legal systems able to protect property rights and public policies that, inter alia, provide educated labour forces. These, along with issues of access to the largest markets, provide some of the reasons why foreign direct investment (FDI) by multi-nationals is concentrated in North America, Europe, and Japan. This is not to deny that multi-nationals have also located in areas of cheap labour, or conducted resource-extraction in poor under-developed countries ruled by corrupt regimes with whom some accommodation is reached to protect mutual interests. What is significant in either case is not the disappearance of the state, but the making and re-making of states that suit particular global and national interests. The only systematic anti-state interests are probably to be found in the orbit of organized crime, notably the inter-national drugs trade, which seeks to de-stabilize the capacity of nation-states for law enforcement.

Economic globalization may also not be the sole aspect of globalization that impacts on nation-states and processes of state-building. Global concern for human rights was one major element in inter-national debates and actions around the recent establishment of the independent state of East Timor. Here colonial independence from Portugal had been followed by imperial annexation by Indonesia, and a new independence struggle. This had the support of some external groups, movements, and individuals, the number of which swelled after the UN supervised vote for independence. Many of these interests, including the UN and the Organisation for Economic Co-operation and Development (OECD), have become involved in the process of state-building and reconstruction of civil society in the aftermath of the armed conflict between East Timorese and Indonesia. The significance of this issue is both that the formation and development of the new East Timorese state required inter-national intervention to succeed, and that this intervention was legitimized in relation to both the trans-national idea of human rights and the notion of national self-determination. In this case we are dealing with an inter-national project to globalize the nation-state rather than abolish it.

A further way of thinking about the interconnection between large 'macro-level' global processes, and smaller 'micro-level' local processes is introduced – based on the ideas of the 'Glocal' and 'Glocalization'. To be 'glocal' means the combination of global and local elements within human activities. Examples include local marketing by global corporations, or the environmentalist practice of thinking globally but acting locally. Glocalization, meanwhile, is the process whereby glocal fusions take place.

The idea of Glocalization is a very striking and productive way of moving debate away from *first-phase* theories pitting the global against the national and local as alternative, contrasting, and conflictual forms of social organization and cultural life. The term 'glocal', while not widely used in academic or popular debate, nonetheless has a significant presence in a range of areas from business and management, to city-to-city collaboration and social movements seeking to empower civil society to combat market-based globalization and the power of multi-national corporations (the Google search engine on 8 December 2003 throwing up about 28,700 instances of the term).

Amongst the disparate array of examples are The Glocal Forum and Annual Glocalization Conferences within which city mayors from around the world seek to encourage city-to-city collaboration between richer and poorer cities in collaboration with agencies like the UN Food and Agriculture Organization (FAO), and the WB. For Uri Savir, former head of the Israeli Foreign Service, co-architect of the Oslo Peace Accords, and founder of the Glocal Forum, glocalization is a process that re-inserts local concerns and networks within global arrangements that have hitherto excluded too many sections of the world's populations (Savir 2003).

In Chapter 5 we pursue the question of how useful it is to think and act glocally. Could the idea of glocalization be a coherent and useful way of drawing attention to fusions of global and local institutions and activities, whether states, cities, or social movements as much as business strategy, cultural identity, and social movements? Thinking glocally would in this way avoid the excessively polarized assumptions associated with ideas of the global and globalization, whereby the global and the local are seen as mutually exclusive and necessarily in conflict. This would, at the very least, prevent the polarized discourses of first-wave thinking, whereby hyper-globalizers foreclosed the long-term viability of the nation-states and nationalism at the same time as the realist school of political science foreclosed the possibility that trans-national developments were creating anything significantly new.

Global civil society

In Chapter 6 we move on to look more directly at the idea of global civil society and the people that constitute it. This term, as John Keane (2003: 1–2) has recently pointed out has entered the vocabulary of globalization both in the West and beyond. The term itself has been used in a number of ways, both analytical and normative. These may be linked, as in the idea that global civil society is co-terminous with a global citizenry that somehow stands above national or ethnic divisions (e.g. Akami 2002) – a development that is both real and desirable. This usage draws attention to the ways in which many self-styled inter-nationalists and cosmopolitans have seen themselves as a progressive force over the last 200 years. There is, however, a wider sense in which the idea of global civil society can be used, of which inter-nationalists and cosmopolitans are one important sub-set. This broader approach includes all those people involved in non-state modes of mobility, communication, and exchange across borders. This embraces this world of immigrants and diasporic groups, traders and business people, scientists and professionals, pilgrims and sportsmen and sportswomen. Such people are sometimes autonomous travellers, businessmen and tourists, sometimes workers employed by multi-national companies, and sometimes members of networks of trade, migration, or global crime and terrorism. Activities may be individual and inter-personal or more collective and formal, embracing the writing of letters and emails, making telephone calls and sending text messages, publishing newspapers and books, opening up new markets and conducting global research, or establishing bonds of long-distance friendship and love.

The point here is that it does not take a committed cosmopolitan or world citizen to make global civil society. To restrict attention to the latter is to ignore the paradox already noted above that most globally active people retain ties to one or more particular places and histories. Chapter 6 will then move on to consider the implications of this point for individual identity, and in the process attempt to determine the extent and limits of global civil society.

While there is a literature on the general limits of globalization, there has been comparatively little empirical research into the limits to global civil society. For many, it is sufficient to rehearse general points about the resilience of nationalism and ethnic conflict, or to draw attention to anti-global protest in the name of local community or national democratic institutions – allegiances that are sub-global in scope. The difficulty with this approach is that it fails to take account of the interpenetration of the global and the particular in social life. The most obvious examples of this are where those promoting the particular interests of an ethnic or national or religious group, or simply protesting against globalization, use global 'means' to promote what are seen as 'non-global' or 'anti-global' ends (Keane 2003). Chapter 6 will conclude with an attempt to make sense of this paradox by specifying different ways in which the global and the particular interpenetrate and intersect.

Globalization and its discontents

In Chapter 7 we return to current controversies over globalization and human welfare. Having established the significance of different kinds of human agency in the making of globalization, it is now possible to challenge much of the over-generalized and abstract rhetoric surrounding debates between globalization's supporters and opponents. In place of ideological clamour that demonizes global actors as either elite manipulators or irresponsible activists, a more balanced assessment is possible of the claims and counter-claims advanced by proponents and critics. A number of recent studies have, in particular, picked up the theme of 'globalization and its discontents' (see especially Sassen 1998, Stiglitz 2002) as a way of taking criticisms seriously while equally identifying positive trends and developments. This current of thought has also proven sensitive the many paradoxes and contradictions evident in the development of global processes. Foremost of these, as pointed out by Amartya Sen, is the co-existence of a world of 'unprecedented prosperity' and 'staggering inequality'.

Within this context, the angry clamour of anti-globalization protest has increased rather than decreased since the Seattle protest of 1999. And criticism is not confined to pressure from below. If a global elite had been running globalization according to what came to be known as the Washington Consensus of free-market policy-settings and privatized loosely regulated economic activity, then even key elite figures such as George Soros, the financier, and Joseph Stiglitz, former senior WB advisor, have broken ranks to call for fundamental reform of global economic architecture. There is thus a widening agenda of both failures of economic globalization, and policy changes required for reform. Elite opinion cannot provide a unitary front on global policy issues, and can no longer dominate the discussion of where globalization is and should be heading.

Chapter 7 starts off by reviewing the literature on global inequality, poverty, and economic welfare, so as to identify the interplay of opportunity and constraint in the ways in which the global economy operates. An outstanding issue here is the unresolved debate as to why economic growth is capable of increasing overall prosperity, but is unable, by itself, to guarantee freedom from poverty, hunger, insecurity, and arbitrary and oppressive government. Attention then turns to the operation of global economic institutions, notably multi-national corporations and regulatory organizations; two of the more contentious elements in the global arena. What objectives, policies and visions animate key actors in such institutions, do they operate uniformly or in a variety of ways, and how far do they enhance or constrain opportunity and a more equitable distribution of global wealth? And how far, lastly, have Soros or Stiglitz type reforms progressed?

Such questions about economic globalization are not of course purely economic. They are intrinsically connected with both the politics of global governance and government, and the cultural variations in the *ends* that individuals, organizations, and a diverse range of social groupings set themselves. One influential way of thinking about modern society is through notions of differentiation and integration. Differentiation of economic, political, and cultural activities arguably allows specialization of functions through distinct institutional forms (e.g. markets, democratic political organizations, cultural activities freed from state controls) and greater capacity to meet different kinds of objectives. Nonetheless, differentiation brings with it challenges of integration. How far, for example, can markets be left free from political or cultural regulation? How far can a pluralistic or multi-cultural set of cultural objectives be promoted through market-based means, and what are the limits to markets as guarantors of human welfare.

Attention shifts in the second part of Chapter 7 to the broad policy positions that are evident within practical debates and controversies over globalization. Here may be found a contrasting set of answers to the question 'What should be done about global inequality and injustice?' The responses of human actors vary from continued enthusiasm for market liberalism and isolationism, to statism, global reform, and support for alternative versions of globalization. These options are evaluated in the light of the arguments developed and evidence presented in the body of the book.

The argument of the book

Chapter 8 returns to the leading themes of the book and re-affirms the importance of the major themes of this study. The first of these sees globalization as a set of processes that do not add up to a singular inte-grated system, but are better understood in terms of a multiple set of processes that inter-relate but sometimes conflict with each other. Put another way, forms of economic globalization are by no means identical to forms of political, cultural, or technological globalization. One conse-quence of this line of argument is that the polarization of political and policy debates over globalization into simple dichotomies – for and against – is profoundly misconceived.

The second theme emphasizes that globalization, in its various mani-festations, is a product of human agency, reflection and activity, and conflict and co-operation. This point arises from both long-run historical approaches to globalization and analysis of the contemporary world. The kinds of globalization we have may not always be the products of human intention, but they are capable of re-shaping and even reversing under certain circumstances. This leads into a third theme, namely the dynamics and limits to globalization processes, and the possibility of resistances and reversals as much as a continuation, ever onward and upward of the kinds of globalization we currently have. Globalization processes, insofar as they widen the differentiation of economy from polity and culture, have created enormous social strains. These have produced both a crisis of legitimation for economic globalization and anti-global reactions that may well usher in a phase of de-globalization. Meanwhile, the fourth and final theme is the emphasis given to reformers and re-shapers of globalization, forms of action that may help to create an alternative to de-globalization in the search for the construction of a more just, sustainable, and secure global world.

2

When did Globalization Begin?

David Hancock (1995), in his study of globally active London merchants in the 18th century, describes the visit of a Swedish botanist to a West African slave factory in Sierra Leone towards the end of the century. This impressed the visitor, neither for its barbarity nor for its ordered discipline, but for the entertainment available to Europeans seeking relief from 'tropical discomfort'. This included team golf played by Europeans in cotton clothing from India, served by African caddies dressed in tartan from Glasgow. This vignette may be seen, in Hancock's terms, as a 'bizarre un-self-conscious parody of African territorial conquest' (2). But as he goes on to explain, it is also an indicator of the global stretch of expanding mercantile activities. By 1785 the London merchants who operated the enterprise had trading stations from India and Jamaica to Nova Scotia and Germany, together with plantations in India, the West Indies, and the North American mainland.

The images of economic expansion, social injustice, and Western cultural dominance evident here pose a number of challenging questions. When did the global processes described here originate, and does globalization always take this form? What kinds of social actors have been involved in the making of globalization and have traders and manufacturers typically driven globalization across time and space. When, in short, did globalization begin?

Movement across political and cultural borders has also been going on for millennia. We have always been, as Kwame Anthony Appiah (2003: 192) points out, a 'travelling species' ever since the forebears of the present world population left Africa. Phenomena such as population movement in search of food, land, and freedom, conquest of land and slaves, or trade between tribes, city-states, and regions go back a long way in human history. In this very long-term sense, the history of the human species may be regarded as a process of globalization (ibid.: 193), and one which has no necessary connection with Western expansionism.

Many of the earliest imaginings of space and time, by contrast, linked groups to particular places and environments and were thus typically local rather than global in focus. Australian aboriginal stories of the dreamtime are a case in point. Such cosmologies were locally embedded rather than outwardly engaged. Over time a broader sense of the cosmos and the place of humanity within it emerged primarily within religious and spiritual thought. Environmental awareness of planet Earth based on a systematic global sense of inter-dependence between biosphere, geosphere, and atmosphere was slower to develop, though an awareness of the adverse impact of humankind on the natural environment was evident in ancient Greece, Rome, and India (Grove 1995: 6).

But are these satisfactory answers to the question 'When did globalization begin?' Many feel globalization began far more recently. Specific answers still vary, however, from the late 15th- and 16th-centuries voyages of discovery and conquest symbolized by Christopher Columbus sailing to the Americas, the 19th-century expansion of European commerce and Empire, or the post-1945 epoch of multi-national corporations, and more recent phases of technological change in information-processing and communication. In this chapter we review a variety of answers put forward, and suggest ways of considering the historical sociology of globalization as a multi-dimensional set of processes with different origins and often quite contrasting types of human actors.

For the reader unfamiliar with debates about world history, what is required here is neither the absorption of large amounts of detail nor a model of history in two simple stages: before and after the onset of globalization. Nor again is it obligatory to think of globalization arising first in the West, thereafter spreading outward to the rest. What is required here is the willingness to think in terms of broad often multi-centred trends which may be spread in time across centuries and millennia, and in space across all continents rather than Europe and its overseas extensions alone.

Exploring the history of globalization

While humankind has indeed a long history of population movement, much of the earliest movement was into previously unoccupied land, and early forms of trade took place at boundary markets between territories (Curtin 1984: 2). Increasingly over time, land became occupied and movement across borders expanded. However, the very existence of socially constructed boundaries may be seen as a claim to exclusive use or control over territory, and as a cultural marker separating different groups. In this sense, human history may equally be seen as a process of particularization and localization.

Metaphorically we may say that fence-building and bridge-building are both features of the human condition, and there is no good general reason to suppose that one is more likely to predominate than the other.

The mere existence of movement across borders may then be more of a necessary rather than a sufficient indicator of globalization. Movement may be episodic, involve relatively few people, and have few consequences for social groups not involved with it. The crucial indictors of globalization may then have more to do with the second and the third elements of the definition provided in Chapter 1 – namely closer inter-dependence between spatially separate social organizations, together with a sense of the world as a single place or community.

Having to take account of global inter-dependencies which typically involve cross-border movements is perhaps a rather passive or involuntary sense in which individuals encounter or become enmeshed in globalization. It has the quality of becoming globalized through external constraint, or globalized by default. This is how many anti-global critics interpret the world. Lack of choice or democratic consultation about patterns of globalization is the source of much global discontent. There are, however, two alternative ways in which individuals may relate to the processes that constitute globalization.

The first involves participating actively in cross-border processes, inter-dependency and/or the global imagination, whether as trader or pilgrim, explorer or migrant, multi-national manager or world musician, colonizer or environmental activist. Activity of this type involves some kind of enlarged cross-border orientation, whether citizen of the world or Imperialist, Christian or Muslim, free trader or member of a worldwide diaspora.

The second, less overtly global orientation, involves all of those who make use of material and symbolic resources and repertoires that have an origin beyond their own people or country of origin, whether technology, foodstuffs, political institutions, or religious practices. Involvement in these social patterns may require no especially global orientation, or even awareness that most human groups have met their needs through the selective borrowing and adaptation of ideas, institutions, and resources from elsewhere (Curtin, ibid.: 1). And such ideas, institutions, and resources may themselves have a long pre-existing syncretic cross-border history, whether we are talking about key concepts in mathematics, forms of economic organization, or world religions.

What then are the most useful analytical tools with which to analyse the historical emergence of globalization? Two important sets of concepts are worthy of mention here. One involves the idea of modernity associated with notions of social differentiation; the other, now somewhat discredited, looks at world history through the analysis of civilizations.

For many analysts, globalization is associated with the rise of the West and the development of modernity. Thus for Giddens (1994: 96) 'the first phase of globalization was plainly governed primarily by the expansion of the West'. One can either see this process stretching across centuries, as in Wallerstein's (1974) focus on expansive cross-border processes of agrarian and mercantile capitalism, or link globalization with the more recent processes of market integration discerned by O'Rourke and Williamson (1999) from the mid-19th century onwards. One common feature of the range of thinking linking globalization, modernity, and the West is the idea of social differentiation.

The idea of differentiation was originally developed as a way of referring to processes of institutional specialization. Modernity, in this view, means the differentiation of society into specialized and autonomous spheres (e.g. economy, polity, culture) each with their characteristic institutions (e.g. markets, governments, value systems, etc.). Free trade and worldwide capital mobility, for example, reflect a differentiation of economy and society, whereby economic processes are not set within tight controls imposed by tradition, religion, or law. The contrast between undifferentiated and differentiated social arrangements has also made use of parallel concepts of embedding, disembedding, and re-embedding (see especially Polanyi 1957, Granovetter 1985, Giddens 1994). While economic life is constrained by cultural norms (such as a just price or a fair wage) and political controls, the economy is said to be embedded in society. Where economic autonomy is greater, notions of disembedding are brought into play.

Differentiation rarely occurs without pressure to re-embed (or re-integrate) spheres of social life previously separated from each other. This is evident in the classic 19th-century 'social' and 'socialist' reaction against individualism and *laissez-faire*, which led in part to the development of welfare states and community-focused approaches to social problems (Polanyi 1957). It is also manifest in the recent reaction against forms of global differentiation that are felt to privilege economic processes and institutions over personal security, cultural integrity, and human rights.

Globalization, especially in its economic manifestations, may be seen as one form of disembedding, and possibly the most radical, insofar as it necessarily means engagement with the world outside hitherto self-contained groups. The forms globalization takes, whether free trade, mass migration, or cross-border movements of ideas and affiliations, typically pose new challenges to social stability and integration. Responses typically take one of two forms. Protection from the 'intrusion' of global processes is the first of these, whether achieved through protection of product market from competitors, or restriction of inflows of immigrants. The other response is to develop new forms of integration, harmonizing existing social arrangements with global change. An example of this is the integration of migrant settlers into their new society through granting of citizenship rights.

Free trade represents a profound differentiation of economy from direct social and communal control. But what happens to those like unskilled or very poor who lack effective market access to jobs and consumer goods, and how are market instabilities and dislocations to be handled. In such situations the question 'Has (economic) globalization gone to far?' arise, a question that is essentially about integration problems generated by an excessive disembedding of economic from broader social institutions.

Other examples of globalization raise questions about the disembedding of experience. Where processes of global migration and settlement are concerned, profound questions of human identity and security are posed just as much as issues of material welfare and social progress. If we become increasingly aware of and connected with the world outside our original points of local reference, then who are we and where do we belong?

Historical processes of disembedding or differentiation are, however, far more complex, uneven in speed and scope, and subject to reversals (re-embedding), than schematic accounts of this kind suggest. They also tend to skew analysis to more recent phases of history, and by-pass the possibility that globalization began far earlier in history and in a multi-centred form, well before what is conventionally regarded as the onset of Western modernity.

An alternative set of reference points for the longer-run analysis of globalization may be found in recent work in the genres of historical sociology, and world history. These are typically multi-dimensional in form, examining political and cultural as well as economic processes. They embrace empires, religions, and migration as much as trade and capital movement. The concept of civilizations, much criticized for pro-European bias, is also more typical in historical work as a way of thinking through large cross-border patterns of relationships and interconnections.

Some world historians, such as Arnold Toynbee (1934–61), have interpreted the development of human history in terms of a sequence of dynamic centres sufficiently distinct to qualify as discrete civilizations. History then moved forward, as it were through the dynamic genius of ancient Sumer (Mesopotamia), Egypt, Greece, and Rome, to be followed by the Chinese empires, medieval Islam, and so forth. Each possessed a distinct innovatory capacity, some of which was diffused to the others. The early work of 20th-century world historian William McNeill (1964) also tended to see civilizations as relatively distinct.

Such approaches make a good deal of sense where levels of interaction and inter-dependency between different regions or civilizations are low. For example, if cross-regional trade is restricted to luxury products consumed by small elites, it may have little impact on systems of subsistence agriculture or localized mercantile activity. Similarly if communications linkages are weak and episodic as a result of natural barriers, material poverty, or geographical ignorance then trade, migration, political contact or cultural exchange are not likely to be of major significance to processes of social development. This does not, of course, prevent the slow diffusion of ideas or technologies, but it does impede the scale and intensity of interactions.

Openings to an understanding of more profound inter-dependencies are evident in much 19th-century and 20th-century thinking. Examples include Marx' work on the capitalist mode of production and Toennies' (1911) emphasis on global inter-dependencies created by scientific and professional networks and the development of the press. Nonetheless, much thinking about globalization remains dominated by Euro-centric presumptions in which global developments reflected the diffusion of Western institutions, technologies, and world-views. Some neglected contributions to the historical sociology of globalization are evident in the work of non-Europeans, such as the African-American writer William du Bois. Like the Bengali writer Brajendranath Seal (see Chapter 6), he had been influenced by the epic quality of Hegels' philosophy of history, but was nonetheless dissatisfied by the exclusively European focus of Hegel's account of human progress. While Seal (1994 [1903]) was to produce an alternative account of the progressive cultural development of India, du Bois (1939) attempted the same for African peoples.

A greater interest in inter-civilizational relations has, nonetheless, developed in the last two or three decades (for a more elaborated discussion see Holton 1998: 24–33). Work by Marshall Hodgson on Islam (1974) focused on issues of inter-dependency as well as parallel development between the four traditions centred on the Chinese, Indic, European, and Nile-to-Oxus long-run civilizational complexes. Such inter-dependencies created an Afro-Eurasian Oikoumene, linked together by commerce, art, religion, and science. Within this entity in the medieval period, Islam was very much the central hub, while Western Europe was relatively marginal. William McNeill (1990), in a later long-run overview of world history, identified conquest, migration, and expansive religious movements as sources of cross-border movement, challenging local unities with new forms of mobility and poly-ethnicity. Wilkinson (1987) more radically has proposed that a 'Central Civilization', that emerged first around 1500 BC in West Asia, Egypt, and Sumer, has now expanded to form a 'single global civilization'. This has embodied a variety of economic, political, and cultural institutions but these varied from time to time, place to place, and thus are reducible neither to market exchange nor to politically centred institutions.

Some of the most ambitious attempts to produce a long-run historical account of interaction and inter-dependency have been produced within the broad tradition of world-system theory by Andre Gundar Frank and his associates (Frank 1990, Frank and Gills 1993). One of the most radical claims here is that the world system is around 5000 years old rather than 500. This proposition rests on evidence such as long-distance trade, market exchange, and forms of capital accumulation. Frank's main aim here is to demonstrate the existence of an expansive capitalist core within world history. This position is significant for two reasons. First, it revises Wallerstein's argument that the capitalist world system originated from the 16th century onwards with mercantile and agrarian developments that created a dynamic and extensive inter-national division of labour. Second, it emphasizes the non-Western origins of the world system, and a sense of the 'unity and indivisibility of Afro-Eurasian history' (ibid.: xv).

Some kind of distinction is helpful here between world-system theory and globalization. Wallerstein's work makes a contrast between the longer history of the world empires of the ancient world, tied together by military and political bonds, and the more recent capitalist world system. While 'world-empires', such as ancient Rome, were expansive beyond their original central core, they nonetheless failed to sustain expansiveness, unlike the more robust capitalist world system. The main theme here is, therefore, a discontinuity between the older and the more recent forms of 'world' organization. The problem with Frank's discussion is not so much the very long-run historical focus, as his belief in a strong sense of capitalist continuity over time. The difficulty here lies in defining capitalism merely in terms of long-distance monetary exchange of goods. On such a definition, as Weber (1978: 17) pointed out long ago, the expansive drive to acquisition through trade is age-old.

Janet Abu-Lughod (1993) has produced a more balanced account of continuities and discontinuities in world-system development. Her argument is that a world system predated the post-1500 European system identified by Wallerstein. This was constituted through eight overlapping circles of long-distance exchange that linked China in the East with Western Europe (Abu-Lughod 1989). These exhibited high levels of inter-dependency such that changes in Asia or the Middle East were as capable of affecting all other circuits as changes in the West. This was a period when for a number of decades China traded extensively with East Africa, and where cosmopolitan currents circulated in the Arab-Islamic world. Such multi-centred developments have perhaps been obscured by the tendency of Wallersteinian world-system theory to think in terms of core-periphery models rather than multiple networks of interaction. Abu-Lughod's argument is also consistent with Mazrui's (1990) observation that for much of human history, the Chinese, Indian, and Islamic worlds have been net exporters of innovation to others. For Abu-Lughod the fall of the East preceded the rise of the West. There was, in other words, no intrinsic logic which predestined the West for global success and the East for global subordination.

The tracing of patterns of global or interregional inter-connection, conflict, and synthesis over long stretches of time has involved the intersection of several intellectual currents. World historians, civilizational analysts, and world-system theorists have played important roles in the process. The very recent emergence of what might be called a multicultural global history that is *trans*-national and inter-cultural in scope (see especially Hopkins 2002a), as compared with the *inter*-national and comparative focus of world history, is also of major significance, as we shall discuss below. But beyond this, further significant intellectual currents within discourse analysis, cultural studies, subaltern studies and postcolonial theory have also been important, especially to the critical assessment of power and hegemony, conflict, and dialogue within the ways in which global interconnection has been understood.

For Edward Said (1991 [1978]), following Foucault, the discursive structures of language constitute power relations through forms of knowledge and action. This applies both to processes of nation-state building studied by Foucault as much as interactions between Europeans and the world beyond. The very language of terms like 'The West' or 'The Orient' is, for Said, implicated in power relations rather than constituting a neutral objective scientific language within which analysis can spontaneously emerge free from power contamination. Western ideas of Orientalism are less empirical descriptions of reality than sets of assumptions that construct the 'Orient' not just as distinct from the 'West', but its very opposite or 'Other'. Where the West is seen as rational, controlled, dynamic, and born to rule, the Orient or East is represented as its obverse – irrational or mystical, erotic, idle, enveloped in stasis, and born to follow.

Discourse analysis of this kind has often led its adherents away from historical or empirical analysis that seeks out the truth of propositions. Since all knowledge is rhetorically constituted, the claim is that the conditions that establish its truth are wholly internal to discourse rather than externally generated through broader social processes amenable to empirical analysis. Such epistemological assumptions do not, however, necessarily follow. This is, I believe, the logic of Said's position, his claim being neither that the Orient does not exist nor that the insiders have a privileged view of their own worlds (ibid.: 322). His point is rather that there are fatal inadequacies in the view that 'there are geographical spaces with indigenous radically different inhabitants who can be defined on the basis of some religion, culture, or racial essence proper to that geographical space'. If this interpretation of Said is valid, we may incorporate a critical approach to language and discursive constructs within historically informed inter-cultural analysis. One important consequence of this approach is what Dipesh Chakrabaty (2000) calls the 'provincializing of Europe', de-throning Europe, as it were, from the status of unitary prime mover of global history.

In so doing, it is possible to retain an actor-centred mode of analysis which is interested in the voices and actions of those involved within global interconnections, whether as masters or slaves, Europeans or non-Europeans. Paul Gilroy (1993) has offered an impressive demonstration of this in his path-breaking study *Black Atlantic*. This is a study of 'Black people' involved in cross-Atlantic movements of people, ideas and music, racist conflict, and inter-cultural engagement. His approach is founded on a critique of the presumption that world history is constituted through the collision of 'fully formed and mutually exclusive cultural communities' (ibid.: 7). To think in this way not only makes the dubious assumption that cultures are highly integrated, but also neglects the analysis of inter-cultural relationships. This encourages dichotomous thinking, in which races or ethnic groups are invested with separate and distinct characteristics, histories, and traditions. As far as the Black Atlantic is concerned, the effect is to see European slavers, traders, and colonists as the makers of global modernity, drawing on their own singular traditions and resources. This leaves Black ex-slaves, immigrant settlers in Britain, and African-American intellectuals as either intrusions from traditional worlds or exemplars of a separate racial consciousness, rather than inter-dependent co-actors in the unfolding of modernity and globalization, in their political, economic, and cultural manifestations.

Gilroy's perspective elaborates an argument previously developed by du Bois *in The Souls of Black Folk* (1993) [1903]. 'I sit with Shakespeare,' wrote du Bois, 'and he winces not' (ibid.: 88). Du Bois' evocation of the worlds of Black Folk sees a duality within, between being an American and being a Negro, 'two souls … two unreconciled strivings' (ibid.: 9), yet both equally part of the modern world. This duality can only properly be understood through the construction of a world history in which the African has a presence. It was this project that du Bois developed further in *The Negro* (1915) and *Black Folk: Then and Now* (1939). Here he constructed a more Afro-centric historical sociology, though one that somehow avoided much of the romanticism and partisanship that has sometimes rendered later histories of this kind poor history as well as re-assertions of an essentialized identity (Howe 1998). Emphasis was placed both on the physical harshness of the African environment and upon African political and cultural achievements prior to the dislocations of the slave trade, as well as the African contribution to modern America.

Gilroy's strategy for overcoming global histories organized around notions of essentialized differences between peoples represents an auspicious moment for the development of a global historical sociology. It offers one way of moving beyond the rather programmatic manifestoes of post-colonial theory into the terrain of empirically plausible analysis exploring historical data. Any such enterprise must, however, deal with a number of critical objections that may be levelled at any such undertaking.

The first is the problem of teleology, in particular the idea that globalization is somehow the underlying purpose of history. This assumes that history somehow contains an inner developmental logic leading inevitably from past origins towards the globalized present, and some kind of future globalized end-state. The major difficulties here are, first, that philosophical ideas of historical necessity are difficult to confront with evidence and, secondly, that they presuppose a given logic to history that is inexorable whether in the face of contingency or human intervention. In the particular case of globalization, there is no way of knowing whether or how far the set of processes will develop, be reversible, or be replaced by alternative trends.

The second challenge is the problematic notion of civilization. From a discursive viewpoint, the term 'civilization' has often been tied up with a triumphalist Western sense of superiority over the rest of the globe. This may take several forms, whether the overtly racial sense of superiority widespread in the 19th and 20th centuries, or the rational-technological sense of superiority widespread among those who have sought to promote Third World development in the last 50 years. For many, these associations mark out the language of civilization as untenable. The difficulty, nonetheless in disposing with the idea of civilization altogether, is that it robs our conceptual vocabulary of a key term useful in encapsulating large influential entities that extend over political boundaries and which contribute to the repertoire of human social and cultural practices, whether through religion, science and technology, military or economic organization, or some other salient legacy. Robbed of the term 'civilization', we are left with geographical Continents, indeterminate regions, or spheres of influence. This may suggest why the term continues in use, and why it may prove valuable to retain, provided ethno-centric teleological baggage can be identified and controlled for.

The third, following the work of Tilly (1984), is the problem of what might be called 'marginal' or 'trivial' interconnection. This may arise when the significance of evidence of interconnection is blown out of proportion. When the discovery of an artefact made in one place is found in another far away, or where a traveller from one continent visits another, there is perhaps a temptation to exaggerate the scale, intensity and impact of interconnection. One is then on a slippery slope in which 'we will most likely discover.... The world has always formed a single system' (ibid.: 62).

One way of dealing with this problem is to set higher thresholds of significance for forms of interconnection, such as proportion of population affected. An example of this may be found in the work of economic historians looking at the functioning of markets across borders. While long-distance trade through markets has been around for millennia, a stronger test of market interconnection is convergence in the price of commodities across space and time. The more integrated the world market, the more prices for the same goods in different markets will converge. For many commodities, this has only really occurred in the last 150 years (O'Rourke and Williamson 1999) and has depended, amongst other things, on transportation improvement. In this example, interconnection has only recently become of a sufficient intensity to also mean inter-dependence. Tests of interconnection may typically be less onerous than tests of inter-dependence.

A similar problem of potential vagueness and possible triviality arises if we add into the analysis the third definitional layer in account of globalization, namely conceptions of the world as a single place. What would count here as an example of this kind of orientation? The kinds of empirical phenomena that have often been linked to this kind of global consciousness are typically religious or cosmopolitan world-views (Robertson 1992, 1995). The minimal analytical requirement seems to be (a) that global imagining means reaching beyond the local and particular to some larger trans-local orientation, and (b) that orienta-tions of this kind are salient to human actors, rather than merely attrib-uted to them. However, just as forms of global inter-dependence are less well understood than global interconnection, so forms of global imagining have, until very recently, been even less well studied than the other two.

Wills (2001), in his 'global history' of the year 1688, points out that as late as the end of the 17th century, global awareness was comparatively limited. A few European scholars, missionaries, and travellers had perhaps the widest knowledge of literate sources of evidence though large components of the world continents had as yet to be explored and colonized by Europeans. The Islamic world stretching from 'Beijing and Mindanao to the Danube and the Niger' (ibid.: 3) was trans-continental in scope but lacked extension to the Americas. The Chinese emperor, according to Wills, had some knowledge of Europeans on the edge of the Chinese world, but far less of Africa and the Americas. China had of course banned maritime trade two decades before Wills' cut-off point, and had previously traded directly as far afield as the coast of East Africa (van de Ven 2002). Similarly West Africa, at the beginning of the 17th century, was by no means cut off from developments elsewhere, mediated in part through the great trans-Saharan caravan trails. Yet, as Davidson (1998: 131) points out, little or nothing was known of the world outside. These considerations should alert us to the comparatively recent preconditions for forms of global imagining based on some kind of global knowledge rather than religious metaphysics.

Global imagining is, of course, simultaneously a matter of global representation. Terrestrial globes were known in the ancient world, but it was only in 17th and 18th centuries with European expansion that more accurate mapping of the world developed. In the hundred years or so after 1688, enormous changes were evident in the capacity of Europeans to imagine the wider world. Exploration and Empire encouraged a 'cartographic consciousness' (Ballantyne 2002: 121). Thus 'the new world of knowledge was made available through maps, books, libraries, and collections of curiosities' (ibid.). These became available not simply to individual scholars but also to new middle-class reading publics via the diffusion of the printing press.

Towards a history of globalization

Globalization in World History (Hopkins 2002a) provides a tentative yet very plausible historical typology of globalization over the very long term. The regional specialists on Asia, Africa, Europe, and the Americas who have put together this work do not necessarily agree on all the essentials of this typology. Nonetheless, the arguments within the book do offer a relatively cohesive organizing framework that has helped move the debate forward.

This features a fourfold typology of types of globalization. Figure 1 combines a brief outline of this typology, to which I have added some examples of actors involved in activities that had a globalizing thrust.

That part of the typology on the left-hand side, derived from Hopkins (2002a), is not organized around a single prime mover responsible for globalization, such as trade, technology, or an expansive drive to control resources. Nor does it assume that all phenomena across history can be arranged neatly in a set of boxes. The typology is rather suggestive of the range of cross-border processes and ways of imagining the world across time and space, organized into broad patterns with distinct features of their own. These patterns typically combine different economic, political, cultural, and technological characteristics. The history of globalization cannot, if one takes this view, be summed up in a single formula, such as the progressive expansion of capital accumulation or the predominance of free trade. It also follows that the question 'where did globalization begin?' depends on the type of globalization in question.

In the case of the first *archaic* form of globalization, salient institutions include trading diaspora, empires, and religious movements able to generate significant forms of interconnection, and inter-dependence. Long-distance traders like the Venetian Marco Polo, mobile warriors like Genghis Khan, and cross-border proselytizers like Saint Paul symbolize the mini-globalizations of this phase. Bayly (2002: 50–57) also draws attention to what might be termed archaic forms of global imagining in ideals of cosmic kinship and cosmic religion during this phase. Emperors from within the Manchu, Mughal and Ottoman

Archaic	Pre-dates industrialization and nation-state	Associated with empires, cities and trading diaspora
	Asian and African, as much as Europe	Actors involved include kings, warriors, priests, and traders
Proto	Emerges between c.1600 and 1800, with state reconfiguration and commercial expansion	Multi-centred sources of indigenous change, including improved management of seaborne commerce
	Europe, Asia, and parts of Africa	Actors include explorers, slave traders, merchants, and pilgrims
Modern	Conventional Western-centred phase, post-1800, associated with industrialization and the rise of the nation-state	Involved both free trade and imperial expansion, and improved manufacturing military and communications technology
	Increased involvement of non-Western nations in latter phase	Domestication of earlier forms of cosmopolitanism
	Emergence of global civil society	Actors involved include imperial colonizers, manufacturers, scientists, activists from non-government organizations
Post-colonial	Post-1950 emergence of a de-colonized world, with new types of supra-territorial organization and regional integration	Post-imperial revival of cosmopolitanism
	Continuing non-European sources of globalization, including Islam, as well as syncretic inter-cultural fusions like jazz and world music.	Actors involved include business & political elites, migrants and asylum seekers, global civil servants radical social movement activists, virtual networks around the Internet.

Figure 1   Four historical types of globalization

Source: Derived in part from Hopkins (2002a).

worlds may have from time to time seen themselves as world conquerors, but they also cherished men from afar, drew up inventories of universal knowledge, and encouraged forms of luxury consumption reliant on long-distance trade (ibid.: 51).

Such patterns are found across and between many parts of Asia, Africa, and Europe. A number of these ventures of course collapsed (e.g. the ancient Middle Eastern empires) or became more insular over time (e.g. China after 1500). In this sense, archaic globalization has an episodic or ruptured trajectory to it, rather than leading smoothly into more modern forms (ibid.: 49). This reflects in part the tendency of Empires to overreach their economic and fiscal sustainability. The slow pace of communication between major centers of power and authority also meant that inward withdrawal remained an option.

Their longer-term legacy was nonetheless significant for what came later. Braithwaite and Drahos (2000: 480) in their study of global regulation point to other legacies of this phase linking different regions through which organizational and technological innovations were diffused. Their list includes coins and paper money and complex bureaucracies that could carry commands over longdistances (China), monetary policy and commercial credit (China–Arab), the Arab system of number that enabled double-entry system of bookkeeping and bills of exchange (India–Arab–Islam), and maritime regulation (Rhodes, the Phoenicians, and Alexandria). Many later aspects of globalization can be said to have begun in this archaic phase, as urban communities of traders, scholars and administrators developed new forms of cross-border diffusion of knowledge, power, and faith.

The shift from *archaic* to *proto-globalization* between c. 1600 and 1800 involves a 'developing symbiosis between emerging state systems and growing cosmopolitanism' (Hopkins 2002b: 24) within a historical epoch that predates the more familiar emphasis on industrialization within nation-states. Beginning with an epoch in which explorers and colonizers were leading agents of globalization, new institutional arrangements like the Atlantic plantation and slave system represented major forms of economic globalization. These linked commodity production, large labour forces, and chains of consumption (Davidson 1998: 187–205). The expanding mercantilist states of Europe, especially Britain, also consolidated cross-border power and constructed intensified webs of spatial inter-dependence during this phase.

Meanwhile the human actors, involved whether through intention or coercion, involved traders, scientists and colonizers, map-makers and translators, slavers and slaves, sea captains and their crews, and those seeking religious freedom in another land, all of whose numbers tend to increase as a result of processes of outward-expansion and improvements to seaborne communication. Very diverse forms of human agency were involved here. A case study of colonial expansion and the diffusion of knowledge provided by Richard Grove (1995) in his study 'Green Imperialism' is both fascinating in itself and a warning against stereotyping global relationships in this period as the simple expansion of Western dominance.

Grove examines the flows of botanical and medical knowledge arising from patterns of exploration, trade, and conquest by Portuguese, Dutch, French, and British from the late 15th century onwards, with particular reference to engagement with India and traditions of Persian and Arab knowledge diffused there. A significant global actor, in this context, was the 16th-century Portuguese physician Garcia da Orta, resident in the Indian region of Goa. Orta compiled the first major European book on Asian botany published in 1563. Through the patronage of a local ruler, he accumulated a knowledge of Muslim and Hindu ethno-botanical knowledge. This not only fed into the recon-struction of existing European botanical classification systems on Indian lines, but assisted in the transfer of ideas of the botanical garden together with plants and drugs from the East to the West. Orta's work thereby prefigured interactions in succeeding centuries, such as the role played by European physicians to Indian potentates in diffusing indigenous technical knowledge to Europe. There is also a line of continuity here to the later development of botanical gardens in Leiden and later in Kew, and to the work of better-known actors like Joseph Banks. The most striking discontinuity, nonetheless, according to Grove, is that global networks of this kind became increasingly dominated by Europeans as colonial power became consolidated.

Previous archaic forms outside Europe were often savagely chal-lenged, but by no means obliterated during the traumatic impact of colonization that led to the incorporation of South and Central America and parts of Africa and Asia into Empires with global reach. Asian and African state consolidation and mercantile expansion also continued. In India, China, and parts of Southeast Asia, state-building between 1600 and 1800 was stimulated by long-distance trade and by improved military technologies of Asian as much as European origin. Bennison (2002: 80–81), in particular, points out that the 17th and 18th centuries saw an expansion of Muslim trade, cultural influence, and political authority in Africa, the Indian Ocean, and Indonesia. Such developments often included the same trends to 'plunder, colonize and civilize' as may be found in European expansion.

Through such processes, Islam as a universalizing religious movement 'incorporated large sections of the globe into a system of shared values and cultural practices, which represented a very dynamic form of archaism' (92). This proved robust through post-archaic forms of Western globalization both before and after 1800, serving both as a source of cultural solidarity and as a basis for political legitimacy for both Islamic traditionalists and modernizers. Islam has retained this role even in contemporary post-colonial setting as a continuing aspect of political and cultural globalization.

Hopkins' emphasis on cosmopolitanism during the phase of proto-globalization refers to the ways of seeing and acting that are outward-looking as yet not strongly nationalistic, a process associated far more with the 19th century. He is here reminding us of the dangers of reading nationalism too readily back in history. While national affiliations and pride are to be found in the 17th and 18th centuries, they had not as yet crowded out, or become incompatible with more outward-looking affiliations to humankind as a whole. Cosmopolitan humanism perhaps saw a heyday in the 18th century where ideas of reason and science attracted scholars and statesmen, explorers, and colonizers.

While West and East both saw expansion during the proto-phase, by the mid-18th century the capitalist economy in Europe and North America was beginning to pull ahead of Indian, Chinese, and Arab (primarily mercantile) capitalism. Capital, labour, and, to an increasing extent, land too were organized as commodities, capital accumulation and economic productivity were increasing, and new middle-class consumer markets were helping to fuel global expansion.

It is only with the third type of globalization – the *modern* – that attention shifts to institutions and the time period after 1800 that sociologists typically associate with globalization as a Western project. We are talking in other words of the European and North American global expansion and world dominance of the 19th and 20th centuries. Within this phase, the emphasis is very much on the combination of qualitative and quantitative changes in cross-border activity, inter-dependence, and global imagining. The commercial, political, and cultural developments of the *proto* phase were now extended and transformed by Western nation-states.

This involved shifts from state mercantilism to global free trade, and changes in production and communications technology (ibid.: 28). Transportation improvements, to take only one element in the picture, both increased the speed and reduced the costs of transactions, whether for goods or people. From the point of view of global domination, free trade and Imperialism could and did go hand in hand (even if ideological tensions between liberal cosmopolitans and imperialist globalizers were real and widespread). Both required strong nation-states to enforce and/or institutionalize their functioning. They also stimulated expansion in the range and numbers of global actors including entrepreneurs and colonial administrators, engineers and doctors, missionaries and explorers, anthropologists and linguists to participate in globalizing projects. This apparatus incorporated many members of subaltern colonized groups, especially the educated, primarily in lower to middle levels of administration (Anderson 1992).

A seeming paradox at the heart of the *modern* form of globalization is the centrality of the nation-state. This may seem puzzling from an early 21st-century viewpoint, where much debate has taken place around the idea that globalization is undermining the nation-state. What is seen in the 19th and 20th centuries is what might be called the global diffusion of the nation-state as a social institution. The ideal here is the development of territorial control, legal and administrative coherence and predictability, and the integration of a people into relatively stable forms of political culture. The underlying cultural norm here is that each people should have their own state.

The paradox underlying this process is that globalization is both a cause and a consequence of nation-state development. Global opportunities seized through free trade or Imperial conquest, and models of state organization, borrowed or adapted from other countries or regions, helped certain nation-states to consolidate and expand, reinforcing rather than undermining nation-states. Greater levels of state power and capacity in areas like revenue raising and social pacification more easily enabled nations to take on outward-looking expansive global projects in trade, conquest, and the diffusion of Western 'civilization'.

Similar paradoxes are evident outside Europe. On the one hand, global Imperialism and colonization inhibited local state formation. Yet on the other, anti-Imperialist nationalism and post-colonial state-formation depended to a significant extent upon Western notions of state-building and national independence, as well as indigenous institutions and practices that pre-dated the Western presence (Appiah 1998). Print-capitalism developed first in the West also helped in the global diffusion of local vernacular languages and the capacity to imagine the post-colonial nation (Anderson 1983). Meanwhile Western educated lawyers, priests, and other professionals from Africa and Asia analysed and researched national and regional traditions (Hayford 1903, Sarbah 1906, Agbebi 1911, Seal 1994 [1903]). These very often fed into political and cultural mobilization aimed at independence.

A final dimension to the *modern* phase is the development of both inter-national and trans-national organizations, governmental and non-governmental, and the growth of a globally oriented set of professionals, technical specialists, and officials. These populated new organizations like the International Telegraphic Union and World Meteorological Organisation, the International Committee of the Red Cross, attended inter-national scientific and professional conferences, and became officials of the League of Nations (1919) and the United Nations (1945). Many of these bodies were constructed by sets of nation-states to resolve common issues of world security and an expanding agenda of social and economic issues that could not apparently be resolved by nations acting alone. The modern global paradox is, nonetheless, to be found on the trans-national level too, namely that institutions set up by nation-states develop trans-national characteristics. One aspect of this is the development of a trans-national officialdom or bureaucracy.

Dag Hammarskjold, UN Secretary-General, in an important speech in the early 1960s, emphasized the significance of what he called 'the international civil servant' (Hammarskjold 1962: 330–332). This new type of actor was distinct from the conventional diplomat. International civil servants represented no particular country, even though serving bodies composed of such representatives. In the 40 years or so, since this was said, the numbers and autonomy of actors of this kind have expanded markedly. The secretariats of bodies like the International Labour Organization, the World Health Organization, and the International Atomic Energy Agency have more than a thousand staff each. Size, as Braithwaite and Drahos (2000) point out, does not, however, necessarily equate to power. The WTO, for example, has a relatively lean secretariat of around 200 professionals (ibid.: 196), yet has far more regulatory power than the United Nations Conference on Trade and Development (UNCTAD) whose secretariat is over five times larger (ibid.: 486). Whereas UNCTAD was set up very much as a vehicle for the views of developing countries and the Soviet bloc in the 1970s, the WTO, successor to the GATT, is dominated by the Quad (ibid.: Ch. 10), involving the US, EU, Japan, and the Cairns group of agricultural exporting nations.

Taken together the development of post-colonial states and trans-national organizations and officialdom represent two processes which lead us beyond the modern towards the most elusive and possibly the most controversial of the forms of globalization developed by Hopkins and his colleagues. And they are paralleled by a continuing expansion of both non-government organizations and more informal networks within civil society, that is outside the direct orbits of states. We consider these developments in much more depth in Chapter 6.

Whereas many treat globalization from around 1800 onwards as a single phase of Western market–led development, Hopkins conjectures that another shift to a *post-colonial* globalization occurred during the second half of the 20th century. Although he has greater discomfort with this label than the other three, the contrast being drawn here is between a phase of globalization organized from within leading industrial nation-states, and one based increasingly on 'new types of supra-territorial organization... new forms of regional integration' (ibid.: 7) and re-emergent 'supra-national and infra-national affiliations' (Hopkins 2002b: 25). This embraces both institutions such as the WB and the EU, and cultural processes such as growing trans-national networks among diasporic populations like the Chinese and the Indians, and the development of innovative outward-looking currents within Buddhism and Islam (Bennison 2002). Broader cultural aspects of globalization are significant here, some involved with computer-mediated interaction through the Internet, but many related to exposure to a diversity of cultural influences through popular culture and the global media. While many discern cultural Imperialism at the heart of this, anthropological work also stresses inter-cultural fusions, including notions such as hybridization and creolization (for further discussion see Chapter 5).

In discussing this fourth contemporary phase of globalization, it is possible to bring together the long-run historical analysis of globalization with the far more widespread view that there has been a new and distinct change in global arrangements over the last few decades. A number of scholars have attempted to encapsulate this change, ranging from Urry's (2000) emphasis on a radically new pattern of mobilities and fluidities, and Castells' (1996) emphasis on network society, to Beck's (2000) emphasis on globalization as a new cosmopolitan mode of modernity. Compared with these emphases on social and cultural dimensions of change, use of the term 'post-colonial' suggests a more political emphasis that is not easy to connect with such wider debates in any straightforward way.

From the viewpoint of the history of relations between Western and non-Western worlds, emphasis on the *post-colonial* makes a good deal of sense. Whereas *modern* forms of globalization in the third phase rested largely on the domination of the West, subsequent processes of de-colonization constitute a new phase in global history. Representatives of post-colonial states and post-colonial intellectuals became more prominent global actors, but so did bankers, development economists, and military experts based in Western countries and Western-dominated institutions like the WB, active in re-shaping the post-colonial order.

It is therefore unclear how far the notion of post-colonial carries any strong substantive content of its own, in terms of a new pattern of relations between the West and the rest. How far, for example, have formally independent peoples and nations been able to take new initiatives independent of the richer and more powerful Western nations, or forge new linkages across the previous colonial divide with the former colonial powers? Such questions are not pursued very far by Hopkins and his associates, though Harper (2002: 141) notes the continuing sense of a North–South divide, manifest in occasions such as the South Summit in Havana in April 2000. Here leaders such as Mahathir of Malaysia and Castro, the Cuban host, reiterated the continuing significance of fundamental inequalities of power within the global arena, articulating a typically first-wave account of globalization as Western economic dominance, corrosive of national sovereignty while tending towards cultural homogenization.

A major line of objection to the idea of *post-colonial* globalization is the recent revival of Imperialism. Following Huntington's (1996) notion of a contemporary 'clash of civilisations' between the West and the emerging Islamic–Confucian axis, it is by no means clear that the US global policy has abandoned the imperial ambitions to command and control the global order characteristic of European thinking in the 19th century. Rather the idea of an 'evil empire' or 'axis of evil' has resurfaced as a negative trend requiring a positive coalition of 'willing' opponents of evil. This quasi-Imperialist coalition is the vehicle whereby the US and her allies aspire to wage global war against 'terrorism', with or without approval of the raft of trans-national bodies or the EU. This in turn involves forms of human agency associated with warriors, technologists of modern warfare, and engineers of post-conflict reconstruction, as well as investigate global journalists and human rights activists. At the time of writing, with the US and her allies occupying Iraq it is unclear whether this proposed venture is the last gasp of *modern* globalization (in Hopkins' terms) or its revival. If the latter, then the theory of a fourth phase of globalization beyond the modern is put in doubt.

Another line of argument that projects us back to realpolitik is the idea of 'regressive globalization' advanced by Shaw (2003) and further elaborated by Kaldor *et al.* (2003). This is less concerned with changes in the anchorage of global institutions that foster trans-national processes, and more interested in what might be called the realpolitik of the global order. For Shaw, regressive globalization carries a normative connotation, standing as a contrast with 'progressive globalization'. The more negative connotation is associated with US policy post-9/11. Here 'the war on terror' is seen as an emergent axis of global authoritarian power 'linking Washington with Moscow, Beijing, Islamabad, and New Delhi' (Shaw 2003: 36). This is significant for Shaw because it severs the previous connections between global political elites and civil movements oriented to global human rights and inter-national law. If regressive globalization is the leading trend, then it is greater global authoritarianism that beckons. What is also significant in this scenario is that former colonies appear on either side of the conflict, both within the US-led coalition and among its opponents.

Kaldor *et al.* (2003) take the argument in a more generic direction, seeing regressive globalization as a way in which the more powerful interests, be they 'individuals, firms, businesses, or governments', use globalization when it suits their interests but not when it does not. This perspective is also corrosive of the idea of an emerging post-colonial and increasingly trans-national globalization. It is also a response to the rapidly evolving contemporary world situation, the direction of which is hard to determine with any confidence.

A further dimension to contemporary globalization processes is the emergence of global civil society. This term has no precise meaning, but has risen to prominence as a way of thinking about social and political activities that are somehow beyond both top-down state initiatives, and market-based transactions. It embraces, as we shall discuss in more depth in Chapter 6, a range of trans-national social movements like Amnesty International and Friends of the Earth, as well as many more informal networks. These extend from the more political-driven activists, through a range of social and cultural activities and pursuits in fields such as music, religion, and contexts such as global migration and multi-cultural settlement patterns. Some of these activities have been seen either as 'globalization from below' or as an alternative to elite globalization.

We now widen the analysis of recent patterns of global history to suggest that de-globalizing reversals may be as significant a matter for debate as depiction of the latest phases of global development.

Globalization and de-globalization in recent world history

During the last 10 years, a number of accounts of the recent history of globalization have appeared. Robertson's multi-dimensional listing of global developments was in many ways pioneering (1992: 58–90), especially for its inclusion of examples of global imagining which treat the world as a single space. Here are included both world religions and ideologies, as well as what might be called 'global moments', such as the conferences on slavery or religion, world exhibitions, prizes (e.g. Nobel), and contests (e.g. the modern Olympics), as well as diplomatic moments around the formation of the League of Nations or United Nations. Few of these can be regarded as 'extra-national', even if they invoked new senses of a world community and global public sphere. Most involved the waving of nations flags, literally or metaphorically, whether the forms of nationalism involved are intense or banal (Billig 1995).

Narrower but analytically more focused work has been done primarily by economic historians interested in economic globalization. O' Rourke and Williamson (2002), for example, focus solely on inter-national commodity trade, using this as a paradigmatic test for global integration. On the basis of this measure they identify a watershed in the history of globalization in the 19th century when price convergence for commodities suddenly became a dramatic reality. This signifies a wider transformation in the way goods are produced (highly differentiated manufacturing using a series of new technologies), resources are allocated, and demands for new skills increase. Directed at longer-run theories of an earlier watershed around 1500, this essay is interesting for its more modern periodization of a global 'big bang'.

This argument may be linked with the earlier discussion of social differentiation and the disembedding effects of globalization. The account of *archaic*, and *proto* phases of globalization by Hopkins *et al.*, indicates that disembedding is not an entirely modern phenomena dependent on the 18th-century industrial revolution in the West. Archaic trade, conquest, and religious confrontation could equally challenge existing social organizations through the impact of cross-border influences and the questioning of old practices and affiliations, even if the new ones often re-integrated with 'tradition'. In the sphere of mercantile law, for example, historic problems of piracy or disputes between parties to long-distance trading succeeded in creating a shared, rational, and trans-contextual regulatory framework in Roman times (Braithwaite and Drahos 2000: 418–419).

It is, nonetheless, arguable that the global economic big bang of O'Rourke and Williamson was of an extremely radical kind in relation to both interconnectedness and inter-dependence. Henceforth, international price competition has been a profound force affecting not only production and consumption, capital and labour, but also economic policy and ideals of sovereignty. Since this time, price competition has been capable of enriching mobile factors of production and impoverishing those unable to shift industries or geographic location. Occupations sensitive to world market prices have been most vulnerable to depression, creating crises on occasion for both industrial workers and farmers, unless protective measures could be erected. This new milieu has encouraged mobility of capital and labour, creating further pressure on public policy options available to national Governments. The resultant challenges have included demands to both restrict immigration from outside and limit the flight of capital to external locations. Economic globalization has in short created conditions under which anti-global or de-globalizing forces have been engendered.

This analysis suggests that more is needed than a typology of the most recent phases of globalization. James (2001) has observed that recent history has been punctuated by alternating cycles of global and anti-global development. While the mid-19th century saw the development of free trade and high levels of global migration of capital and labour, even before 1914 certain counter-trends were evident. These included economic protection of key industries, immigration restriction, and the origins of many national central banks to manage and, where possible, control fluctuations and instabilities in economic activity. Symbols of this period included the more systematic use of passports to control borders, and the development of country of origin branding to identify preferred home-produced goods. Somewhat paradoxically, these were introduced in a period usually associated with openness and cosmopolitanism.

As is very well known, trends towards protection and nationalism (economic and political) were magnified in the inter-war period as the global economy moved into crisis, and nation-states generally became more introverted. These may be interpreted as forms of re-embedding of economic activity or ideology into nationally focused endeavours. Though paradoxically again, many of the origins of the renewed post-war development of globalization were incubated at this time, whether through consolidation of multi-national companies or the institutional-ization of initiatives that led to the subsequent foundation of bodies like the IMF (Pauly 1996) or UNESCO (Renouliet 1999).

This was also the period in which Communist Internationalism sought to revive on a global basis after the debacle of 1914 when the largely European Socialist International failed to prevent war. This variety of inter-war developments have perhaps been overshadowed by the failure of the League of Nations to guarantee inter-national security and the subsequent Second World War. They may, nonetheless, be indicative of a diverse set of attempts to provide alternative sources of re-embedding or re-integration of social arrangements on some kind of inter-national or extra-national basis.

A similar set of alternating phases may also be detected in the period since 1945. First comes the renewed expansion of the global economy, the creation of a far wider set of inter-national and supra-national organizations, and new forms of global imaginings around the environment and human rights. Such organizations and global world-views did not, however, succeed in embedding the rampant global economy within a stable or legitimate set of globally acceptable rules. Regulatory bodies such as the IMF had not been designed to prevent national crises of indebtedness and capital flight, nor have they seemed able to find ways of alleviating crisis that are politically acceptable to the populations of the countries affected (Stiglitz 2001). Meanwhile, UN organizations are generally weaker and perhaps hard for individuals to feel adherence to. The net effect has been the so-called anti-global backlash with which this study commenced.

This argument has several implications. One is a crisis of global legitimacy that will be explored later in the chapter on globalization and its discontents. Whether or not economic globalization enhances economic welfare in aggregate or in most though not all locations, many do not believe the process is fair or accountable to any kind of transparent political or moral regulation. However, effectively or ineffectively, many global economic activities are regulated (for the complexity of this issue in areas such as food safety or environmental impact, see Braithwaite and Drahos 2000), it is widely believed that they are either unregulated or that regulatory bodies have been captured by venal corporations. These perceptions will not be easily changed nor are they easily addressed through academic research.

But nor are they necessarily anti-global. Protest is more diverse, and sometimes more ambivalent than this, inasmuch as alternative models exist for the re-embedding or re-integration of global economic practices within processes of social accountability. Such models include new forms of cosmopolitanism, or glocalization, as much as older visions of nationalism or local community-centredness.

Conclusion

Historical perspectives on globalization are central if we are to understand its many functions, dynamics, and limits. They help to identify the multiple processes involved and the different types of human agents who have participated, often unwittingly, in the construction of globalization. Long-term perspectives also help us to see patterns of social change in the present in a more informed way. Globalization is not essentially a Western project, even though contemporary structures of power and influence are largely concentrated in what are conventionally referred to as Western hands. This dominance may already be eroding with the rise of East and Southeast Asia, and parts of Latin America. But insofar as this proves to be the case, should this be seen as further proof of global Westernization as diffused to the world beyond, or something more complex?

One major difficulty raised in this chapter is unease with the conceptual language within which we understand relations between different peoples and regions of the world. Dichotomous concepts of the West and the rest derive historically first from attempts to mark a civilizational boundary between the classical world of ancient Greece and Asia (Said 1991: 56–58), European Christendom and Islam (Delanty 1995) and then, in the 19th century, from racial senses of the superiority of white races over others. Latterly, the distinction has been constructed in terms of economic and political distinctions between market-economies and democracies on the one hand, and command economies and authoritarian polities on the other. The problem with such distinctions is not that they have no empirical purchase, but rather that they discourage any exploration of commonalities or cross-currents. In addition they tended to stereotype forms of interaction either as a one-way process from more to less advanced or as domination by the powerful over the victim.

An alternative perspective, as we have seen, is provided by Gilroy. He emphasizes the importance of multiple inter-cultural encounters, conflicts, and forms of co-operation as a theme in global history. It is not merely that interaction goes from slave to master as well as the reverse, but also that the very entities that interact are not homogenous. Global migration, new information technology, and the impact of globalized cultural styles have created increasingly polyglot popula-tions. In addition earlier traditions and resources developed in dynamic pre-modern phases of globalization outside the West continue to have a longer-term salience, whether in the form of older legacies of state-building, technological innovation, or universal religious aspir-ation. In the case of technology, for example, the point here is not simply that parts of Asia have been net exporters of technological and organizational innovation for much of world history, but also that since the profound 'modern' impact of 'Western' industrialization over the last 150 years, they have continued to do so in areas like electronic products and forms of work organization.

So, taking all this into account, when exactly did globalization begin? The argument in this chapter is that there is no single answer to this question. Since globalization is a set of processes rather than unitary phenomena, the answer given depends very much on the particular type of process in question. If we see globalization primarily in terms of free trade and price convergence in commodity markets, then the answer centres on the19th century. But if the focus shifts to imaginings of the world as a single place, then the answers project backwards in time over millennia during which the world's great religions and cosmopolitan thinking emerged. Emphasis on technologies of global communication, meanwhile, provides a further set of answers, where greater emphasis is given to very recent late 20th-century changes including the Internet and digitalization of information.

A final twist to the argument is that aspects of globalization are reversible. To the extent that de-globalization is possible, we may say that globalization may be un-made, possibly to be re-made later. From this perspective answers to the question 'when did globalization begin?' cannot simply assume that a search for historical origins will be sufficient. Un-making and re-making also matter. Where re-making does take place this may project answers to the question into the present or very recent past. Examples of this include the intensified post-war development of both global regulatory institutions and reforming social movements. In the former case, the development of institutions like the WB and WTO may be seen as contributing to the re-making of the global economy, after de-globalizing tendencies associated with the economic nationalism of the inter-war period. Many reforming social movements dealing with human right and environmental sustainability, insofar as they think globally, do so in attempts to re-make globalization on a basis other than market freedom and corporate dominance. In these ways human agency continues to matter too, whether in making un-making or re-making, as we shall discuss in more depth in Chapters 6 and 7.

We now turn to the many competing attempts to understand the underlying logic or logics to processes of globalization. This discussion starts with the powerful notion of globalization as a unitary and systematic structure of social relationships, and moves on to explore why alternative more multi-dimensional and more flexible accounts of globalization have arisen, placing greater emphasis on human agency.

3

Global Patterning: Systems, Structures, Fields, Networks, Webs, and Flows

Metaphors abound in the study of globalization. Some of these have been transferred from broader areas of scientific enquiry such as structure, field, and network. Others, including webs and flows, have gained much of their current resonance from a more specific and intimate connection with global phenomena such as the Internet, or the intensified movement of people, products, and messages across space. Such metaphors attempt to encapsulate the patterned nature of global arrangements, varying according to a range of connotations. These include spatial forms, levels of causal determinacy, degrees of complexity, and issues of continuity and change.

Although world-system theory developed immediately prior to more recent discourses on globalization, it stands nonetheless as a major example of system theory applied to global processes of economic, political, and social life. System stands here as a metaphorical representation of strong patterns of causal determinacy. The emphasis is on a single system logic that generates and reproduces a hierarchical pattern of social relationships and institutional arrangements. For Wallerstein (1984, 1976) and Chase-Dunn (1989), the drive to capital accumulation, operating within increasingly global markets, creates and re-creates a singular global division of labour. Whereas world Empires of the past were centred on a single economy and polity, the world capitalist economy that emerged from the 16th century onwards (Wallerstein 1974) was structured in terms of a spatial hierarchy and multiple political centres. Global inequality is an intrinsic feature of the system both in a spatial sense and within countries. Within the world system as a whole, unequal exchange through the market is sustained through a core of metropolitan states and regions which dominate a periphery of underdeveloped and a semi-periphery of partially developed states and regions.

Economy, polity, and culture are structured according to the world-system logic, although cultural integration is not required for the system to function. For Wallerstein, 'the world-economy is a complex of cultures – in the sense of languages, religions and ideologies – but the complex is not haphazard' (1984: 14). This is because a strong world-view of domination ('Weltanschaung or imperium') is present, alongside cultures of resistance. Culture, for Wallerstein, arises from the development and tensions within the world system (1990a: 42–44). Two dominant examples in his view are universalism and racism/sexism. Universalism arises from the geographically expansive character of the system, serving either as a form of deception that the system operates for universal benefit or as an ideal that the weak think they can use against the strong. Racism/sexism, meanwhile, functions to justify hierarchies of dominance and control across different states and peoples.

Nonetheless, while inequality generates antisystemic sentiment (Wallerstein 1984: 130) and conflict, this has not so far fundamentally modified the characteristics of the system. Hence, while Wallerstein continued to perceive structural crisis in the world system throughout the last 30 years of the 20th century, this state of affairs appeared unrelieved by radical social change. Structures it seems continue to dominate antisystemic cultures.

Chase-Dunn's version of world-system theory retains an emphasis on structured patterns of relationships between economy and polity, but seeks a more nuanced and less 'totalising' account of its component parts. To think of world systems dominated by a single mode or production is to give undue weight to production. He thinks instead of 'modes of accumulation' defined as 'the deep structural logic of production, distribution, exchange and accumulation' (Chase-Dunn and Hall 1997). Such modes of accumulation are not features of whole systems or even whole societies, but may exist at different levels of the system. Kinship, or tributary-based modes of accumulation, for example, may co-exist with capitalist types. Such amendments to the Wallersteinian model are interesting, but once again a comparatively silent on the dynamics of human agency within world-system development and transformation.

World-system theory has undoubtedly changed much of the intellectual landscape around the study of globalization. Wallerstein, as noted in chapter 1, has done most to challenge the convention that endogenous analysis of politically bounded entities, such as Empires and nations, should be the fundamental unit of social analysis. The shift from a national to a world focus represents a major methodological advance in those types of modernization theory which assumed that developing countries simply needed to adopt Western institutions in order to achieve take-off into self-sustained growth, nation by nation. For world-system theory, by contrast, it is the capitalist world system which structures the economic and political life of nations, regions, industries, and households. The inter-national division of labour, and global markets are, nonetheless, multi-centred, operating through hierarchies of exchange and political power distributed across space. Economic power has been both partly dependent upon and efficacious for political power, while cultural arrangements are profoundly marked by global political economy. All of this is common ground for many global analysts. Yet there remain difficulties.

The main general problems with systems thinking in the social sciences are twofold. One is the over-deterministic approach to analysis centred on a single systems logic. This tends to downplay complexity, the possibility of multiple logics, the presence of counter-trends, and funda-mental elements of disorder and anarchy. Thus in world-system theory, there is typically only one system logic and one overarching dynamic. This leaves no significant space for loose coupling between institutional features of the system, and no serious consideration of the possibility of multiple globalizations based on different logics. Capital accumulation is taken to dominate everything else, leaving other globalizing logics such as the drive for human security, the search for a meaningful and valued way of life, or the construction of a just world order based on human rights and environmental sustainability, all subordinate to a single unitary logic. It also has little place for the possibility of fundamental disorder leading to a fragmented anarchy. It is assumed that systems may be crisis-prone, but will typically either transform themselves or re-structure to survive.

The unitary nature of world-system theory rests on claims about the predominant power and robustness of the capitalist system over economy, polity, and culture. It is, however, a huge leap from asserting the reality of this power to asserting its omnipotence. This leap simply by-passes the question of counter-vailing power or alternative logics without adequate empirical scrutiny.

The second problem with systems approaches is the downplaying of social action and analysis of the strategies and impact of social actors. Although social science has generated systems theories that incorporate action and actors, world-system theory is generally conducted without attention to the meanings that actors give to their actions or to normative aspects of global governance. Wallerstein does usefully distinguish between two senses of culture: the one associated with harmony, the other with difference. However, beyond that, culture is quickly subsumed into ideology (see especially Wallerstein 1990a: 31–55). Culture must function, according to this view, to deal with the exigencies and tensions of the unitary social reality generated by the world system. As ideology, it is involved with either deception and hypocrisy from above or the pathos of failed attempts at resistance from below. Capital is typically treated as an impersonal force, whose dynamics require no particular account to be given of the cultural world of its agents, or the normative framework of economic life. Resistance, meanwhile, is typically doomed by the dominance of the system. It does not go far enough to overthrow it (ibid.: 53).

This very profound functionalist devaluation of the cultural domain is likened by Boyne (1990) to the construction of a framework of analysis with no inner substance. World-system theory, in this respect, 'is like a house without glass in the windows, fuel in the fireplace, food in the cupboards, or beds upon which to sleep' (ibid.: 61). In more concrete terms, this devalues human accomplishment, failure, spiritual joy, and pain as epiphenomena. It is telling that Wallerstein (1990b), in his rejoinder to Boyne, asks why so many people wish to defend the concept of culture as an analytical category, and ventures the answer that this is because culture is seen as an expression of human freedom. This is essentially a moral-political interpretation, where culture functions solely as a value – may have some purchase in some empirical cases, but it denies the sociological premise that culture is an irreducible element of social action. Culture here is taken to embody meaning and knowledge through the human repertoire of material and symbolic resources that may be deployed in meaningful action.

World-system theory is perhaps the most inflexible example of a broader mode of analysis that might be termed 'structuralist'. What unites structuralist accounts of globalization is the focus on a clear ordered pattern of global relationships and institutions. This kind of thinking varies a good deal, however, on what it takes the driving forces and key institutional features of globalization to be. It also varies in terms of the types of linkages that are taken to be present within and between economic, political, and cultural phenomena. Some significant example of this broader structuralist approaches include work on the development of a global capitalist class (Sklair 2001), and the emergence of world cities as strategically focused concentrations of producer services (Sassen 1994).

Within the Marxist traditions, the work of Gramsci has helped to create space for a less deterministic and a more nuanced analysis of structural complexity, with greater interest shown in social agency in the making of global arrangements. Cox (1981, 1992) has argued for the importance of 'historical structures' within the global political economy that function as configurations of 'ideas, institutions and material forces'. Rival structures are possible, and the analysis of how structures emerge, conflict, and evolve involves empirical accounts of human agency. Collective action appears in this kind of analysis in the first place through the metaphor of organization. Organized interests enter the analysis, whether class-based, inter-governmental, or non-governmental in form. This creates space for the analysis of institutional patterns. One leading example of this is the argument that neo-liberal institutions such as the IMF and WB provide political hegemony to complement the economic hegemony of global corporations (Cox 1987, Gill 1990, 1992).

Another example of the openness of some structural arguments to empirical complexity and human agency is the debate over the existence and dynamics of a global capitalist class. Among first-wave contributors to the analysis of globalization, Hymer (1979) had argued that an inter-national capitalist class was emerging, whose interests lay in the world system as a whole not particular nation-states. This proposition was not, however, well grounded in empirical evidence, and it has taken another 20 years for this to emerge (e.g. Sklair 2001, Carroll and Fennema 2002, Carroll and Carson 2003), alongside further theoretical elaboration.

Overbeek (2000) has argued that while mechanisms of global trade and investment provide the structural basis for such a class to emerge, what was also required was strategic vision. In this way the role of human agency in the making, criticism, and re-shaping of the global order is highlighted while structural forces and system imperatives are mentioned less. Similarly, Sklair's (2001: 1–2) study of trans-national class formation is founded on the proposition that 'globalization is driven by actors working through institutions they own and/or control'. The 'global system' is constituted through 'transnational practises' articulated through corporations and 'a globalizing elite of corporate executives' (6–7). Agency is important not simply in the sense that the trans-national capitalist class works 'consciously' to produce profit, but also because global capitalism can only sustain and reproduce itself if the mass of people are convinced that consumerism offers a meaningful way of life.

Using data from interviews with executives from 80 major global corporations, Sklair makes three important substantive points. First, corporate executives increasingly see their activities shifting from state-centred *global reach* to a more profoundly trans-national *global shift* (ibid.: 81ff.). The distinction here follows Dicken's (1998) attempt to differentiate between inter-nationalization and globalization. This trend is not complete, nor does global reach mean that nation-states and national jurisdictions have become unimportant. Second, global reach does not necessarily reproduce the top-down quasi-Imperialist forms of domination, in which local partners get the worst of the deal. Rather 'globalization creates new forms of class cleavages globally and within countries, regions, cities and local communities...' (75). The dynamic here is that it is more profitable to work with rather than against global allies, including emergent entrepreneurs, businesses, regulators and social movements, at regional or urban as much as national levels. Within this process, globalizing politicians and professionals as much as corporate executives operate in an increasingly trans-national manner, subsuming norms such as national competitiveness and national standard-setting into global norms such as world's best practice and benchmarking, under the stewardship of global corporate citizenship. This form of global activism from above also faces problems, challenge, and crises. For Sklair, these centre on the problem of global poverty in the midst of increased wealth, and the problem of long-run environmental sustain-ability (we return to these questions in Chapter 7).

As empirical debate over the existence of a global capitalist ruling class has developed, increasing use has been made of the ideas of network and community. Carroll and Fennema (2002), in a study of 176 corporations between 1976 and 1996, identify two interconnected layers of class activity. One is the development of a trans-national business community active on both a policy and an ideological front (further data on five elite policy-planning groups are provided in Carroll and Carson 2003). This is primarily trans-Atlantic in focus with little input from Japanese, Korean or Brazilian multi-nationals. The other is a more nationally focused cluster of networks around specific corporations. These are, however, constructed by looking at interlocking directorships and membership of organizations, which may tend to understate global linkages of a less formal kind. Whilst this debate continues, what we note for present purposes is the shift from structuralism to a more actor-focused approach.

Sassen's work on global cities, the development of global regulatory organizations, and immigration patterns is even more striking for its combination of structural themes with human agency, and serious engagement with the empirical. Her work on global cities set out from issues of decentralization and centralization with the world economy. New information technology has helped to make possible the de-centralization of certain forms of economic activity, such as the instantaneous transmissions of finance through multiple money markets or the relocation of production outside previous production centres. However, what is equally striking is the centralization of strategic global command centres in a set of global cities such as New York, London, Tokyo, Sao Paulo, Hong Kong, and Sydney. Whilst the concept of an inter-national division of labour generated interest in dispersed activities such as export-processing zones in developing countries or offshore banking centres, the centralization of strategic command functions represents a counter-trend, albeit one that embraces cities within both the developed and the developing worlds.

These observations are crucial for several reasons. First, such a centralized pattern of control over dispersed activities 'does not come about inevitably as part of a "world system"' (Sassen 1998: xxii). If we ask 'How does the "world economy" cohere as a system?', says Sassen, any systemic features cannot be assumed simply because of the large volume of transactions. Transactions require an institutional framework within which they are co-ordinated and in which risk is reduced. Amongst other things what is required is a set of inter-dependent specialized services, telecommunications, infrastructure, and industrial services. These are not wholly contained either in multi-national corporations or in states. But they are concentrated in cities, and in networks of control across space. Global cities, in short, are made by lawyers, entrepreneurs, IT professionals, bureaucrats, financiers, advertizers and politicians, rather than arising spontaneously from world-system imperatives. Second, within this new geography of power, space and spatial hierarchies still matter. Globalization has not obliterated geography, but it has created new hierarchies in which cities are key centres, operating horizontally across space, as much as vertically within nation-states (for further discussion of global cities, see Chapter 4).

Sassen's approach to global structures, like that of Sklair, has the merit of treating capital as a form of agency, bringing intention, strategy, institution-building, and problems of cultural meaning into the analysis. Whether or not Sklair exaggerates the extent of global shift, global system theory in his hands has moved a long way from a deterministic system dominated by functional imperatives to an action-centred system driven by human actors. The global economy is in this way a product of human endeavour which embraces the construction of trans-national organizations and social activities. The system is actively made and re-made rather than emerging through structural imperatives.

Even so the metaphor of structure and the analysis of formal organizations have their limits, as ways of bringing human agency back in. One of these is the very thin account offered of culture and cultural meaning, restricted in the main to economic culture.

Another is the excessively formal approach to social life and social interaction. Large-scale organization is clearly a vital part of the global institutional arena, but what of the less formalized and more fluid interactions at work in economic, political, and cultural domains. Alternative metaphors such as network and web have emerged to describe this kind of activity, which offer more scope to capture elements left out by examining formal organization.

In what follows, we shall explore two major alternatives to system thinking. The first more theoretical contribution is Roland Robertson's conception of the global field. The second more empirical input is the burgeoning literature on networks and webs.

The global field

The field metaphor has been used in social analysis to free thinking from excessively deterministic or structuralist perspectives. Social fields contain a range of entitites, the interaction between which produces complex sets of outcomes, rather than effects that can be read off from a knowledge of social structures (for an important sociological example see the work of Bourdieu 1993). Robertson's approach to globalization and his depiction of the global field operate very much in this manner. They are founded not on some strong sense of structure but on the idea of a 'global-human condition' in which different 'forms of life' interact with each other (Robertson 1992: 27). Consciousness and meaning are thus built into the foundations of the approach, rather than being responses to economic forces. This reflects Robertson's previous work on the sociology of religion and religious life, and also the influence of Talcott Parsons.

Parsons (1951), noted for some of the most abstract versions of social system theory ever devised, was nonetheless concerned to bring human action into his system. He also sought to produce a multi-dimensional account of social life which, put simply, included normative issues as well as economic ones (for more elaboration see Alexander 1984, Holton and Turner 1986). The values and rules embodied in social life were as important, perhaps more so, as economic and political considerations. Whether Parsons ever succeeded in bringing human agency back in, in any empirical sense, is most debatable. Robertson's approach, while it retains strong Parsonian echoes, has thus abandoned the system metaphor, while seeking out an action-based account of the patterns evident in the global field. This is composed of four elements:

1. Selves
2. National societies
3. The world system of societies and
4. Humankind.

These elements are for Robertson not structures but 'forms of life'. They interact with each other and also serve as reference points for the way human actors think about the world. Interestingly they are not subdivided into differentiated functions such as economic, political or cultural, but into forms of life with a potential for action, whether as individuals, states, or trans-national institutions such as world religions. Rather economic, political, and cultural activities are expressed through interactions between all four forms of life.

Robertson's global field has been justly criticized for underplaying economic processes and conventional political-economic accounts of globalization (Friedman 1994: 195–197). It has also been claimed that he has failed to explore whether culture could be successfully integrated into political-economic world-system theories. Whether or not this will prove to be possible is not at all clear. Meanwhile it is worth pointing out that Robertson's cultural approach was designed precisely to produce a more balanced account than that on offer among political economists in the early 1990s, bringing the cultural domain back in as a central rather than derivative feature of the global human condition (Robertson 1992: 29). What is perhaps even more important is the way this is done. The cultural domain is not treated as a unifying normative force or global culture in some kind of quasi-Parsonian manner. Rather cultural issues are played out in a complex manner through the interaction of the four component parts.

Individual selves, for example, inhabit forms of life in which nation, the world of societies and humankind are elements. Such orientations might play out in different forms of balance among individual orienta-tions. Put very simply these might range from nationalists who combine suspicions of the United Nations as a form of world government but equally remain members of the Catholic Church supporting its world mission. They might also include self-styled cosmopolitans working in an inter-national aid agency, but tuning in to the radio each week to catch up with local football scores from their home town, and Islamic migrants from the Middle East to Australia with dual nationality.

One of the core insights in Robertson's discussion is then that much that might be called global or local may better be regarded as a syncretic mix of global and local elements, creating glocal rather than global relationships. In other words, the global and the local interpenetrate rather than maintaining a distinct free-standing character.

The idea of a glocal level of social life is a key example of a more general trend which Robertson refers to as *relativization*. This involves the combination or interpenetration of what he sees as 'universal' and 'particular' aspects of social life. The core of this idea is that it is impossible to live and function without recourse to both universal and particular aspects of life and experience. Universalism, in the form of general world-views, allows us to place ourselves within the cosmos and within global society, stressing what is or should be common features shared by humankind. However, this is too abstract a way of living since social action is also profoundly enmeshed in the particularities of time and place within which individuals live, identities form, and social institutions emerge. The universal in short is typically relativized in terms of a particular context, and this is especially true under conditions of globalization where the universal and the particular come into closer and more intensified forms of interaction. Just as it is difficult for individuals to conceive of themselves without reference to a number of global, national, and local aspects of the global field, so it is difficult for institutions and world-views of humankind to function under conditions of globalization without similar forms of relativization.

The idea of relativization can be illustrated through several examples. The first involves interaction between national forms of citizenship and the more global notion of human rights. While human rights thinking grew in large measure from national sources of liberal-democratic citizenship such as the French Revolution or European movements for the equality of women, universalizing as it were the particular, so national jurisdictions have not necessarily proved able or willing to secure human rights. An obvious case of exclusion is that of refugees in camps outside their country of origin, but lacking citizenship rights in any other jurisdiction. Here the problem is that of getting particular jurisdictions to adhere to human rights norms, responding, as it were, to the challenge of particularizing the universal.

Another example, drawn from a key issue in the sociology of religion, is the so-called revival of 'fundamentalism' (ibid.: 168–170). In contrast to those who see in religious fundamentalism a return to 'local', 'indigenous', or 'authentic' spiritual traditions, Robertson, following Stauth and Abaza (1990), sees such practices arising within an increasingly globalized frame of reference in which inter-cultural exchange, conflict, and diffusion are crucial. Local knowledge in this sense has already been affected by global relationships, including those between the East and the West and, equally important, global perceptions construct the very perspectives within which apparently 'local' knowledge understands the world. One form of this is the very distinction between the East and the West, sustained not merely by Western notions of the Oriental 'Other', but by parallel Eastern notions of the 'Occidental' (Ahmed 1992). Each reacts to its Other, to the extent that any sense of the pure indigenous locality is culturally constructed rather than an empirical reality.

Behind Robertson discussion of global–local fusions, then, stands a more ambitious theory of social life as fusion of the universal and the particular. Social life is localized or particularized in time and space, but it is equally implicated in globalized or universalized discourses about the nature of the cosmos and humanity, embracing fundamental questions of meaning. This way of thinking has also opened up productive ways of thinking about the inter-relations between the global, the national, and the local levels of activity. Robertson, who may be seen as an early exemplar of third-wave thinking, thinks in terms of both trans-national and national elements within the global field. Trans-nationalization is not sweeping all before it (first wave), but neither the nation-state nor the system of states are the predominant component in the global field (second wave). Both are co-present. But he goes further than this, to argue that the two may fuse. This argument is pursued through the process of glocalization (see also Chapter 4).

Glocalization involves the interpenetration of global and local (defined in a broad sense to include sub-global forms of life) (Robertson 1992: 173–174, 1995). Many of his first formulations of the term were drawn from the Japanese context. In a business setting the idea of *dochaku* was transformed during the 1980s from its original meaning as 'living on ones own land' (1995: 28) to a broader sense global localization. This became a widespread marketing concept, where global production was tailored to niche of micromarkets, that is adapting global strategy to local conditions. Another example is drawn from a religious context of a syncretic combination of religious sources from within and beyond

Japan. A characteristic of Japanese religiosity, according to Robertson (1992: 85–96), is the borrowing of elements from different religions – notably Buddhism, whose influence came to Japan from the Asian mainland, and Shinto, the Japanese religion. Individuals may use both for different purposes rather than being either Buddhist or Shinto in affiliation. Syncretism in a more general sense has characterized the drive to industrial development combining imported technologies and management techniques with Japanese spirit.

A recent discussion of management challenges in Malaysia makes a similar point in relation to the perceived need to combine imported technical management practices aiming at combining efficiency with Islamic principles (Abdullah 1996). The result would be forms of management that allow an enterprise to be both globally competitive and sensitive to religious context. In some cases this may require what is somewhat alarmingly termed 'cultural surgery'. This may arise when rigidities arising from religious culture obstruct effective management. Making the glocal, it seems, may involve tensions such as those experienced in conflicts between 'modernizers' and 'traditionalists' in developing societies. For Robertson, however, these are likely to be seen more as conflicts between glocal strategies rather than between global and local strategies.

Robertson has done most to include conceptions of the world as a single space within contemporary definitions of the global. In this respect his key concepts are ontological, that is pertaining to human social being or, as he puts it, aspects of the human condition. Glocalization is so to speak our human fate, for while being profoundly local we cannot understand our fate without an increasingly and equally profound engagement with the global. We cannot, however, do this without relativizing general issues within a local context. This framework necessarily elevates culture and religion to a central role in the discussion of globalization.

From a theoretical viewpoint, it is important that Robertson be understood as dealing with ontological rather than epistemological issues. When he speaks of the universal and the particular, he does not mean to give the universal a higher epistemological status. Put another way, the universal does not provide a higher order of truth than the particular. Claims to universalism by world-empires, world religions, world economic discourses, or any other overarching social entity remain claims by particulars. His argument therefore lacks any philosophy of history, whereby the path to universalism is identified with the agency of a particular country, class, or scientific movement. The task is rather to trace more complex global–local relationships among individuals, national societies, the world system of states, and conceptions of the human condition. This non-teleological approach may be appealing in that it avoids any return to an evolutionary account of global history. There is, nonetheless, a huge empirical research programme to be followed through to assess its coherence and explanatory power (for further discussion see Chapter 4).

Robertson's work has been discussed at some length because he has made the most elaborated challenge to economic and political-economic approaches to globalization. While there is good reason to suppose that this normative-cultural approach is fruitful when applied to empirical analysis, most analysts place far more emphasis on economic, techno-logical, and cognitive aspects of globalization. And they do so in a manner that has left highly abstract theoretical schema behind. Robertson's work is therefore inadequate by itself to understand both the political economy of globalization, and the relationship between economic, political, and cultural aspects of globalization. It is also difficult to establish the limits of globalization in his approach, given his emphasis on global–local fusions rather than global–local oppositions. We return to the broader issue of inter-relations between global, national, and local intersections and conflicts in Chapter 5.

Analytical attention now moves on from the fruitful idea of global fields of interaction to the widespread practice of understanding global-ization through the metaphors of network, web, and flow.

Networks, webs, and flows in the study of globalization

Use of the network metaphor has received a major boost with the emergence of Manuel Castells theory of Network Society. For Castells (1996, 2001), globalization is not only characterized by mobility and fluidity, but has also depended on new possibilities for multi-centred activity based on new information technology. The network metaphor emerged in a context where new information technologies made possible new flexible and adaptive modes of managerial control, thereby challen-ging the more centralized command and control hierarchies characteristic of organization. 'Flows of capital, flows of information, flows of technol-ogy, flows of organizational interaction, flows of images, sounds, and symbols' are for Castells the defining feature of current arrangements. They are in one sense closely connected with structures being 'purposeful, repetitive, programmable sequences of exchange and interaction between physically disjointed positions held by social actors in the economic, political and symbolic structures of society' Castells (1996: 412). As such they represent the manifestation of dominant social processes, for flows are organized as part of a hierarchy. Castells identifies this as the space of flows, layered in three ways.

Borrowing metaphors from information technology, the first layer is a 'circuit of electronic impulses' (412) associated with microelectronics, telecommunications, computer processing, broadcasting systems, and high-speed transportation. These serve to co-ordinate dominant practices within a network. The second layer is composed of 'nodes and hubs' (413) such as global cities or networked workplaces within a firm. These are spatially dispersed but, nonetheless, hierarchically organized according to their relative weight within the network. The final layer involves the inter-personal networks of the managerial elites who are the dominant actors in the overall network. Network society thereby becomes a network of networks. In all of this, network is a metaphor that captures fluidity, multi-centredness, and complexity, but it does so without denying hierarchy or conflict within network arrangements.

Taken overall, the approach is less deterministic and its elements more loosely coupled than world-system theory. In attempting to connect social arrangements with spatial inequality, for example, Castells identifies a cleavage between the space of flows and the space of place. The former is dominated by cosmopolitan global elites, incorporated into the physical, virtual, and cultural world of flows. Theirs is the space of limousines, business class hotels, and air-conditioned offices. The latter space incorporates the life-world of those outside the elites, whose restricted mobility chances provide greater adhesion to local place and community. Bauman (1998), in similar vein, speaks of a dichotomy: 'globalization for some, localization for others'.

Whereas world-system theory assumed the homogenization of social actors, whether pro- or anti-global, into the ideological system logic of liberal individualism (Wallerstein 1990a), Castells sees polarization and alternative currents. These typically take the form of 'resistance identities' united in their opposition to the global order. Ethnic groups, or fundamentalist religious movements are two major examples.

Castells' substantive contribution is thus to loosen the deterministic grip by treating structure as a set of somewhat autonomous networks rather than a system. Yet the treatment remains at a high level of generality, with somewhat speculative gestures towards social action. This is because Castells retains a version of structuralism, albeit a looser one, in which the morphology of networks remains 'predominant over social action' (1996: 469). This in turn creates a weakening of civil society. This shrinks in significance as the logic [*sic!*] of power networks becomes disarticulated from 'the logic of association and representation in specific societies and cultures' (Castells 1996: 11). These propositions allude to the phenomena of contemporary life, but remain speculative and unconnected with any convincing body of empirical data. The complex and diverse mobilities of the contemporary world involved many non-elite segments (e.g. migration chains and diaspora), while social movements and NGOs for human rights and the environment have penetrated the agendas of the elite world and become part of prominent networks of regulation.

For Urry (2000), the contrast between the networked space of flows and the space of place is insufficient to come to terms with the patterns of contemporary globalization. Using metaphors from medicine, he thinks rather of global flows and fluids as well as global networks. His sociology of global fluids, which may involve cross-border flows of people, information, money, and images, is designed to emphasize 'heterogenous, uneven, and unpredictable' forms of mobility. These have no clear point of departure, have no necessary end-state or purpose, possess different kinds of viscosity, and operate through 'capillary-like relations of domination/subordination' (39). These have 'heterogenous, overlapping, and unintended effects' (ibid.). This approach appears at first sight to break with both system theory and with Castells' network logics.

Urry identifies several examples of global fluids, including the Internet, images of Western consumerism as perceived in Eastern Europe, and oppositional counter-cultures (ibid.: 38–45). As is well known, the Internet has evolved from its origins as a state-financed search for modes of intra-state communication sufficiently robust to survive nuclear attack. It has grown over time into a profoundly decentralized plurality of electronic connections. The Internet, which enables all online users to communicate with each other electronically through applications such as email and the World Wide Web, is not controlled by any single or dominant centre. Governments find it impossible to control the web content due to both the multiplicity of points of access and the de-territorialization of virtual systems. Compared with telephone or terrestrial television communications, the Internet is far harder to monitor and impossible to censor.

The fluidity of the Internet is both a function of its multi-centredness, its de-territorialization, and its relative plasticity as a mode of communication. Billions of messages are sent and received from millions of points of origin, while applications and usages are constantly shifting and evolving. Users can browse information and consume entertainment, or engage interactively with others via text, audio, and video, as individual citizens and consumers as well as in a workplace context. Forms of virtual interaction are emerging, such as chat-rooms, in which individuals can play with and simulate identities, becoming, as it were, 'digital nomads' (Makimoto and Manners 1997). Such forms are also constantly evolving, and a significant element of uncertainty exists as to both future technological development and its effects on individual world-views and behaviour. And yet it is not altogether clear that the Internet lacks systemic patterns.

For Castells, its characteristics are those of an open system able to sustain a myriad decentralizing uses and end-states. These may include those seeking or simulating a search for love or friendship, more mundane purchase of groceries or books, and also communication between employees of corporations and government, and forms of intra-professional communication. In this sense, the Internet is not simply an underground unofficial world of fluid encounters, but a vehicle for official and inter-organizational communication. Urry recognizes this, in drawing attention to Internet markets for commodities, mediated through organizations including social movements as well as profit-seeking businesses (2000: 44). Sassen (1999) has drawn attention, in more comprehensive fashion, to several types of limits on openness and de-centralization. One is the issue of privileged commercial access to the faster more reliable lanes of the information superhighway. Another is the growth of corporate Intranets protected by firewalls, which limit and filter rather than encouraging interconnectivity.

Emphasis of fluidity and flow is a very useful counter to the deterministic excesses of system theory, and provides a highly appropriate representation of major empirical trends in economic and cultural globalization. Such metaphors, drawn in part from medical representations of the body, do however invite further questions as to the nature of obstacles to flow, the development of residues and their location within the world of flows, and lastly the generation of, as it were, stocks of fluids available for circulation.

The collapse of Communist states in Eastern Europe, Urry's next example, is a very strong example of global flows penetrating borders and the structures of state control. Here the impact of Western consumerism on production-centred societies opened up the consumer imagination, perhaps even more so than the political imagination. Through media advertising, shopping trips to Western Europe, and smuggling, populations had already been sensitized to the desirability of an alternative social system, well before the velvet revolutions and demise of the Berlin wall at the end of the 1990s. And yet this period of extreme fluidity has been succeeded by a phase of institutional reconstruction with external intervention by global bodies such as the WB, and the drive to meet EU accession criteria and gain admission. There is then a danger that insistence on fluidity, even when mediated through networks, leads to an underestimation of the formal institutional context of life-world processes. Urry's argument runs the danger of sacrificing institutional analysis for a one-sided emphasis on fluidity.

The dialectic between fluid and often illegal population flows and state-based immigration controls is another cautionary example of the difficulty. Here a quite justified emphasis on capillary-like flows of people regulated by micro-level illegal immigration networks is part of a broader picture in which the richer nations seek ever-tighter immigration controls and enforce narrow definitions of refugee status. Fluids and barriers co-exist, albeit in a dynamic process subject to continuing change as new flows emerge and new controls strive to contain them. In addition, whether or not capital in particular locations would welcome and utilize new flows of cheap labour, national Governments and large sections of public opinion would not. The example of illegal immigration flows is therefore difficult for both fluid network theories and world-system theories to come to terms with.

Networks and governance

The shift from seeing networks as part of an organized system (Castells) to seeing them as nodes with a very fluid, mobile, and uneven set of flows (Urry) is a very radical one. These two contrasting approaches do not, however, exhaust the multiplicity of ways in which the network metaphor has been used in social enquiry. There is, for example, a widespread emphasis on networks amongst those who study the global polity (Keck and Sikkink 1998, Coleman and Perl 1999, Stone 2000a). Here an array of policy, knowledge, and advocacy networks have been identified.

One of the origins of this work is associated with shifts from primary emphasis on government to new forms of governance. In the former case, attention centres on the formal politics of sovereign bodies such as parliaments and law courts. In the latter, by contrast, the emphasis shifts to the ways in which activities are regulated by more complex sets of institutions, actors, and norms, many of them not formerly part of government. Governance has many shades of meaning, but for Rhodes (1997: 15), it is usefully defined as 'self-organizing and inter-organizational networks characterised by inter-dependence, resource exchange, rules of the game, and significant autonomy from the state'.

Governance within the global polity is by no means fluid and free-floating, though it does involve multiple actors and types of network. State-centred Government does, of course, include extensive forms of lobbying and public enquiry whereby non-state interests seek to influence policy. Governance, however, typically embraces non-state actors in a more intimate way in formulating and implementing its rules. This is very clear wherever government seeks only an indirect or arms-length relationship with economic and social regulation. Here the popular notion of liberal economic de-regulation is something of a misnomer. In this context de-regulation more often than not means less direct state regulation, rather than an abandonment of any regulation. Meanwhile, parallel changes in public-sector management including the outsourcing of expertise and service delivery in private directions also encourage governance.

In economic affairs, less state regulation may result in increased self-regulation by corporations, but it may equally lead to the development of regulatory regimes where other kinds of non-state networks become involved. These may include the knowledge networks of think tanks and professions, and advocacy networks populated by activists and campaigning NGOs. Struggles for inclusion in governance arrangements are no less evident than for conflicts over access to government itself. Much of this conflict is driven by struggles for greater public accountability, and greater corporate responsibility for the ethics of their operations.

O'Brien (2003) has identified four major categories of players within governance: governments, world companies, organizations of civil society, and illegal networks. This categorization focuses on an amalgam of types of institutional membership of networks, and, in the last example, modes of operation. The inclusion of illegal networks allows a focus on both criminal (e.g. drug cartels) and terrorist networks (e.g. Al Quaida).

Governance also comprises both networking *between* these entities (inter-category networks) and networking *within* (intra-categories) them. Inter-category networking has become increasingly important as a result of a number of intersecting social changes already noted above. One is the increasing importance of regulation of economic activity outside the formal apparatus of Government, but embracing government officials, companies, and various kinds of expert knowledge. This is especially evident as a global and regional level, where the period since the Asian economic crisis of 1997 has seen a growing realization that the institutional architecture of the global order is currently unable to guarantee stability and accountability to the world's populations (for further discussion see Chapter 7). Such trends intersect with pressures for greater inclusion of non-state actors other than business and business-oriented professionals, and with the agenda of concerns of such actors.

Controversies around the WTO and the desirability of including labour, environmental, and other social issues within its trade policy remit are one of the more central examples of inter-category networking. Here, we may find efforts by at least some more reform-minded NGOs to break into hitherto elite forms of inter-category networking between government and companies such as the World Economic Forum. Other major examples of inter-category networking include debates over the relationship between public need and private intellectual property rights arising from the HIV/AIDS crisis in Africa articulated at the 2002 summit in Johannesburg. These involved dialogues between governments, companies, and NGOs, with a view to reform the current rules governing trade and intellectual property.

O'Brien argues that intra-category networking is sometimes less well recognized or studied than inter-category networking. This applies to many economic processes such as intra-company trade or regional networks of central bankers. In the former case there is general awareness of the use of internal transfer-pricing as a means of avoiding taxation, but comparatively little public understanding of the sense in which firms act as networks rather than centralized entities. This issue leads on to the ways in which global and local issues are balanced within intra-firm networks, and the extent to which decisions are decentralized. As far as central banks are concerned, a European network of central bankers pre-dated the establishment of the Bank for International Settlements (BIS) in 1929. Part of the role of the BIS was to develop and extend the work of this forum of bankers, which, over the years came to include a wider non-European membership, and to establish committee work on issues of mutual interest. The European Central Bank grew out of one such committee.

The continuing importance of national and local influence is to be found in regional banking and economic policy-making as much inter-firm networks. Networking styles in a European setting clearly vary by national tradition. Thus, the people of Germany are used to a federal network of governance, the French are long used to a more centralizing structure.... And the British apparently have an innate fear of the word federal despite having been a union for three centuries (and that network is evolving too with devolution) (2003: 3).

O'Brien's is not the only typology of networks (see also Boerzel 1998, Struyk 2002). A range of criteria have been used to differentiate the enormous diversity of networks from objectives and membership basis to incentives for participation and type of network coherence. Within any typology of this kind, research has focused on both *horizontal* issues (how networks operate and with what success) and *vertical* issues (how networks operate and are stratified in terms of power and access to decision-making. More radical critics of much network analysis have, however, claimed that greater attention has been given to the horizontal over the vertical. This reflects, at least in part, a suspicion that global networks are typically of an elite character. Against this, the horizontal focus has been an important way of bringing agency back into accounts of elites, as well as directing attention to claims for inclusion by groups hitherto left outside network membership.

One important type of network is what might be called the 'network of networks'. Amnesty International is an important example of a network of networks operating from below via professionals and a range of activists. Founded in 1961 as an international non-government organization (INGO) dedicated to the promotion and defence of human rights it has developed a membership and activity structure based on both autonomous national sections and specialist networks. There are around eight of the latter. In addition to the Urgent Action Network which is designed to produce inter-nationally co-ordinated mass protest to stop or prevent serious human rights violations such as torture or medical neglect (Amnesty International 2003a), there are seven additional thematic networks. These comprise the following:

1. The Amnesty International Health Professional Network comprises of individuals, groups and networks of doctors, nurses, mental health specialists, and other health professionals in more than 30 countries. This network 'campaigns on behalf of prisoners who have been subjected to violations of human rights that have a health-related perspective, such as deprivation of medical care and breaches of medical ethics' (ibid.).
2. The International Lawyer's Network made up of members of the legal community from national lawyers groups representing over

40 countries has worked for lawyers at risk of human rights violations, established the International Criminal Court, and began a special project 'justice without fear' for the legal community in Guatemala.

3. The Military Security and Police Network focuses on the account-ability of governments and businesses involved in the manufacture and trading of arms and security equipment, and those providing police or security training. It has worked to develop the text of an International Arms Trade Treaty and helped to promote the creation of a UN Rapporteur on Small Arms and campaigned for better weapons collection and destruction programs in Afghanistan, Angola, and Sierra Leone.

4. The Business and Economic Relation Network has been working on strengthening corporate accountability. The Network has urged companies doing business in the Russian Federation to protect and promote human rights and called on companies of the extractive sector – in particular, diamonds and oil – to account for the impact of their activities on human rights.

5. The Children's Network works for children's rights in all regions. Concerns worked on during 2002 included the killing of children in Israel, the Occupied Territories, and the Palestinian Authority, abuse of children in detention in Burundi, and treatment of children with mental disabilities in Bulgaria.

6. The Women's Network took action on a number of issues during 2002, including application of the 'Sharia penal code' in Nigeria and continued existence of discriminatory laws in Pakistan that fail to tackle the violence which affects a high proportion of the country's women.

7. The Lesbian, Gay, Bisexual and Transgender (LGBT) Network has recently campaigned on behalf of those persecuted for their actual or perceived sexual orientation, in a range of Middle Eastern and Latin American countries.

This network of networks has been outlined at length to emphasize attempts at the making of globalization from below according to a range of human rights norms whose violation implicates governments, corpor-ations, and cultural assumptions across the globe. This not only links a range of human rights issues and campaigns together across national frontiers, but also engages with inter-national agencies and national Governments. These in turn play a major part in the emergence of global civil society, a theme which receives more detailed discussion in Chapter 6.

Networks take many forms operating from the bottom upwards as well as from the top downwards. One useful way of thinking about networks, power, and governance is through the notion of multi-track diplomacy developed by Diamond and McDonald (1996), and more recently by Kraft (2002). Diplomacy, here, has come to be extended far beyond its conventional elite-based meaning. Overall, three tracks have been identified. The first is state-centred focusing on official government channels for dialogue and direct negotiation. The second, developed to make sense of networks that operated in parallel with the first, might be called unofficial channels. Here discussion is off-the-record, is meant to be more open-minded, and involves non-state actors (such as experts or NGOs) as well as officials. Track two diplomacy may include policy analysis, policy advocacy, and policy formulation. Track three diplomacy, by contrast, is NGO-based and has a critical edge being unconstrained by official involvement. It tends to feature trans-national advocacy of norms (e.g. human rights), and focus on particular campaigns. It does not negotiate policy, but seeks to influence the climate of opinion in which policy is set.

Kraft (2002) develops the three-track approach in an analysis of regional diplomacy over human rights in Southeast Asia. Here within the Asian and South-East Asian Association of Nations (ASEAN), track-one diplomacy founded on the principle of non-interference in each other's affairs meant that one nation-state could not, amongst other things, criticize the human rights position in other member countries. Track-two networks, such as the ASEAN Institutes of Strategic and International Studies (ASEAN-ISIS), have emerged to discuss issues such as regional security, where officials require expert knowledge to assist in the formulation of policy options. However, concern among Southeast Asians over human rights abuses in East Timor or Burma could not be pursued down either track. In 1991, human rights and development organizations had already set up Forum Asia to strengthen collaboration between them. In 1993, activists also set up the Asia Pacific Coalition for East Timor (APCET) as a regional advocacy and pressure group. Conferences of this body in the late 1990s, were either cancelled or obstructed by host states, but the media impact of the cause being pursued was, if anything, magnified by such actions. This helped keep the issue on the regional and global agenda. In this sense it may be seen as a type of diplomacy, albeit one that neither participated in subsequent policy changes nor left a strong organizational legacy behind.

In terms of sovereign power, then, track-one diplomatic networks are firmly under state control. Nonetheless, the more complex and intellectually demanding challenges of a global scale of operations require states to have increasing recourse to track-two mechanisms. These lack formal sovereign power, but have considerable cognitive and normative influence as well as enhancing the capacity of governance mechanisms. Even so, wider inputs from civil society tend to stimulate track-three mechanisms. These may be repressed or ignored, but they equally influence agendas, not only through impact on media comment, but also by influencing tracks one and two. In the case of the APCET, Kraft suggests some evidence showing that track-three mechanisms can be used as a source of ideas by tracks one and two. Such organizations have little, if any, power, but may possess cognitive and normative resources that when taken up by states have an impact on policy disproportionate to their power.

Another useful way of thinking about different networks or multi-track processes is provided by Braithwaite and Drahos (2000). They take up the metaphor of 'webs', developed in earlier discussions of the global polity by McGrew (1992) and elaborated by Holton (1998). Two types of web are identified, namely webs of power and webs of dialogue. Webs of power represent what many critics see as the unacceptable face of globalization. Examples of webs of this kind would include the kinds of elite networks of business and government officials noted above, as well as webs linking these with military and intelligence networks. Other powerful webs include global legal communities around bodies such as the International Criminal Court. In some cases webs of power involve cross-over between legal and illegal activities, as in the use made by the Bank of Credit and Commerce International (BCCI) by Governments to channel funding of paramilitary groups. In all such cases there is some linkage between each web and forms of sovereign power held either at national, regional, or global level.

Webs of dialogue, by contrast, suggest the possibility of a more positive face based on co-operation and sharing of knowledge. They exist wherever various sets of governments, organized interests, and social movements believe, or are persuaded, that there are cognitive problems that obstruct the resolution of particular problems. One leading example of this is the issue of global warming. Is this really happening, for what reason, and at what rate? Answers to such questions influence policy options. Another prominent example is the search for more effective policies of global development built, in part at least, on a wider sharing of knowledge between local interests (governmental and non-governmental), as well as economists and officials of global agencies. The launching of the Global Development Network (GDN) by the WB in 1999 is the most obvious example of this approach (for further commentary see Stone 2000a). One of the emphases underlying such initiatives by the Bank was the encouragement of social capital as a means of capacity-building in developing countries.

One difficulty from a policy point of view is that global governance cannot be neatly separated into webs of power and webs of dialogue. The two intersect and intertwine. Dialogue by itself may never get close to influencing policy, while sovereign power without dialogue may become illegitimate and be unable to secure economic and social cohesion. There is moreover a further complication, namely the import- ance of forms of power that subsist with prevailing sets of ideas or discourses, rather than depending on the sovereign power of institutions. A criticism made of many webs of dialogue is that they continue to embody powerful discourses such as neo-liberal economics, sociological modernization theory, or liberal-democratic political science rather than being open to insights from a wider body of thought. Discursive power, following a line of thought developed by Michel Foucault, does not necessarily depend on macro-level institutions for its execution, but operates at a micro-level, affecting the way individuals understand and construct their social worlds. If discursive themes such as the rationality, self-interest, utility-maximization, and individual rights dominate dialogue, the policy outcomes will be skewed to conventional Western nostrums, however wide inclusion in the membership of the web is drawn.

In the case of the GDN, the objective of building a network of think tanks and research initiatives from across the globe has necessarily faced this kind of challenge. Johnson and Stone (2000) in their keynote paper note criticisms that much of its think-tank membership appeared based on 'a rather technical form of neo-liberal analysis' (15). Nustad and Sending (2000) argue that the very notion of 'governance' has gained the connotation within development discourse of identifying the ways in which Western interests may legitimately intervene in developing countries perceived as lacking good governance. The danger here, at least in part, is that of failing to listen to other voices, including those of the potential sites of intervention. One sub-set of such voices is that of research institutes in developing countries. Johnson and Stone (2000: 7) report the testimony of researchers from both Bangladesh and Uganda, which suggests that governments in such countries have become so intellectually colonized by external experts that they have become sceptical that any worthwhile policy innovations can emerge from local sources.

Conclusion

Global analysts have been less and less convinced by theories of global-ization derived from simple structural propositions about capitalism and the world system. In reviewing the array of metaphors of system, structure, field, network, and flow in this chapter, our intention is not so much to describe different ways that globalization has been understood, as to investigate the relative merits of the different approaches. The first general conclusion to be drawn from this endeavour is that a major shift has occurred in the ways in which globalization has been understood, from system theory and structuralism to a less deterministic emphasis on fields, networks, and flows.

This shift has two further characteristics. One is the greater substantive focus on human agency and intention in the making of globalization in its different forms. This applies from above as in the example of corporate and regulatory networks, and from below as in the case of NGOs and, to a certain extent, in conflicts and interactions between elites and grass-roots activists. Much of the chapter has been concerned with organized action and formal institutions of this kind. But it is equally important to emphasize that global human agency also involves broader cultural world-views and cultural practices whereby human actors seek to find meaning in the world, and seek to improve their welfare; issues discussed by Robertson, which we return to in later chapters.

A second methodological aspect of the shift in thinking from structures to networks is a growing preference for middle-range theory, which we have argued is increasingly characteristic of third-wave approaches to globalization. Many analysts of globalization have become dissatisfied with highly conjectural approaches that assert general propositions about global trends, devoid of serious empirical analysis. We have noted a number of examples in this chapter, including work on the empirical structure of corporate power, Japanese religious syncretism, Internet chatrooms, and global knowledge networks. What unites this seemingly disparate array of topics is an interest in testing out general speculative arguments about globalization, whether these take the form of debates over the existence of a global capitalist class, global cultural homogeneity, the Internet as a form of democracy, or the role of knowledge-holders in global governance.

Work of this kind has enabled a more complex picture of global interconnection and inter-dependence to be elaborated, while not excluding the analysis of power and inequality. It has also opened up the cultural domain to closer inspection, while treating cultural processes as connected with economic and political life. And yet middle-range theories still beg questions about the possibility of a more integrated approach that somehow draws the complex threads together. If world-system theory is too deterministic, then Robertsons' global field might seem a more promising resource, provided its cognitive/cultural focus can somehow be reconciled with political-economic processes. For the moment, however, this theory has been largely by-passed. While some eschew grand theory altogether, many global analysts now operate with theories of modernity as one of their principal intellectual resources (Giddens 1994, Beck 2000). Here globalization is treated either as a form of modernity or as a process driving modernity.

In the next chapter we discuss two major issues that connect globalization with important social changes associated with modernity. The focus here is on changing forms and experiences of space and time.

4

Globalization and the Transformation of Space, and Time

Much recent attention has been given to innovations in global communications technology and the profound social changes with which they are associated. The digitalization of information, and its virtually instantaneous transmission across the globe has, for example, been seen by many as ushering in radical transformations in the spatial and temporal organization of social life. Just as virtual communication through the Internet and the mobile phone reduces spatial barriers to communication, so the time frames within which social life takes place seem to have speeded up. A range of debates have ensued as to the meaning of such changes. Does globalization of communications mean the end of geography, as distance matters less and less to the capacity to communicate? And if so, does this indicate a growing cosmopolitanism divorced from any close tie with particular spatial locations? Meanwhile, does the virtually simultaneous access to information spread across multiple sites bring with it a speeding-up of social learning and interconnection, and also perhaps a greater capacity for powerful interests to control and shape the direction that interactions made possible by new technology may take?

In this chapter we look in more depth at spatial and temporal changes associated with globalization, and their connection with human agency. Space and time are interpreted not simply as natural processes within which human life takes place but also as socially constructed ways of understanding and organizing social life. From this perspective the challenge is to understand how different conceptions of space and time have emerged, how they have been embodied in social institutions through human agency, and what light such conceptions shed on globalization.

Time–space compression and processes of globalization

Space and time are both fundamental categories of thought, and key elements of social experience. They involve social interactions with the natural world, whether conceived of as mastery of, or harmony with, nature. They link the physical distribution of natural resources, the spatial settlement and mobility of populations, technologies for communication and movement across space, and a variety of temporal ways of organizing and giving meaning to cultural life. Twentieth-century physics came to see space and time as conjoint features of the universe, such that matter moved and forces operated in space–time. Space and time in this world-view are intrinsic to physical processes rather than containers within which processes operate (Urry 2003: 19–20). Alongside this the physics of sub-atomic particles increasingly emphasized uncertainty, fluidity, and virtually instantaneous processes.

Just as in modern physics, social scientists have linked time and space together as conjoint features of social life, and argued that they are intrinsic to social life rather than mere containers, as it were, within which social processes operate. There is, as we shall see, a parallel emphasis on issues of fluidity and uncertainty associated with the new ways that global communication takes place. Much of this is associated with the idea of time–space compression within global processes developed by David Harvey (1996). Following Le Goff (1980) and Landes (1983), Harvey links globalization of time and space with the dynamics of capitalist globalization which are thought to underlie this process of compression. New technologies linked with the capitalist organization of production and exchange both speed up temporal aspects of life and reduce spatial barriers to economic activity. These processes have been going on for a number of centuries. In the time dimension they are associated with the much more common use of the minute and second from the 17th century onwards, together with an intensified time-conscious regime of industrial employment and work discipline. In the spatial dimension they are asso-ciated with technological changes in transportation and communication that reduce spatial barriers to communication and exchange. This process has been dramatically intensified with contemporary information technology enabling the transfer of any information capable of being digitalized across national borders. This has become a vital feature of global finance markets, news services, and multimedia transfers, as well as inter-organizational and inter-personal communication.

As time-based processes speed up and spatial barriers are eroded, time–space becomes, as it were, compressed into shorter periods operationally across global space. In one sense this may be referred to as 'the annihilation of space by time' (Harvey 1996: 241). Nonetheless, this does not usher in the end of geography because space remains a crucial dimension of social life. Rather particular forms of space–time are now deployed in new geographies of power. These, from Harvey's neo-Marxist perspective, emanate from processes of capital accumulation that drive newly shortened time-horizons for decision-making, shorter product and fashion cycles, and, for some at least, changed structures of feeling that emphasize the short-run and ephemeral.

Such ideas also connect with recent theories of the evolution of modernity and post-modernity. One line of connection is through Giddens' notion of contemporary (or high) modernity as a process of de-traditionalization. Part of this involves the disembedding of social relations from local contexts and their transposition across globalized tracts of time–space (Giddens 1991: 18). This transposition may alternatively be taken in a post-modern direction whereby space is transformed from a real to a virtual status as hyperspace or a world of 'non-places' (Augé 1995). Many such notions, it should be noted, have emerged from highly generalized conjectures obsessed with the profound novelty of virtual communication, but elaborated with relatively little empirical or historical depth.

The idea of time–space compression, the notion from which much speculative thinking set out, undoubtedly has much purchase on social life. This is evident in popular senses of the world becoming a smaller space as a result of various changes in the speed of communications. In the 19th century, as is well known, the coming of the railways created a strong feeling among social observers that spatial barriers to human interaction had been profoundly undermined. The result was a sense of the speeding up of social processes, symbolized in new railway timetables.

The creation of standard national, and eventually world, time depended to a significant degree on a pressing need to standardize a multiplicity of local times. In the 1870s, as Blaise (2000: 72) points out, two cities on the American continent 100 miles apart typically maintained an 8-minute time separation. The growing network of railways originating in different cities with timetables set in different local times made it impossible for travel between railway systems to function effectively. The Prime Meridian Conference of 1884, which established a standard world time divided into 24 time zones based on a 24-hour clock and with Greenwich at the longitudinal meridian, was very much based on ideas developed by a coalition of railway managers, engineers, and astronomers led by Sandford Fleming.

Fleming, a Scottish-born Canadian, is a striking example of a global visionary. A surveyor by profession, he not only played a key role on the achievement of a standard world time, but engineered both the trans-Canadian railway, and the trans-Pacific telegraph system linking London with Canada and Fiji. Individuals are of course embedded in broader networks and communities of human actors. Fleming's involvement in the 1884 Conference may in this respect be interpreted in terms of the operation of a epistemic community, that is a community of practical knowledge-holders seeking to apply knowledge to the making of improved global communications and inter-connection. Haas (1989) has advanced a more general argument as to the importance of such communities, alongside states and economic interests in the development of technical standard-setting and regulation on a global scale. The example of Fleming, above all else, demonstrates the importance of a particular kind of knowledge-based and technically competent human agency in the social organization of global time. Such developments cannot, in other words, simply be read off from general propositions about the logic of capital accumulation.

Whereas the title of Jules Verne's novel *Around the World in Eighty Days*, published in 1873, was taken at the time to refer to an almost unthinkable and possibly unachievable feat in personal travel, the world of Verne and Fleming is separated by little more than a century from the even more radical achievement of instantaneous time. Based on a set of technologies involving telecommunications delivery and the digitalization of information, the spatial constraints on the speed of communication were now reduced to virtually zero, creating the possibility of virtually instantaneous transactions. By contrast with clock time, which as Urry (2000: 113) points out involved forms of measurement and timetabling around calendars, diaries, and alarm clocks, instantaneous time has the effect of breaking down distinctions previously measured by the clock such as night and day, the working week and the weekend, and home and work.

The speeding up of technical interactions has also been connected by some with two further kinds of processes involving human actors. One is the incorporation of individual users into a world of virtual communication spaces, virtual relationships, and a virtual sense of personal identity. For some this emphasis on cyberspace and cyber identity creates cyborgs, that is a new type of social actor, whose life-world is dominated by, if not exactly fused with, technology. Another parallel process concerns the institutional framework in which the technology is embedded, notably media businesses in globalized communications. Communications media are typically organized through multi-national corporations. The older spatially limited print media companies either transform themselves into multimedia operations across a range of global spaces or decline in significance. This process, typified by Rupert Murdoch's *Newscorp*, involves film and video production, television delivered by satellite or cable, and sometimes the acquisition of transmission hardware itself. In this way a potent convergence between the media content provision business and the service delivery business is achieved in the one organization. The net result is the capacity to deliver both information and entertainment across regional, national, and local spaces, at the same time delivering information in virtually instantaneous time. A similar example of a convergent multimedia business organization is *AOL Time Warner*, where print, film, and Internet delivery become fused.

Does globalization 'annihilate space'?

With the technological capacity to show events from anywhere on the globe instantaneously, commentators like Virilio (2000) see a world in which virtual global mega-cities dominate flows of images. This leads, so it is said, to cities becoming virtual hyper-centres (11), rural life being desertified, and the decline of medium-sized towns who lack information infrastructure. As particular places wane in importance under the impact of media constructions of space, visual contiguity is believed to take precedence over territorial contiguity. This has two kinds of effect. One is the development of a 'global perception market' in which 'we all observe each other and compare ourselves with one another on a continual basis' (112). The other, bringing in the dimension of media power, is the idea of 'tele-surveillance'. This is seen as a 'systematic snooping operation' (108) which destroys the foundations of 'truth' in professional ethics and press freedom and allows an uncontrolled manipulation of sources of information.

Thinking of this kind is certainly not short of creative verve. Nor is it held back by scholarly caution, waiting for plausible evidence to ground the very long chains of speculation involved. If we start early on in the chain of reasoning with Harvey, the idea of the annihilation of space by time has attracted criticism. At their most general, sceptics sees such arguments as folk-myths of modernity, whereby every new innovation is invested with almost demonic dynamism capable of transforming all that goes before. Street (2003) sees the 'space annihilation thesis' as a form of technical fetishism in which changes in technology produce strong and direct effects on human perception and identity.

The same general line of criticism can be mounted against theories of the domination of virtual hyperspace. Although phenomena like online chat rooms and virtual relationships founded upon them are a significant feature of contemporary life, it seems dubious to regard their operation as a key element in a new social order. Large sections of the world's population lack Internet access. Even for those that do, there is evidence of widespread mistrust or resistance to virtual communications. This is reflected in the very slow take-up of most forms of e-commerce bar pornography and perhaps bookselling.

Another way of seeing use of the new information technology is not as a displacement of reality into virtual space, but as a pragmatic means to achieve some other end. The Internet and email, for example, may permit information gathering or co-ordination of activity between NGOs on the ground. It may also permit the ordering of books or downloading of music or sporting fixture lists for personal use in some other context. It is not simply an entry point to chat rooms and virtual relationships.

Perhaps the major criticism of theories of the annihilation of space is simply the material and symbolic resilience of space, and the cultural robustness of place as a central feature of how life is lived and experienced. Harvey makes the very useful point that place represents, so to speak, forms of relative stability in an increasingly mobile world (Harvey 1996: 295ff.). The coming of instantaneous time certainly introduces new kinds of social process and experience, and gives contemporary forms of globalization a somewhat different character to earlier forms discussed in Chapter 2. The time frames of social life prior to the global present were clearly based on longer time cycles set by the seasons and agricultural year, and later by the speed of a ship, camel, or horse, prior to the 19th-century advent of the telegraph and the train.

The point remains though that even instantaneous time does not annihilate space. This is largely because many social processes work on far slower time cycles. While digitalized information may move at the speed of light allowing financial transfers and real-time global TV, the production of most goods, city life, flows of migrants, national Parliaments, deliberations of the WB, or the diffusion of new cultural repertoires typically occur at slower rates. Successful diffusion of change or effective communication based on trust may take far longer than the transmission of information and images. As we shall discuss further below, there remain multiple social times even within a global environment.

Space and place then remain intact to the extent that material and symbolic life are not conducted instantaneously within central places, but are diffused across time and space. In the material world of production, even within global businesses based on software engineering with high levels of IT use and staff mobility, O'Riain (2000) has shown that place still matters. His study of a team project, linking an Irish subsidiary to a US multi-national, found that time–space relationships may become intensified where managerial deadlines are tight. Nonetheless, even software engineers do not find themselves being dissolved into cyberspace. Rather they are both tied together as a workgroup creating co-operative technical networks with a particular local space, and are subjected to pressures towards individual spatial mobility that are characteristic of career paths in this sector of the industry. Globalization therefore does not mean an end to place even though the inter-connection between places is profoundly altered by global processes.

Globalization, identity, and territorial space

Meanwhile, within symbolic life it is very clear that first-wave assumptions of a growing homogeneity in global culture around consumer consciousness fed by global media have proven grossly exaggerated (Holton 1998). The picture, as we have already noted, is far more complex. One set of writers have stressed polarization, as in Barber's (1996) celebrated confrontation between the global consumer capitalism of McWorld (an amalgam of McDonalds, MacIntosh computers and MTV) and Jihad, symbol of holy war in pursuit of fundamental values. Another equally influential current stresses inter-penetration, fusion, or creolization of culture under global conditions (Hannerz 1990) – the product of inter-cultural engagement, conflict, and borrowing. Theories of polarization and hybridization give certain kinds of agency back to human actors, in the sense that global consumer consciousness is not seen as an all-enveloping outcome of corporate marketing strategy built around global brands.

The complexity of the debate about culture and globalization has nonetheless left understanding of space, in the sense of territory and territorial identity, in a rather confusing state. Has globalization de-territorialized or re-territorialized populations? If plenty are wedded to local identities and ways of life, is this a continuing tribute to the robustness of particular territorial spaces or adherence to new globally constructed notions of localized space? Or, are such questions excessively polarized and simplistic, unable to do justice to glocal flows? And where are the characteristic personality types of modernity to be found in all of this? Would they be found rejecting locality for cosmopolitanism, or celebrating the complex flows of multiple glocalized images and products that permit either combinations of identities or the freedom to switch identities at will? None of these questions is anywhere near to resolution.

On the one hand, local and national identities retain a considerable hold on popular consciousness. Following Anderson's (1983) notion of imagined communities, it is clear that national and local imaginings remain very significant, and that these attach to a range of symbolic representations of territory, its flora and fauna, history and formative moments of war, occupation, liberation, and success. One reason for this is that global imaginings and identities, while not absent, seem to lack the particularities of time and space that go to make cultural affiliation, and for which individuals are often prepared to risk their lives. Another reason may be the search for re-territorialization as some kind of anchorage in a sea of global flux.

On the other hand, the mobility and fluidity of social life, representation, and contemporary media products has created spaces for new forms of cultural imagination. Appadurai (1998) sees the combined effect of mass migration and the electronic mediation of information as ushering in profound changes in forms of the cultural imagination. Mass media changes both widen access to a range of cultural resources and create new disciplines 'for the construction of imagined selves and imagined worlds' (ibid.: 3). They offer both access to the romance of cosmopolitan celebrity and the immediacy of news and documentaries. At the same time population movement and the creation of new diasporic groups stretched across space create forms of life that are equally not bounded by the nation-state. Thus:

> As Turkish guest workers in Germany watch Turkish films in their German flats, as Koreans in Philadelphia watch the 1988 Olympics in Seoul through satellite feeds from Korea, and as Pakistani cabdrivers in Chicago listen to cassettes of sermons recorded in Pakistan or Iran, we see moving images meet deterritorialized viewers. (ibid.: 4)

The line or argument is persuasive as far as it goes. Once again we see the return of human agency, which in Appadurai's terms may involve resistance to, or irony about, received mass-media images, as well as audience selectivity in what is consumed (ibid.: 5). There remain, nonetheless, problems with the assumption of de-territorialization. How many of the world population are immigrants or closely implicated in the world of migrants? The answer at any particular moment may be in the order of 1–2 per cent (Castles and Miller 1993: 4). The proportion who have emigrated at some point in their lifetime would be greater, and the number of those with family or friends involved greater still. If one guessed that one-quarter of the world's population were connected in one shape of form with global migration, we may still ask how far mobility and de-territorialization are able to meet questions of human security and welfare? De-territorialization may occur over the short-run, but re-territorialization, as we argue below, is often restored, albeit in somewhat different forms. Are not the de-territorialized viewers cited above re-territorialized through diasporic networks and imaginings?

As it happens, this line of critique is not incompatible with Appadurai's position. What he calls de-territorialization is really concerned with the demise, as he sees it, of national territorial boundaries, rather than territoriality *per se*. What he believes is happening is a shift from national to trans-national public spaces that in some senses transcend the salience of the nation. These may be occupied by migrants, but they may equally be occupied by activists, students, and intellectuals. Within this context the term 'diaspora', conventionally applied to mobile and dispersed groups, becomes a kind of metaphor for imaginative movement across and beyond national spaces.

Limits to global fluidity

Returning to the long chain of reasoning with which this chapter began, a major difficulty affecting literature on global fluidity including that of Appadurai is the tendency to elevate mobility into some kind of axial social principle. This difficulty is greatest for theories of post-modernism organized around the adage 'all that is solid melts into air'. John Urry's *Sociology Beyond Societies* (2000) is a brilliant statement of the new centrality of mobility to social life under global conditions. However, this work is stronger as a critique of methodological nationalism, based on the assumption of society bounded within the nation-state, rather than as free-standing theory of the social. The difficulty with theories that centre on mobility is accounting for relatively permanent features of social life, that is the patterns of residues and resistances that in some sense channel or resist flows and fluids. As Harvey (1996: 18) has pointed out 'while it is true everything can be reduced to flows . . . we are in daily practice surrounded by things, institutions, discourses and even states of mind of such permanence and power that it would be foolish not to acknowledge these evident qualities. . . .'

Street (2003) has developed an empirical research agenda focusing on what might be called the stabilization of fluids. This is offered as a corrective to 'theories of globalization which end up with little to say on the manner in which, among the fluxes and flows of the social, stable regions and networks are maintained...' (13). This requires more work on the 'heterogenous and complex ordering processes and practises of polymorphic social networks'. This argument is followed through in analysis of the legal stabilization of intellectual property rights in plants and biotechnology. This has been achieved, in part at least, through the integration of many US and Canadian farmers into social networks dominated by corporations. By these means, life science companies have sought to create an intellectual property regime which stops farmers selling or saving their own seed, in order to avail of the alternative bio-technologies made available by corporations. This offers a case study of the importance of studying stabilization, and the role of specific networks in mobilizing law to achieve this.

One difficulty with the project of reconciling mobility and fluidity with residue, resistance, and the search for stability is that of excessive disciplinary specialism. While the field of cultural studies has done most to emphasize, if not celebrate, new mobilities and cultural ambiguities, areas like legal studies and political science have been more concerned with the institutionalization of social life. These two bodies of thought rarely intersect. Instead, the insatiable habit of cultural speculation is left intact, without coming to terms with the formal world of legal regulation and the world of work. Whereas production once received far more attention than consumption, the tables are now turned. One casualty of this shift is any sustained engagement between the heady worlds of cultural self-expression or imagination and the 'dull compulsion of economic circumstance'.

Another problem in reconciling these matters is that the forms of life involved are in one sense moral choices as much as sociological trends. Moral choices are most explicit perhaps in the cultural domain than elsewhere, though omnipresent in global economic and political arrangements also. Robertson, in his discussion of the global field (1992: 28) argued that global complexity – or the irreducibility of self, nations, the world of states, and humankind to one another – should itself be welcomed as a value. The moral connotations of mobility and stability, or fluidity or resistance, are hard to disentangle, encouraging speculative assertion and counter-claim. To the extent that personal global movement is a choice rather than forced, is it a nomadic betrayal of community and homeland in search of personal welfare or global power? Or, are trans-local attachments a superior form of allegiance, a move away from local prejudice to a more humane and tolerant one? What should moderns want? Would opting for one or the other free us from such haunting questions?

We turn now from these unresolved issues to consider the spaces and times of globalization in further depth.

Naming spaces

Systems of names, as with any system of classification, blend technical, moral, cultural, and political elements. This is as true of the world's spaces as any other form of classification. Here broad civilizational entities like 'the West', or 'the East', geographic expressions such as 'Africa' or 'Europe', vie with a host of national and local forms of naming, arrived at for different purposes and from different vantage points. To overlay all these on top of each other would create a mental map that would be so complex as to be unworkable.

Nation-states are still the conventional basis for naming global spaces. This is most clearly symbolized in the opening ceremony of the Olympic Games, televised across the globe, in which each team marches behind a national flag and is identified by a text sign. Seating in the United Nations is marked in a similar manner. Nation-states themselves embody collective expressions of national self-ascription developed historically. As such they claim to act as both political and cultural boundaries that contain distinct sets of economic and legal activities. For many purposes, however, individual nation-states are aggregated either by themselves or by others into supra-national entities (such as regions, or even civilizations), as well as disaggregated into sub-national regions, cities, and localities. What matters in all of this is how far national spaces adequately reflect the spatial character of social life, and whether certain activities may be more effectively labelled in other terms.

The distribution of economic activity may still be understood as stratified by space. An inter-national division of labour exists, though this is constantly evolving in a dynamic way as market opportunities open up, costs of capital and labour change, and regulatory arrangements prove more or less conducive to investment decisions. Different regions, nations, cities, and other localities gain or lose in relation to each other. The poorest nations twenty years ago, mostly in Africa, remain the poorest, even though some nations in the East and Southeast Asia (such as China, Malaysia and South Korea) and Latin America (such as Brazil) have made significant developmental advances. And within the wealthier group, income inequalities persist within nations and cities, to the extent that it is sometimes said that urban neighbourhoods possess 'Third World' living standards. Meanwhile, 'world' or 'global cities' have emerged in many nations across the apparent divide from New York and London to Rio de Janeiro and Shanghai. These typically play a key economic role, as we have seen in global service industries (Sassen 1994), as well as participating in up-market cosmopolitan consumer cultures. They nonetheless confound spatial distinction between rich and poor in the sense that both are typically found within one city, performing different, though inter-dependent, functions.

These complexities have made it harder to think in terms of a simple dichotomy between a rich developed First World and a poor Third World. There are gross disparities in global wealth, but these do not easily approximate to conventional spatial categories. Such distinctions now serve no useful analytical purpose, although they remain the stuff of political protest, and underlie the approach of many anti-globalization activists.

Magyar cites data on the global distribution of wealth, whereby the First World of OECD countries comprise 16 per cent of the world's population but generate around 72 per cent of the world's wealth. Nonetheless, divergence is evident both within and between the large regional and continental categories within which space is usually distributed. While the rich–poor divide is associated spatially with First World–Third World divides, it remains impossible to accurately characterize how the world's peoples live across these internally divergent highly aggregated spatial categories.

For these reasons, a number of analysts have spoken either of the 'end' of the Third World as a useful concept (Kamrava 1995) or of the need to restrict its use to a very specific set of historical phenomena (Berger and Dore 1996). For Magyar (1995: 707), five sub-divisions need to be made to encapsulate the diversity of trajectories of countries labelled Third World. These involve distinctions between the following:

  (i) newly industrializing countries, for example Brazil, Malaysia;
 (ii) major surplus oil producers/exporters, for example Iran, Libya, Venezuela;
(iii) countries where economic growth exceeds population growth rates;
(iv) countries where economic growth equals population growth rates; and
 (v) countries where economic growth is lower than population growth rates, for example Somalia, Haiti, Burma, Chad.

This type of disaggregation is useful, but the question remains as to what this widely divergent group have in common. Unless it is presumed that the more economically successful countries will tend to slip back into the least successful categories, this exercise in disaggregation seems to undermine the continuing usefulness of ideas of the Third World.

The terminology of developing and underdevelopment is also problematic, in that it encourages a morally loaded divorce between optimism (developing countries are on their way and will surely get there soon) and pessimism (underdeveloped countries will remain so, as long as developed countries exploit them). There is a heavy ideological investment in these scenarios, but each has problems.

What has been called the 'development paradigm', whereby countries would successfully modernize and achieve developed status if only they adopted market economies and liberal-democratic polities, has proven impossible to apply as a set of general nostrums across all cases. The oppressive heavy-handed use of conditionality by the IMF and WB to secure such reforms generally failed (WB 1999). Social learning theory, as Schon (1971) has pointed out, suggests that any successful example of transplant from one context to another is really a local form of discovery. Stiglitz (2000) interprets this to mean that knowledge needs to be localized and placed in context to be effectively utilized. His advice then is 'scan globally, reinvent locally' (31).

Such criticisms of the development paradigm as implemented by global regulatory bodies through the 'Washington Consensus' do not, of course, mean that all market-based routes to development are singularly problematic. For what is equally important is the creation of a suitable institutional framework that is effective in a given space. To the extent this is provided, spaces of opportunity, capacity-building, hope, and success will tend to open up.

Meanwhile, assumption of 'dependency theorists' that under-underdevelopment cannot be overcome unless dependency is challenged also lacks general applicability as a development strategy. This does not mean that global inequalities of income and life conditions are being steadily eroded by economic globalization. Indeed the failure to make significant inroads into the poverty of the poorest parts of the world population, or to avoid famine, is an indictment of both global institutions and local elites alike (for further discussion see Chapter 7). It leaves intact spaces of misery, premature death, despair, and abuse.

Alongside the economic 'spaces' of investment, production, and consumption, political 'spaces' also persist under conditions of globalization. The robustness of the nation-state and citizenship has confounded first-wave predictions that the state was being either fundamentally eroded or hollowed out by de-regulation and the dominance of markets (see Chapter 3). This does not mean that all nation-states are robust. A number of post-colonial states established according to politically arbitrary forms of spatial sub-division have functioned more like 'quasi-states' (Jackson 1991). They may have possessed legal sovereignty and a seat at the UN, but lacked internal legitimacy, the will to create stable representative political institutions, and the internal capacity and resources to deliver the efficient administration of taxation and a social infrastructure. The result being the creation of spaces marked by civil war, inter-communal violence, poverty, disease, and human rights abuse. Political spaces, then, like those of the global economy, vary profoundly in character.

Alongside robust nation-states and disintegrating 'quasi-states', continents, regions, and cities, a further type of political space has emerged around what Beck (2000: 68–69) calls a burgeoning 'global subpolitics'. This is based around civil society and expressed in social movements and NGOs. The term 'activist' has come to refer to actors mobilized in campaigns of direct action. In this manner a sense of global political spaces has widened from debate and decisions made within global organizations, parliaments, elite fora, think tanks, and the political press to sites of environmental, human rights, and feminist political mobilization. Typical campaigns in these sub-political spaces include Greenpeace's 1995 bid to prevent the multi-national Shell oil company from disposing of the Brent Spar oil storage platform in the North Sea.

Alliances between global sub-politics and direct action, emphasized by Beck, do not, however, mean that such political spaces lack continuous organization or dispense with more conventional types of lobbying. As Yearley and Forrester (2000) point out, Shell has been targeted by a range of organizations, including Amnesty International and the World Council of Churches for a number of years in relation to a range of its worldwide activities. These include drilling plans and practices in rainforests in South America and West Africa. In Nigeria, human rights abuses were alleged as government and paramilitary forces suppressed local opponents of oil drilling and extraction. Shell subsequently withdrew from most of its Nigerian operations. In such cases sub-political campaigns include both analyzing and publicizing claims of environmental and human rights violations and abuses.

Nonetheless, Yearley and Forrester also argue that such campaigns remain hard to co-ordinate and sustain over time. Some successful campaigns, such as the Brent Spar, have the advantage of striking imagery, such as boarding parties occupying the platform to capture the public imagination, as well as being targeted on a specific issue. As a general rule, however, campaigning organizations do not have the resources or organizational structure to function as NGO 'mirror images' of multi-nationals such as Shell (ibid.: 140).

It is also important to stress that sub-political activity may also generate involvement with and incorporation into formal politics as a means of widening its influence. In some respects strong connections have grown up between formal politics and NGO activity, especially where NGO activists become involved in electoral politics (e.g. through Green Parties in Germany and Australia) or within policy and knowledge networks. Some state and UN bodies create political spaces for NGO participation. In other cases, the formal and the sub-political proceed in parallel. A good example of this is the alternative feminist political space established by NGOs at the 1995 Fourth World Conference on Women in Beijing. Here the UN-sponsored Conference was paralleled with a Forum of (Hsiung and Wong 1998). It is estimated that the Forum was attended by 35,000 women from around the world. The discourses of the Forum were intended as more open than and less bound by concerns of Governments anxious to use the Conference to emphasize the successes of their respective policies affecting women. The alternative political space of the Forum enabled global linkages between NGOs, networks, and individuals to be formed, extending the scope of women's access to global spaces.

The cultural spaces of a globalized environment, many of them closely entwined with political life, are similarly far more complex than first- or second-wave theories of homogenization indicated. They include seemingly boundless global as well as regional, national, and local spaces. World religions, based on the idea of a single cosmos subject to divine will, co-operate or vie with each other, often as a kind of glocal fusion of one world thinking as interpreted for particular local populations. Varieties of self-styled national and local religious activity also proliferate, sometimes as resistance to the materialism of economic globalization or the militarism of global imperial aspirations. World music also grows in stature, though again typically as a glocal fusion of different styles from a range of cultural settings (Frith 1989).

Such spaces may be open or closed to 'Others' of various kinds, and their occupants may at least attempt to regulate who may, and on which criteria, become accepted users of space. Closure may be found especially among those culturalist movements that seek to mobilize cultural difference as a basis for identity politics. Examples include French speakers in Canada, Pakistanis in Britain, and Algerians in France. All seek not simply cultural recognition in daily life, but political rights embodied in the rules of citizenship and allocation of political resources between communities. These may create educational and administrative spaces reserved for particular kinds of minority language use, as well as an opening of access for minority practices in relation to literature, dress, forms of worship, and rituals of burial, to public spaces.

Inter-national population movement – forced or voluntary, long term or shorter term – creates a variety of social spaces, both alongside and often in interaction with existing populations. Such migrant spaces have been referred to variously as trans-national, diasporic, or multi-locational. The spaces of population movement are very much a complex heterogenous matter rather than the repetition of a single pattern of spatial movement over time (Castles and Miller 1993). They are affected by a number of factors, including the conditions under which people leave their countries of origin or residence, the resources to which they have access during the process or movement and settlement, and the balance of opportunity and restriction in their destination countries. Opportunities may be created by Government schemes or through buoyant economic conditions, while restrictions include popular opposition, discrimination in employment and access to political rights and resources, and, at the most extreme, forcible expulsion by Governments.

The spaces of the migrant experience are thus varied and contrasting. On the one side, they include the abject high-risk world of illegal tran-shipment and abuse, de-moralizing refugee camps which potential countries of asylum either ignore or cherry-pick for human capital. On the other, they involve chain migration networks linking extended families and community members, as well as the fast-track mechanisms open to business migrants. Somewhere in between are included the short-term passages of temporary workers, both highly skilled and unskilled, who form an increasingly significant part of what Sassen (1998: 5–30) refers to as 'the transnationalization immigration policy'.

Settlement experiences may be equally varied both in terms of location within economic life and in social and cultural terms. In the economic sphere, much attention has been given to immigrant incorp-oration in relatively low-wage manufacturing and service work, ranging from car assembly plants and food processing to domestic service, small-scale retailing, office cleaning, and restaurant work. This emphasis is largely justified, though it is equally important to avoid stereotyping immigrant economic status and human capital endowment as low grade.

A significant aspect of the spaces of immigrant employment is the incorporation of women from poor developing or underdeveloped countries into wage labour in rich countries. Sassen (1998: 111ff.) argues that this process is not simply kin-related, but stems from an expansion in demand from industries whose occupational niches are conventionally sex-typed, but which cannot be met from local sources. Using US data from the 1980s, Sassen finds that the proportion of immigrant women holding operative jobs is three times greater than 'native women' across the five states where most immigrants live (New York, California, Florida, Texas, and Illinois).

In broader social and cultural spheres, the spaces of immigrant settlement are again multifarious. As far as social organization is concerned, and as is well known, successful processes of settlement often depend on the availability of networks of ethnic solidarity and community formation to provide mutual aid in the daily exigencies of life. Recreational and associational life may also be organized in these terms. Such patterns may be reinforced over time by levels of in-marriage within groups, as well as by continuing flows of new migrants from countries of origins. But they may equally be eroded by out-marriage, by increasingly privatized modes of family-living and by the weakening of ethnic ties between generations as identity ceases to be based on daily interaction of a practical kind and shifts towards more symbolic characteristics (Gans 1979). Continuing global connections with the country of origin or with other centres of ethnic diaspora may, however, give continuing succour, and sometimes even re-invigorate trans-national ties of solidarity within groups. Here the phenomenon of long-distance nationalism takes root (for further elaboration see Chapter 6).

For all these complexities, elements of re-territorialization are crucial to the immigrant experience. They may take the form of cultural assimilation or pragmatic social integration within new countries of residence including the taking up of citizenship where available. Hyphenated identities (e.g. Greek-American, Lebanese-Australian) combining elements of two spaces may also develop, whereby links are formed between two spaces. In such a way partial integration into the new country of residence may be combined with continuing identification with country of origin, and/or specific spaces within it – spaces called 'home'.

Longing and nostalgia for 'home' may play a key part here. It may remain an 'ache in the heart' as in the testimony of a Welsh migrant from rural Wales to Australia, who left as an adolescent in a large family group, recorded as follows by Hammerton (2004: 276).

If you can imagine, a scene on the train platform, Neath railway station as a family of *ten* were leaving. We had a lot of friends. There must have been hundreds of people at that railway station all singing: 'We'll keep a Welcome in the Hillside!' ... it brings tears to my eyes now! And one of the lines is 'We'll kiss away each hour of *hiraeth* (Welsh for longing), when you come home again to Wales!' And I still crack up when I think of it.

In other cases, migrants return home for family reunions, including reunions of diasporic kin. Sutton (2004: 249) records an example of a family reunion in the Caribbean island of Grenada in the 1990s. This brought back around 250 people from places such as England, Germany, Canada, the US, and Puerto Rico. The reunion lasted several weeks, with activities including visits to 'family land, and old family houses, parties, and a special church service'.

Trans-national spaces may also also open up as a result of symbolic as much as physical movement in the sense that individuals and groups enter cultural journeys from one space to another. Such journeys arise from a number of sources. They may result from religious conversion and from the choice of an alternative lifestyle (e.g. 'Eastern' rather than 'Western'). Symbolic movement within the imagination is typified in the Rastafarian culture. Here descendants of African slaves, living in the contemporary Caribbean and in global cities such as London and New York, imagine a return to a re-invigorated Africa, restoring a cultural and spiritual completeness severed by slavery and dispersion.

The proliferation of spaces discussed here does not, of course, mean that living in a global world is a necessarily fragmented experience. Inter-connection and inter-dependence remain omnipresent features of life under conditions of globalization. It remains, however, to come to some overall judgement about the nature of these forms of life and their relationship to global, national, regional, and local patterns of institutions. This will be attempted in Chapter 5, after a discussion of the proliferation of times.

Globalization and the proliferation of social times

Time is often thought of solely as a feature of nature. Phenomena such as the seasons, day and night, and lunar cycles seem to provide the temporal framework for life. Beyond these examples, however, different notions of social time have emerged over history, such as clock time associated with factory discipline. Processes of globalization have been particularly connected, as we have already seen, with a sense of virtually simultaneous or instantaneous time, made possible by new information technology. For some, instantaneous time represents global time par excellence. This is a powerful idea, but it does not exhaust the wider range of social times that may be associated with globalization.

One of the most elaborate accounts of social time has been provided by George Gurvitch (1963). He rejects notions of the unity and continuity of time as a singular process. Drawing on Bergson's notions of qualitative as well as quantitative times, Gurvitch argues that a sociology of time involves different types of social flows and varying senses of time. He goes on to identify eight temporal dimensions within social life, ranging from slow-moving time to explosive time. These are itemized in Figure 2. This figure assists in thinking through other potential connections between time and global processes.

Type 1 or 'Slow-moving time', for example, has many common features with what Braudel (1972) refers to as La Longue Durée, and Urry (2000: 157–158) calls 'glacial' or 'eco-time'. In one sense, globally instantaneous time may be thought of as annihilating the slow-moving time of those traditional worlds that were geographically remote from each other. However, in another important way, slow-moving time may be seen as a kind of planetary time, whose rhythms may be affected by human activities such as global warming. This slow-moving time is intrinsically global inasmuch as the geosphere, biosphere, and atmosphere are inter-connected. It is not as yet clear how far the planet is amenable to human interventions, such as reversal of global warming. Nor is it clear what ecological limits there are to global population growth and sustainability. Slow-moving rhythms are then out of synchronization, as it were, with the instantaneous time of the global mass media, and the electoral time frames of political power. They are, nonetheless, as fateful a global presence as any other global influence.

> 1. Slow-moving time
> 2. Deceptive or surprise time
> 3. Time with irregular pulse
> 4. Cyclical time
> 5. Time that goes ahead of itself
> 6. Time that lags behind itself
> 7. Time that alternates between advance and retardation
> 8. Explosive time

Figure 2   Gurvitch: Eight types of social time

Source: G. Gurvitch (1963).

Many of Gurvitch's other types are, as it were, revisions to linear notions of time, where social processes take place according to standardized regular patterns. Two in particular, Type 2 deceptive or surprise time and Type 8 explosive time, may be used to demonstrate further relationships with globalization. In highly interconnected and interdependent world, it is clear that significant events in one place not only become known in many others, but may exert an influence on other locations. This relationship is usually taken to be an example of simultaneity. However, if we study the events of 9/11 and the destruction of the Twin Towers, certain additional temporal processes can be seen at work.

Deceptive or surprise time may be used to refer both to the American illusion that global terrorism could not strike decisively at the US, and to the trauma of shock and horror that the events caused. This is to do not merely with out-of-the-ordinary events, but also with types of global inter-connection and inter-dependence that have the capacity to disrupt social life even in the most militarily powerful of nations. These may be called the globalization of terrorism, but this phenomenon rested in turn on other kinds of cross-border processes. These included (a) the global mobility of students and others seeking training, which made it seem normal for Arab students to present at aviation schools in the US for lessons in flying, and (b) the global mobility of finance that enabled large funds to be made available to sustain terrorist training, planning, and weapons acquisition. Both these examples occurred in sectors of the global economy that were not typically regulated sectors, adding to the surprise of the attack.

Explosive time, meanwhile, seen in a metaphorical sense, is an apposite term for sudden highly significant events that disrupt the linear flow of time. In the case of 9/11 the notion is both literally and metaphorically true, since the event has had very profound reverberations in American foreign policy. These apply both to the 'war on terror' as a war on new forms of globalized non-state actors and to the idea of global war on the so-called rogue states such as Iraq. Behind such notions lie Hobbesian conceptions of the globe as a 'naturally' dangerous and fundamentally disorderly place that require strong political responses to create any kind of global security. To be sure, a single nation-state – the US – is at the forefront of these moves. They might be seen as the continuation of realpolitik by a hegemonic power, able to by-pass the United Nations. As such they have little to do with globalization. Two responses are, however, possible to this.

The first, drawing on the historical analysis of Chapter 2, is that forms of globalization may and often have taken a rather unilateral (or regressive) form. This is especially true of empires, and also applies to proselytizing religions. There is, in other words, no necessary relationship between globalization and multi-lateralism. While forms of multi-lateralism are certainly stronger in areas like trade or scientific and technical co-operation, they are not in any sense universal across all global processes. The obverse of multi-lateral global engagement is not unilateral engagement but national introversion.

A second response is to say that even within unilateralist forms of quasi-imperial intervention, some wider sense of a grouping of global allies has been evident. In the immediate aftermath of the 9/11, the US initially reached out to UN institutions, rejoining UNESCO and paying UN back dues previously withheld. Such a gesture seems now to have been a fleeting moment of multi-lateral re-engagement.

In the recent Iraq war, a more restricted external outreach took the form of a 'coalition of the willing'. While it may be the case that such allies are not strictly needed in a military sense, they were seen as giving some kind of added legitimation to war. It should be stressed that there is a strongly moralistic aspect to the hegemonic discourse of US foreign policy. From a normative viewpoint, this policy may be interpreted as a re-invention of a kind of protestant fundamentalism which distinguishes between the saved and the damned Tiryakian (1984). The saved are our coalition allies, the damned are our enemies. While it is premature at the time of writing to be certain of the consequences of this particular explosive event, it is clear that the profound ripple effects that derive from it have projected debates about global security away from the incremental processes of conventional diplomacy.

Cyclical time is another prominent part of Gurvitch's checklist. For him cycles represented continuity and hence lack of development. This is the time of spirituality, epitomized in the Buddhist cycle of birth and rebirth. It might also be associated with spiritual or religious calendars in which recurrent patterns of devotion and celebration are fixed, and recur in the same form over time. While the content of tradition actually changes over time (Hobsbawm and Ranger 1983), this may not be accepted by the faithful who associate continuity with the integrity of faith, and tradition with purity. To change would be to deny and violate the sacred. Cyclical time, following Gurvitch's line of argument, is then typically sacred, to be contrasted with the profane world of secular activity. The latter is often associated with the global, the former with the local, though it might be more helpful to speak of a contrast between spiritual and secular forms of globalization.

Fatima Mernissi (1993: 130ff.), the Moroccan writer, has provided an interesting discussion of the clash between religious and secular times in the context of contemporary Islamic culture. 'Today', she writes, 'Muslims are exiles in time, and their exile is symbolized by the shrinking of the field of activities that are regulated by our calendar' (ibid.: 131). Western time predominates over the spiritual mastery of time reflected in the Islamic calendar (tarikh) within which human endeavours are structured. Sometimes the two clash as when managers of Moroccan textile factories fail to meet delivery dates set by German customers because the low-wage workforce observes religious holidays. The Islamic calendar is reduced to marking the time of prayer and religious ritual, while universal standardized time dominates economic life and the organization of global mass media including that directed to the Muslim world.

Gurvitch's account of cyclical time may also be seen as rather restricted in that it rules out cycles that are connected with developmental change including intensified processes of global inter-connection and inter-dependence. Cyclical time in the latter sense has typically been associated with economic cycles that emerged as part of the dynamics of market-based capitalist economies. Here studies of economic indicators such as prices, unemployment, capital formation, and inventories have led to the identification of a range of long-, medium- and short-run term cycles. These are characteristics of a dynamic and expansive system, subject to periodic discontinuities and disequilibria rather than cycles without developmental significance. The increasingly global reach of economic activities simultaneously exposes all spaces to this set of economic cycles and the risks associated with them. The times of economic globalization are, in this sense, multiple rather than singular.

At first sight, Gurvitch's other senses of social time raise difficulties because they appear to rely on a sense of evolutionary development. To say that time gets ahead of itself (Type 5) or behind itself (Type 6) suggests a normal sense of time, or at least expectations about temporal processes, from which some phenomena deviate. In this way that which is labelled ahead of itself presumes that the future is starting to emerge in the present, while that which lags is some kind of atavism about to disappear. Such evolutionary presuppositions have attracted wide-spread criticism (Giddens 1981, Holton 1985) for assuming a direction-ality which may be quite arbitrary, linked very often to a teleological account of history that lies somehow beyond empirical analysis. When the expected changes do not happen as soon as expected they are seen as late, while if they appear before expectations, they become premature.

There is, nonetheless, a way of retrieving Gurvitch's categories from this problem, if the qualities 'ahead' and 'behind', 'early' and 'late' are regarded as cultural constructs rather than evolutionary yardsticks. What then matters is how social actors perceive and construct conceptions of time that connect past, present, and future. In the case of time that gets ahead of itself Gurvitch singles out forms of 'collective effervescence' where new ideals and values emerge. The times of global utopianism might be seen as the most relevant contemporary example of this process. Here hopes for a future immanent in the actions of the present propel activists forward as it were. This is in line with Mahatma Gandhi's admonition 'Be the social change you would wish to see brought about.' Activists' time might then be seen as a dimension of Type 5 time. Even so, utopias are, as Hobsbawm points out, some times fertile and sometimes infertile. They may presage the future or they may not.

Type 6 time that is, as it were, behind itself, is associated by Gurvitch with social symbols that crystalize an immediate mood or feeling, but which are subsequently left behind. They are typically associated with the idea of community. Time lagging behind itself, in this sense, may be useful as a way of drawing attention to the uneven impact and reception of certain global products and processes. Much anti-globalization rhetoric calls for the protection of communities, especially local communities who are seen as being ignored, abused, or steamrollered by economic globalization. Such communities are also seen as the bedrock of democracy. The space of resistance, as we have seen, is associated with the space of place rather than the space of flows. But what is the time of place, and how does it intersect with the time of flows? A typical answer would be to identify the time of flows as faster than the time of place. The time of place, from the viewpoint of the time of flows, would be seen as slow, too slow, even dysfunctional to change. The time of democratic deliberation might equally be judged in the same way. This is perhaps why the idea of 'fast-tracking' development projects has emerged as a means of short-circuiting wider community and democratic scrutiny.

From these observations we may conclude not only that multiple times exist, but also that the terrain of time remains a terrain of contest. Just as workers in the Industrial Revolution found themselves confronted with a new factory time that served as a means of work-discipline (Thompson 1963), so both workers and citizens in a global environment experience conflicts over the time frames in which their lives are enmeshed. The symptomatic complaints that life is too fast, or that there is not enough time in the day, may then be indicative of broader global struggles between instantaneous time and community time, between spiritual time and economic time.

Conclusion

Space and time, in their distinct and conjoint aspects, are clearly crucial to any understanding of globalization. The challenge is not so much recognizing this general point, as much as encompassing its complexity. Space is both physically and socially constructed matter, subject to and linked with temporal change and social perceptions. Time and time-measures too are simultaneously embodied in matter and social understandings.

Globalization, in one sense, simplifies understandings of time and space, involving as it does the capacity for communication that is both instantaneous and capable of immediate terrestrial spatial reach. Yet these simple propositions require profound modification because time and space have become configured in a multiplicity of different ways. Not only is time periodized for a range of social purposes, but space itself, that seemingly more tangible entity, may be perceived and acted upon in varying and sometimes conflicting ways.

One unresolved issue in all of this is the relationships that apply between global, regional, national, and local spaces. If the challenge is to recognize both global fluidity of movement with orderly institutionalized patterns, then what exactly is involved in the activities of nation-states, inter-national organizations and governance networks, as well as cultural interaction between groups and peoples.

In Chapter 4 we pursued the idea of global fluidity and the porosity of national boundaries, while suggesting limits to the utility of metaphors of flow and mobility. In Chapter 5 we reverse the approach, as it were, focusing on activities and relationships that occur on a global, regional, national, and local scale, together with the interrelations between them. Are global or regional activities and institutions in conflict with national and local features of social life as so many critics of globalization believe? Or, are there circumstances in which the global and the national or local become inter-dependent, relying on or even merging with each other?

5

Global, National, Regional, and Local: Competing or Inter-dependent?

In the previous chapter attention was given to globalization in relation to space and time. One major theme that remains to be explored further is the relationship between globalizing processes, the spatial scale and stretch of political institutions, and changing ways of life including cultural understandings of the space within which identity and attachment are imagined and practised. There is much debate here surrounding the relationship between four types of spatial location, namely the 'global', the 'regional', the 'national', and the 'local'.

First-wave theories of globalization see 'the global' as rapidly undermining the remainder, confidently predicting the demise of the nation-state, and the erosion of cultural difference bringing with it the decline of national and local identity. Second- and third-wave accounts of globalization have, as we have already seen, challenged a good deal of this kind of thinking. To rehearse the argument sketched in Chapter 1, for second-wave sceptics, the death of the nation-state has been greatly exaggerated; regional blocs, like the EU, have grown in significance between the global and national scales of activity; while cultural resistance to global homogenization has not diminished. In third-wave opinion, meanwhile, two further points have emerged. One is the attempt to develop a more balanced assessment of the scope *and* limits of global economic, political, and cultural arrangements. The second is a growing realization that the global, regional, national, and local often inter-relate and inter-penetrate each other, rather than being separate, incompatible with each other and hence in conflict.

When we investigate this debate further, a number of difficult issues emerge. An initial problem is the yardstick against which the global, regional, national, and local are to be defined. At first sight these may seem simple politico-legal distinctions between physical territories constituted by law and regulated administratively. Nations are perhaps the bedrock of this territorial system, with supra-national regions, such as the EU or NAFTA, agreed inter-governmentally above them, and sub-national regions and localities beneath.

This emphasis on legal jurisdiction is of course a vital feature of any such system of territorial distinctions. It is, however, inadequate by itself to encapsulate the range of meanings found in discussions of the fate of regions, nations, and localities in an epoch of globalization. One major problem is that certain of these entities, notably the regional and the local may refer primarily to spatial or geographical entities that are not co-terminous with territorially defined political jurisdictions (Benko 1990). Some have spoken of mega-regions like sub-Saharan Africa or East Asia, for example, ascribing stereotypical characteristics to these agglomerations, such as a culture of poverty in the former case, or dynamic entrepreneurial 'Asian values' in the latter. Alternatively the historic regions in which the peoples of Africa or Asia have lived may bear no clear relationship with colonial borders imposed on existing patterns of tribal settlement and nomadic migration. Meanwhile, the meaning of locality is even harder to pin down ranging from an administrative unit (e.g. suburb, parish) to a cultural, life-style-based term (e.g. Bohemian quarter, farming township).

Apparently territorial classifications are therefore never exclusively matters of legal or administrative definition, but are equally constituted through cultural perceptions and aspirations. Geography, in short, is cultural as much as political. Many key geographical distinctions are, in other words, matters of cultural discourse raising fundamental questions about the values that are embedded in spatial distinctions within which the world peoples are located. All this adds complexity to the analysis.

A notable instance of this global cultural geography is the ostensibly territorial distinction between the West and the East. While apparently territorial in character, it has proven very hard to pin down whether such entities can be reduced to specific sets of nations, institutions, or whether they draw upon some less tangible set of cultural associations. The notion of civilization may be pressed into service here, but it remains difficult to establish bounded definitions or civilizations and exactly how many civilizations there are.

Is the West co-terminous with all or some European peoples and all or some of their extensions overseas? Does it include largely Westernized regions such as Latin America? Or is it better defined by institutional arrangements, where market economies and liberal democracy apply? Is Japan Western, partly Western, or Westernizing? Are Muslims living in Western Europe, Western or part of an Eastern enclave? More fundamentally what other civilizations are there? Is the only serious contender to the West, what Huntington (1996) has called, the Islamic–Confucian axis? And is this notion convincing as a real cultural entity shared by sets of populations in Asia and North Africa? Or has globalization, in the sense of a growing inter-dependence and increased awareness of the world as a single place, left us with one single 'core' or 'central civilization' (Wilkinson 1987), based on syncretic borrowing and cross-fertilization between regions and localities? If so should this be seen as somehow post-Western and post-Eastern? In which case, what function do notions of the West and the East, or Europe and Asia perform? Are they simply self-serving binary notions, whereby those perceived as 'different' from ourselves are relegated to subordinate status?

One way of conceiving broader global or civilizational entities, as we have seen in previous chapters, is to see them as imagined communities (Anderson 1983). Imagined communities are typically thought of discursively, that is through the language of adherence and classification. These prescribe the boundaries between different civilizations, or identify the contrasts between different conceptions of global order. Examples include the much debated historical Orientalist distinction between the rational dynamic self-disciplined West, and the irrational, static, and erotic 'East' (Said 1991). They also include parallel forms of occidentalism (Ahmed 1992) which contrast the spiritual East and the crass materialist West. The idea of imagined communities can, however, be similarly applied to smaller ostensibly territorial entities. Anderson first applied the term to nations, but it may equally apply to global and to smaller sub-national entities.

Other global examples include religious communities seen as existing under one God, such as Christendom or the world of Islamic believers (dar al-islam). Some may meet personally through pilgrimage or involvement in religious projects of social service and political activism. Most, however, will never meet, but are tied together through the imagination. Anderson cites the vernacular languages expressed within the printed word delivered to large markets through 'print capitalism' as an important example of mechanisms of connection that provided, so to speak, the cultural infrastructure of nationalism. The print media also link a range of political and cultural communities including protest movements, religious communities, and special interest groups such as football supporters and fans of rock bands. Other contemporary mechanisms that link together communities across the globe include video messages and the Internet, as well as news carried through networks of migrants, passed from person to person.

Such communities are imagined but not imaginary, in the sense of being invented out of nothing. They are real but their reality is not primarily based on face-to-face contact. It depends rather on forms of communication which generate and construct a sense of common membership in shared traditions, institutions, and cultural characteristics. Imagined communities are created through active human agency, whether this involves a Manchester United fan in Hong Kong sending an email to the club's website, or an Islamic migrant in New York receiving religious videos from Iran.

The general implication of these comments is that there is no simple and agreed way of defining the global, regional, national, and local as separate and entirely distinct entities. Rather such terms are used in a way that spans a range of politico-legal and discursive cultural criteria.

Beyond the challenges of definition, a further methodological difficulty complicates the analysis. This is the problem of methodological nationalism (Smith 1983). If methodological individualism assumes that social life is ultimately constituted through the actions of individuals, then methodological nationalism is based on the primacy of national societies, each with their own set of institutions and accompanying cultural identities. One of the most influential versions of this kind of thinking may be found within realist accounts of inter-national relations (Waltz 1979, Keohane 1986), where, as Held (1995: 24) puts it, 'the state is conceived principally as a sovereign monolithic entity', pursuing national self-interest in a rational manner.

Similar assumptions are also powerfully represented in media discussions of politics on the world stage. Here it is governments and statesmen who claim and are accorded primacy, and whose activities are often represented in a rather self-serving manner as the work of 'the international community' mobilized against their contemporary foes, such as the state-centred 'axis of evil' and global terrorist networks. By comparison, the more mobile and multi-centred worlds evident among merchants, corporate decision-makers, professional workers and artists, migrants, global regulators, and standard-setters are, in general, far less evident in media representation. This is partly because few crave media attention, and partly because their activities are less easily transmuted into accessible stories for putative national audiences, except perhaps as examples of perceived threat to nations. Illegal migrants and tax exiles are two such examples; the first being perceived as threats to national employment opportunities and cultural cohesion, and the second as threats to the national tax base and the principle of progressive taxation.

Methodological nationalism, however, has now become an outmoded approach. It is simply untenable to regard the relative robustness of the nation-centred world of states and national cultures as unchanging pillars of national sovereignty and cultural identity within a world order of nation-states. This is not because nations and nationalism no long matter, but because other trans-national, regional, and localizing trends are also significant, and permeate national boundaries almost at will. The events of 9/11 symbolize this permeability, as does the detachment of global terrorism from high levels of dependency on any nation-state. Other forms of permeability involve trans-cultural processes in business, among social movements, and cultural affiliations to a single world.

Many critics of methodological nationalism prefer, as we saw in Chapter 3, to think in terms of methodological globalism. This alternative focus treats social life as more than an interaction between bounded nation-states and national cultures. It is a legitimate focus, providing that it avoids the trap of seeing globalization – actual or potential – everywhere. Once we abandon the first-wave assumption that globalization is necessarily incompatible or in conflict with the national, regional, or local, far fewer limits are set to its scope and functioning. These different levels of social activity may collapse into globalization in a way that obscures difference and exaggerates the influence of the global. This is a very real problem, and requires that some attention is given not only to different ways in which the global, national, regional, and local may be articulated, but also to the limits of the global in these processes.

The global and the local

One initial way of simplifying the analysis is to collapse different sub-global 'levels' into one category. 'Local' thereby becomes a discursive metaphor for spatial scales, both material and imaginary, which are less than global, and by extension less than universal in scope. The contrast here is between that which is spatially or metaphorically extensive and that which is spatially or metaphorically limited. Ricardo Petrella (2001) has identified seven ways in which the global and the local, in such a sense, may be articulated (Figure 3).

The *first* mechanism posited here lies at the heart of much 'first wave' thinking about globalization (see Chapter 1), as manifested in the conflict between pro- and anti-global protagonists. Here the global

1. The global predominates over the local
2. The local awakes itself in a globalized or globalizing world
3. The global, bringing opportunities, helps the local
4. The global invents its own local
5. The local struggles for a different global
6. The dialectics of the global and local builds up a new synthesis, the glocal
7. The local sets free the local

Figure 3   Petrella: The global and the local

Source: Petrella (1995) cited in Racine (2001).

typically refers to economic globalization and is seen as leading to the globalization of markets for capital, traded goods, and labour and to the weakening of the local, that is national and sub-national forms of politics and culture. In its strongest form, this argument presumes that economic globalization undermines national sovereignty, political democracy, welfare states, and the particular cultures of nations and localities. In the cultural realm this is associated with ideas like the Coca-Colonization or McDonaldization of the world (Ritzer 1995), where corporate brands symbolize what is taken to be the homogenization of consumer practice and a decline in particular local or indigenous cultural products and industries.

Arguments about the predominance of the global may be pursued both by looking at political issues associated with sovereignty and governance, and through cultural issues to do with identity, expression, and performance. In both cases, it is arguable that there is significant supporting evidence in favour of the global dominance argument, but that there is equally significant evidence of counter-trends.

Global interconnectedness including the interlocking connections between states (Held and McGrew 2003: 13–14), taken together with the permeability of territorial borders by powerful market forces, migrants, terrorists, and cultural ideas, would seem to render inadequate not simply notions of national sovereignty, but also the idea of strong forms of effective state authority. In a world of global terrorism, where borders are highly permeable in ways that sidetrack the conventional state-centred apparatus of armed warfare, states no longer monopolize force within given territories, and hence cannot guarantee geopolitical security. Other examples of this challenge to the effectiveness of state authority are the huge problems even the most powerful states face in policing borders against migrants, and policing the content of electronic communication.

While the point about declining sovereignty is often made, it is equally important to clarify exactly what national sovereignty is taken to be, and hence what it is that is claimed to be under threat.

Braithwaite and Drahos (2000) note at least three analytically distinct senses in which the term is used, namely the sovereignty of state institutions, the sovereign appeal to nationhood and the qualities that make up national identity, and finally sovereignty of the people or democratic sovereignty. All too often, however, such distinctions are not made. One example is the tendency to collapse notions of popular or democratic sovereignty into state sovereignty (the foundation of realpolitik). This conflation is unfortunate inasmuch as elite, democratic, and popular notions of sovereignty and globalization conflict.

A wide range of actors may then defend national sovereignty for different reasons. These may include national politicians unwilling to sign up to UN organizations and conventions. A leading example may be found in US Republican Government and the US Congress, where unilateralist elites wish to resist supra-national control and regulation. This is reflected in refusal to accept the jurisdiction of the International Criminal Court over US foreign policy and the actions of its armed forces, designed to defending US state sovereignty. This type of defence of state sovereignty contrasts with that promoted from below by social movements on issues like opposition to free trade and promotion of human rights (Falk 1995), often supported by large sections of the political Left. Here it is national sovereignty in the form of democratic consent that is being promoted. A third variant of national sovereignty is evident among a range of nationalists, and especially ethno-nationalist groups and currents of opinion. Here national sovereignty is associated with the life and history of a particular people, and the cultural and political assertion of its values, symbols, and interests, whether in opposition to multi-national companies, global UN regimes, or inflows of immigrants.

That there are three such currents defending and promoting national sovereignty against a range of global and supra-national regional processes is testimony not simply to the presence of resistance to globalization, but also to its breadth and diversity. Arguments in defence of national sovereignty are, nonetheless, pursued by interests and groups with very different objectives, and these cannot be expected to coalesce. National sovereignty turns out not to be a unifying yardstick, within which elites and grass-roots activists, cultural nationalists, and civic republicans can easily find common ground. Beyond this pluralistic but fragmented sense of anti-global resistance it is nonetheless the case that nation-states and nationalism remain robust as the prevailing mode of political organization, even if some states in poorer parts of the Third World are very weak and lack any effective capacity to assert their sovereignty.

Having said this, the robustness of the nation-state as a political institution does not depend on possession of some absolute sovereignty, in the sense of an effective capacity to do whatever is wished. This is partly because nation-states, even the most powerful like the US, do not possess the resources to pursue any conceivable project. The recent neo-conservative push in the US to 'end' a sizeable set of rogue states soon ran up against logistical and financial limits evident in the Iraq campaign. Absolute sovereignty within foreign affairs is not only normatively limited by inter-national law, which may be flouted, but represents a form of 'soft power' exercised through the standards of legitimacy promoted by what has come to be called 'the international community'. These cannot be enforced by coercive means, since the UN is not a global state. But they can be articulated by sets of nation-states acting in common as in recent opposition by France, Germany, and Russia to the US decision to go to war in Iraq, and the terms within which the war was fought.

Domestically the idea of absolute sovereignty may seem more plausible, and it is certainly the case that it is national decision-makers that legislate and take executive political decisions. Analysts like Hirst and Thompson (1996) and Mann (1993) emphasize that nation-states, especially but not exclusively in the West, remain significant players within a global and regional context. Key policy areas such as taxation, infrastructural planning, immigration, education, research, development and training, and many elements of social policy remain in national hands. Even when national state functions have been ceded to a higher-level polity, as in the case of monetary policy within the eurozone in the EU, it is arguable that this is contained within inter-governmental structures rather than any trans-national entity. Sovereignty, at least in the form of state sovereignty is pooled rather than lost.

A further point to be made about sovereignty brings together politics and culture. This involves the largely mythical status of notions of a self-governing people. This idea is fundamental to traditions of liberal democratic, civic republican, and ethno-nationalist thought. It relies for much of its integrity on what has been called the Westphalian order of nation-states that emerged from the Peace of Westphalia in 1648 which brought the Thirty Years War to an end. This has been interpreted as laying the legal foundation for the idea that the territorial state had an exclusive monopoly of power within its given territory, grounded in sovereign rights in which empires or other states should not interfere.

For Osiander (2001) this conventional account of Westphalia is very much a myth invented by the 19th-century nationalist ideologues. The Peace Settlement was in fact silent about issues of sovereignty. The ideal of absolute sovereignty enshrined in the myth is, however, a powerful and enduring one that has empowered and energized a range of social actors, from elite statesmen and diplomats promoting forms of state sovereignty, to democratic party political and social movement activists aiming at more popular forms of sovereignty. Such sentiments draw not only on organized interests of nationally oriented businesses and trade unionists seeking economic advantage, but also on cultural images of the nations as bounded historical entities with a vital history of their own, and traditions that should be preserved and promoted in the face of supra-national threats, whether global or regional in nature. Current debates around the new EU constitution, and the emergence of new nationalist parties in Europe such as UK Independence Party (UKIP), include a strong body of opinion that regards the integrity of cultural nationalism as a fact as much as an ideal.

And yet for all the clamour and flag-waving, there remains a mythical quality to notions of absolute sovereignty. This is because external influences, whether political, economic, or cultural, have permeated nation-states and national cultures over many centuries, through externally generated war, invasion, colonization, espionage, free trade, capital movement and fiscal indebtedness to external sources, as well as cultural influences that themselves range widely through consumerism and individualism, to more overt political movements for human rights and environmental sustainability. All sovereignty is in some sense conditional, though this conditionality is greater for the less powerful and poorer countries and regions.

Much debate over the fate of the nation-state has been more specific in focus, centring on the implications of globalization for particular kinds of national institutions and policies. For much first-wave theory, the negative implications of globalization for national political arrangements focused on the imminent decline of the social-democratic welfare state in the face of neo-liberal global forces of de-regulation. The much predicted collapse of welfare states in the face of economic globalization does, however, seem incompatible with expanding welfare-spending in many of the countries whose economies are most open to global influences. Variations in welfare-spending seem more closely related to national political factors rather than globalization *per se*. Swank (2002) distinguished between welfare states that remain robust (e.g. the larger regimes in Northern Europe) and those which do not (e.g. the smaller

versions in Anglo countries). Here the crucial variable is not globalization but the types of citizenship rights, forms of political representation
and policy-making, and levels of centralization and decentralization
that exist within nations.

This optimistic verdict is less easy to apply to many of the world's
poorer countries, especially those who lack state capacity, a cohesive
civil society, and some degree of local control over the development of
economic resources. Their capacity to provide welfare for their populations has been undermined by a range of factors including limits to
social protection arising from the structural adjustment policies imposed
by global regulatory bodies like the WB, and state corruption. The option
of trading their way to market-based welfare has also been undercut in
many cases by low commodity prices and rich country protection of
primary product markets in food (for further elaboration see Chapter 7).

The existence of profound reservations and counter-evidence to strong
arguments about the predominance of economic globalization does not
mean that all versions of the argument are similarly untenable. Free
trade and capital mobility as regulated through institutions like the WTO
and private credit rating agencies like Moody's do reduce the freedom
of manoeuvre of most national governments, even in the wealthier
countries, to set policy priorities without regard to prevailing patterns
of private economic power. This may well mean some significant measure
of 'losing control' (Sassen 1996). Beyond this, every nation is increasingly
enmeshed in multi-level structures of governance and regulation through
a complex set of global, regional, and national bodies.

Some more concrete sense of this complexity can be gained from
Braithwaite and Drahos' (2000: 3) account of how the governance of
standard-setting effects a nation-state like Australia. Thus

> for years, some of Australia's air safety standards have been written by the Boeing
> Corporation in Seattle, or if not…by the US Federal Aviation Administration in
> Washington. Australia's ship safety laws have been written by the International Maritime
> Organization in London, its motor vehicle safety standards by Working Party 29 of the
> Economic Commission for Europe and its food standards by the Codex Alimentarius
> Commision in Rome. Many of Australia's pharmaceutical standards have been set by joint
> collaboration of the Japanese, European and American industries and their regulators,
> called the International Conference on Harmonization. Its telecommunications standards
> have been substantially set in Geneva by the International Telecommunications Union.

Australia, here, stands as a proxy for almost any nation-state.

The concept of governance refers to new ways of governing social life
that stretch beyond the formal governing apparatus of Government

and Legislature. Governance arrangements typically take the form of networks in which organized interests and knowledge holders operate on a 'self-organizing inter-institutional' basis with its own 'rules of the game, and significant autonomy from the state' (Rhodes 1997: 15). Governance might be thought of in terms of de-regulation and the creation of small government, though it would be more accurate to speak of a different mode of regulation to a state-centred focus. Governance may embrace a range of functions from the formulation of policy to its implementation and evaluation. The example of technical standard-setting, noted above, is one of a range of policy formation and regulatory functions, which increasingly cross-borders and operates through multi-level institutions.

The phenomenon of governance offers a further profound challenge to the idea of the integrity of national sovereignty, without necessarily lending support to ideas of a predominant global control over the local. In the case of standard-setting, it is true that some global corporations are so powerful that they can write their own technical standards into global governance arrangements, as in the case of Boeing and air safety. This is not, however, uniformly the case.

The thrust of this discussion of Petrella's first mechanism linking the global and the local is in the direction of a complex set of inter-relations between the global and different types of local, rather than simple one-way dominance of the global. We now explore this issue as it applies to the cultural domain.

Cultural affiliation and globalization

First-wave accounts assumed either a decline in 'local' cultural forms in the face of global economic homogenization, or the co-option and incorporation of local forms into global ones. In this case 'local' stands for all sub-global forms of cultural identity and expression. Under such global pressures, so the theory goes, human agency is either circumscribed in its scope and diversity, incorporated into forms of activity prescribed by economically powerful global interests, or simply ignored through benign neglect. Leading examples of such trends are taken to be the decline of local languages, in the face of an increasing use of a few world languages such as English, the rise of standardized global consumerism, recently dubbed McDonaldization (Ritzer 1995), and the dominance of cultural genres within particular spheres of cultural expression, such as the Hollywood film within cinema (Barber 1996). When movies such as the *Terminator* series or *Titanic* gross millions around the globe, the fear is that patterns of American or Western sensibility are transferred too, as part of the cultural baggage of globalization.

While a good deal of evidence is consistent with theories of cultural homogenization, there is also much evidence that points in different directions. In a critical survey of the literature, Holton (2000) identifies polarization and hybridization as alternative trends to homogenization. This points to the complex cultural trends evident in the epoch of globalization, and a continuing diversity in cultural agency, albeit in evolving forms. Polarization, for example, is reflected in resistance to global homogenization according to secular market-based principles. As already mentioned, the most obvious example of this is radical Islamic hostility to 'Western' materialism and secularization, where two opposing world-views are seen as in collision.

Other versions of polarization are evident in clashes between different global visions or different conceptions of globalization. There is, in particular, a sharp polarization between the world of global civil society activists – many of whom seek a more just and socially sustainable global order – and the world of economic globalizers, for whom enhanced human welfare is primarily a question of enhanced access to global markets for commodities. (The world of global civil society activists is depicted in more detail in Chapter 6.) Activism may also be profoundly local in scope, defending local jobs, industries, environments, and public spaces against threats from outside, and these may be global, regional, and national in scope, especially where corporations and states act in concert. An example here is the Indian protest movement against the construction of a dam that would flood local villages – a project funded by the WB with Indian state support. Polarization is both a counter-trend to homogenization, and clear indicator of the vitality of human agency in a globalizing world.

Hybridization, as indicated in Chapter 4, occurs where some kind of fusion of cultural elements occurs (Hannerz 1992), rather than the predominance of one cultural element over others. In the sphere of language, for example, new variants to English have arisen in former colonies rather than the consolidation of a standard English. Similarly many musical forms are highly syncretic, that is borrowing elements from a range of repertoires. Jazz and much 20th-century popular music combine a range of African, American, and European musical forms and traditions. The term 'world music' has also arisen as a way of labelling inter-cultural musical fusions. Many trends of this kind depend both on the global migration of populations, producing new demographic population mixtures, and on global communications media that diffuse styles and repertoires.

Discussion of the limits of national sovereignty and of cultural homogenization indicate the complexity of relationships between the global, regional, national, and local. None of these is predominant in any simple sense while each retains a significance, albeit in some kind of inter-dependent relationship with the others. It is in this context that Petrella's six further articulations of the global and the local posit some kind of co-existence or inter-penetration, rather than simple binary opposition. Racine (2001), in his commentary on this work, sees this as the limitation or 'hybridization' of globalization with 'local realities: mainly states and regional constructions' (2). In what follows we use Petrella's categories as a way of organizing a much broader debate.

In the *second* posited mechanism, the local is not vanquished by the global but awakens with it. This mechanism is consistent with both second- and third-wave theories of globalization, which share, albeit in different ways, the presumption that the 'local' (i.e. the regional, national, and sub-national) are not destroyed by globalization.

If globalization has not destroyed the nation-state, one reason for this has been the resilience of nationalism, especially in its ethno-nationalist form (Holton 1998). The metaphor of awakening is typically part of the imagined world of nationalist and ethnic revivals. Ethno-nationalism (Connor 1994) is distinguished from civic nationalism by virtue of its connection with the ascribed cultural and historical characteristics of a people (or ethné), rather than with rights-based notions of national citizenship which are indifferent to cultural backgrounds. Since ethno-nationalism regards itself as an organic expression of popular consciousness, it is regarded as rooted in nature as well as history. Metaphors of awakening are thus understood by partisan nationalists as the people resuming their natural dispositions.

Political institutions in an epoch of global challenge

Another broader line of thinking around awakening involves local mobilization to combat or mitigate the effects of globalization in a local setting. This may involve regional or national states protecting aspects of the local economy or culture. One terrain upon which this has occurred is through attempted negotiation of exemptions from WTO free-trade regimes for particular segments of national economies, such as culture industries. Or, in the case of supra-national regionalism, it may mean national pooling of sovereignty to establish regional forms of protection against global forces. The post-1945 re-awakening of Europe as a political region may be read not simply as a strategy for avoiding intra-European wars, but also in part as a response to the global economic agenda of the US.

The point here is not that the US stood unequivocally for global free trade, requiring an awakened Europe to protect its economic interest. The US, while sympathetic to a multi-lateral Treaty opening up world markets, opposed the establishment of an International Trade Organisation immediately after the war (Braithwaite and Drahos 2000: 177). Subsequently it has always combined a strong protectionist regime (e.g. in domestic agriculture) with free-trade regimes elsewhere to suit American multi-nationals (e.g. in markets for manufactures). The point is rather the advantages for European states, producers and European economies in developing a common European market backed up by infrastructural and regional development funds to maximize the potential for economic growth and internal political harmony. This did not mean keeping the US out, but it did mean pro-active institution-building and planning to secure European interests. The launching of the European Economic Community in 1957 and the construction of the European Central Bank and single currency in the last decade of the 20th century represent major steps in this direction.

How then does regional awakening relate to the position of nations in a globalizing environment? There are clearly many dimensions to this question. From the viewpoint of methodological nationalism, attention within Europe focuses on the degree to which individual nation-states may retain autonomy from regional and global forms of regulation. Assessments here may concentrate on the residual functions which EU members currently retain, such as national taxation regimes or legal and constitutional arrangements. They may also take into account the net benefits of membership, whereby a weakening of sovereignty is weighed in the balance against material benefits. One important example of benefits are transfers of EU Structural Funds, whereby initially poorer member states such as Ireland or Portugal have financed infrastructural and development projects that allow national income levels to converge with the EU average. Such regional mechanisms may also enhance the capacity of such nations to attract global investment, though again national policy-making in areas such as business taxation, industry policy, or educational up-skilling are, as in Ireland, equally relevant.

Within a globalizing and regionalizing context, national autarky, as practised by Albania for much of the post-war period, is no longer an option. But it is also very hard for states, even the most powerful, to operate with high degrees of autonomy from trans-national institutional frameworks. Nation-states have undoubtedly been animated in a positive sense by such external linkages. Such institutional evidence of developmental vitality in the EU context does not, however, exclude strong local antipathy towards higher-level institutions at a cultural and political level. This may take the form of minorities seeking national independence from larger nation-states, such as the Basques, Scots, or Bretons.

More diffuse small-area localism also exists as a potent source of resistance, especially where integrity of the local may be seen as threatened by national, regional, and global processes. Nonetheless, even where antipathy does exist, it often re-engages with the global. This may occur where global 'means' (e.g. communications technology) may be used to meet local ends, where certain kinds of global support are accepted, or by becoming involved in constructing a different global. This is famously the case with the Zapatista rebels in the Chiapas region of Mexico whose use of the Internet and integration into global protest networks have received much attention (see, for example, Olesen (2004), and Zapatistas Discussion Group (2004)). The global and the local may thereby become inter-dependent. It is therefore worthwhile to consider certain additional ways of articulating the global with the local.

In the *third* mechanism, the global, seeking opportunities 'helps' the local. A good deal here depends on which 'global' we are referring to. If we refer to economic globalization, then the notion of helping centres on 'help' delivered through the creation of free trade, free capital movement, and multi-national corporations. Here the local may be thought of as the regional or local state, and regional and local populations. However, on a broader approach to globalization, we may be referring first to areas that bridge the economic and political, such as development aid by the WB, and transfers between richer and poorer nations through schemes like the EU structural funds arrangements. Second, forms of political or legal intervention may be designed to 'help' through efforts to create and stabilize local institutional arrangements on a sustainable basis. An important example here is post-conflict reconstruction, whether this takes the form of legal redress for victims of genocide in countries such as Rwanda, as currently being undertaken by the International Criminal Court, or forms of democratic state-building capacity, as evidence in multiple interventions in East Timor. Such efforts may involve both state and non-state actors, whether regional bodies like the EU, global bodies like the UN and its agencies, global organizations of expert professionals, regulators, or standard-setters, as well as private donors and social movements from the non-government sector.

Extreme caution is, of course, also necessary in handling concepts like 'help'. We are dealing not with unambiguous transfers of good things, but with often highly contentious forms of intervention. 'Help' is an evaluative rather than descriptive concept, defined in different and often conflicting ways by different interests, inside and outside the local entity being 'supported'. Motivations for 'help' may include realpolitical calculations of national advantage for donor countries either in the sense of political support from the recipient (especially prevalent in the Cold War), or in terms of the market opportunities opened up for donor country businesses. Where UN is involved, motivations may also extend to normative commitments aiming at the creation of a stable peaceful world. Help made equally have a significant ideological or cultural element, as found where a sense of moral or charitable obligation or a commitment to address social injustice guides helping.

Taking these considerations into account, what may be said in a general way about this type of global–local linkage? Two basic points may be made here. The first is that the argument relies on the assumption that the global in some way supports rather than undermining the local. The second is that economic globalization depends upon or draws benefits from 'local' political institutions of two kinds. The first involves nation-states with resources and capacities that allow a degree of autonomy. These may be concentrated in Europe but not exclusively so. A good example here is that of Malaysia, where local political institutions have helped shape the direction of global–local interaction. Racine (2001: 12–13) argues that Malaysian Prime Minister Mahathir Mohamed has promoted an outward looking export-oriented development strategy that is not constrained by Western hegemony, and involves significant levels of self-determination. Malaysian interests are in themselves agents rather than recipients of an externally imposed globalization.

The second type of political institution is the 'local state', whether city-based or regional in scale. Brenner (1998), amongst others, has argued that states are becoming re-articulated on a range of sub-national and supra-national scales. However, unlike those who see a zero-sum competition between nation-states and sub- or supra-national states (meaning one must lose if the other gains), Brenner sees a more complex set of inter-dependencies. Rather than 'global cities' expanding at the expense of nation-states (Friedmann and Goetz 1982), we find that nation-states promote cities as host sites for 'transnational capital investment'.

Spatial re-scaling of this kind is associated with the decline of nationally regulated 'Fordist-Keynesian' states promoting national industry policies through nationally regulated labour markets. State re-scaling is driven rather through an association between the globalization of capital and the shift to more flexible post-Fordist production strategies. Cities, with particular sets of resource endowments, increasingly become the unit of competition for FDI, and this uncouples urban growth from national growth. This is seen most clearly in the City of London, where a global financial centre operates to a dynamic that is distinct from British manufacturing.

Such global cities are home to specific kinds of human agency and often striking contrasts between rich and poor. They range from highly paid and spatially mobile corporate executives and providers of professional and technical services to large immigrant populations providing low-cost labour as cleaners, security guards, waiters, and small shop-keepers. Politically, meanwhile, city leaders and mayors assume a growing importance as brokers of urban development, often linking with counter-parts in other global cities in policy debate and diffusion of new ideas. Equally, city managers and entrepreneurs compete for the location not simply for new investment, but also for prestige events such as the Olympics and the World Cup.

Debate about global–local articulations has also been influenced by powerful individual examples of a disastrous local impact. The catastrophic health effects of the Union Carbide factory explosion at Bhopal in India are a case in point. Here 47 tonnes of methyl isocyanate were released over two days in December 1984 affecting 200,000 people (Baxi 2000). Another less dramatic, but well-publicized example is the systematic use of low-wage labour in Vietnamese clothing factories producing for Nike (Vietnam Labor Watch 1997). Such events cannot be dismissed as isolated examples of global economic bads. Corporate races to the bottom, as far as labour, health, and environmental standards are concerned, are likely to be a routine feature of unregulated free trade in contexts where local states are weak in comparison with global corporations, even without dramatic cases that reach the headlines. The notion of global 'help' in this context may seem morally repugnant as well as sociologically naïve.

Beyond the fundamental problems created by unregulated trade and production, however, much of the debate concerns ways of striking an evaluative balance between advantages and disadvantages. This exercise involves at least two kinds of evaluative issue. The first compares net advantage with alternative possibilities. The second involves more explicit moral criteria. We discuss the former here, and the latter in Chapter 7.

In providing income, employment, increased technical and organizational capacity, and access to a wider range of goods, the global market economy and supra-national political institutions may be seen both as delivering economic advantages and as doing so more efficiently than alternative systems – whether subsistence agriculture or some version of state socialism and command economy. The comparison with the former is generally of more relevance in discussions of poorer under-developed societies. Here positive interpretations of global economic help are disputed by those who argue that subsistence agriculture was based on diverse local food systems which have generally been under-mined by economic globalization. Also farm protectionism by richer countries inhibits poorer countries exporting agricultural produce, and increases debt burdens. Nonetheless, increased per capita GDP is evident in a number of cases where FDI has been important, including China and a good deal of Southeast Asia. Such advances are not evident, by contrast in much of sub-Saharan Africa where FDI is far lower, even though cheap labour is plentiful. Here post-colonial states have far less capacity to deliver local benefits such as social stability or infrastructural support for economic development.

What then of other kinds of 'help' and global–local processes associated with it?

The robustness of many nation-states in Europe, Latin America, and East Asia in the face of economic globalization depends in the first place on resource flows made available through FDI and from enhanced tax revenues generated by economic growth. Economic globalization may both help in the enhancement of enhanced social, cognitive, and technical capacity and help finance its provision as a public input into national economies. Potentially positive outcomes of this kind are, however, only a possibility not a necessity. They may be undermined for a number of reasons.

First, there may be a problem of the skewing of inputs to activities that benefit external investors more than the internal population. Second, states may benefit or be disadvantaged in flows of development aid, wherever these are granted or denied according to ideological preference or service to the powerful in global realpolitik, or wherever conditionality as in IMF and WB support imposes adjustment costs that de-stabilize nations and destroy state capacity. Third, local states may be unable to rely on resource flows through taxation. This may be due to corporate or popular avoidance, or more radical challenges to state authority and capacity posed by the inter-national drugs trade, organized crime, and system-wide corruption. This clearly afflicts Colombia and certain other Latin American states. Positive outcomes may also be undermined to the extent that local interests divert resources into personal luxury consumption and grandiose projects that have little developmental potential.

Post-colonial states may also have gained independence after periods of war and civil war, in which existing resources and capacity were either destroyed or depleted. Where such states inherited colonial borders that fail to correspond with social or cultural borders, as in many parts of central Africa, inter-ethnic tensions and civil war, fuelled by less than helpful Western arms sales, may also conspire to undermine capacity-building.

The interplay of global and local sources of capacity loss or reduction help explain the plight of weaker or collapsed states, able to maintaining only a charade of quasi-sovereignty, simply as an effect of globalization. Other endogenous influences are clearly important. Nonetheless, the many kinds of global help that may be forthcoming, whether through technology transfer, foreign aid, loans conditional on policy change or military assistance, create a very complex set of global–local articulations.

This third mechanism of global–local articulation is, then, not only sociologically complex, but morally loaded with assessments of the sense in which help can really be said to be beneficial. Help is an inherently normative concept, bound to generate contesting viewpoints based on different evaluative standards. We return to these issues in Chapter 7.

A *fourth* way of thinking about global–local relations is through the notion that the global invents its own local. The theme of power inequalities between global and local is central here, in the sense that the global is able to create the local rather the local operating as a limit to the global. However we are not talking here of mechanism one, where the global predominates. Rather the emphasis is on the discursive invention of ideas of the local which are somehow functional to the interests of the global. This rather abstract way of putting things can be explored through the global invention of Bali as a tourist paradise set amid natural beauty and an untroubled way of life.

The so-called Bali bombing of a Western tourist area in 2002 was taken by the world's press as an example of the intrusion of violent conflicts between radical Islam and the West into this island paradise. This peaceable image does not, however, survive even a cursory examination of the recent history of political violence in Bali. This is reflected in a sustained campaign of colonial violence by the Dutch empire in destroying independent Balinese kingdoms in the first decade of the 20th century (Robinson 1995), and in the mass killing of Communist Party members in political purges during the 1960s. Around 5 per cent of the population, around 80,000 people, are estimated to have been killed at this time. Bali's reputation as an island paradise is not a historical fact, but rather the invention of global interests. The first of these was the global empire of the Dutch who, having destroyed independent politics and achieved pacification, re-invented Bali as a quiet island in harmony with nature. The first tourist development followed soon afterwards. In the second post-Soekarno phase of killing, the invention was re-invented, again as a tourist niche embedded in nature and harmony and populated by exotic others.

At a more general level, the notion of global invention of the local is apposite wherever the global imagines, constructs, or engineers a version of the local which suits global purposes. The Bali example combines episodes of global imperial imagining with the construction of a niche market for tourism. Other examples of global invention may be found where global institutions seek to engineer the shape of local institutions. An important instance of this occurs when global regulatory bodies seek to reshape national economies in a liberal direction. The ideal of the IMF and WB for much of the post-war period was to re-invent state-oriented national economies as market-orientated economies able to de-regulate restrictions on trade and capital, and tailor public-spending to levels and purposes consistent with the ideal. Such processes were also encouraged by the education of many intellectuals from Third World countries in market-oriented economies.

Re-invention strategies are also evident in the articulation of regional and national institutions. In the case of the EU, re-invention is especially evident in the use of membership criteria to re-shape the economies and polities of applicant countries. Ideals of market-oriented economies with low inflation rates and sound public finances are combined with liberal democratic requirements such as the protection of human rights. Applicants must re-invent themselves where necessary to be acceptable as new members.

This mechanism emphasizes top-down pressures to re-invent and re-shape. A *fifth* mechanism of articulation reverses the direction of pressure from top-down to bottom-up, whereby the local struggles for an alternative global. This process can take a variety of forms, including regional, national, and sub-national sources of pressure.

One of the major pressures for an alternative version of the global emanates from those who are critical of market-driven economic globalization centred on multi-national corporations and the global regulatory organizations. These are seen as imposing arrangements on regions, nations, and localities which ignore social justice, de stabilize social and cultural life, and place profit above human welfare. Pressures for greater global justice have come from both government and non-government sources. In many European inter-governmental circles, for example, there is support for the articulation of conceptions of the global order that emphasize social goals such as human rights, personal security, and rights to information. Within the UN, the involvement of Governments outside Europe and North America has involved networks such as the Group of 77 developing countries, and events like the UN Social Summit held recently in Johannesburg where the conference agenda was skewed very clearly to issues affecting poorer countries. Such challenges have not often been successful in effecting radical change. In areas such as the creation of a New World Information and Communication Order (NWICO), for example, debates in UN agencies such as UNESCO, in the 1970s and 1980s, made little progress in the creation of a new information order based not on free markets but on a more regulated set of arrangements (Mowlana 1996: 179–192).

Meanwhile, NGO's and global social movements have, in very prominent ways, championed human rights, environmental responsibility, and projects like the Jubilee moves to reduce the global debt burden on poorer countries. NGO pressures have been brought to bear nationally, regionally, and globally. Events such as the establishment of Civicus ('citizens strengthening global civil society') at the 1993 meeting of 'World Alliance for Citizen Participation' in Barcelona indicate the feeling of many that global issues cannot be solved by Governments or markets alone. Nor, however, can they be resolved by purely national action. It follows that civil society must organize globally and bring its influence to bear. Exactly what civil society means in this context remains to be clarified (see Chapter 6).

In the meantime, an instructive example of global civil society thinking is that of the Philippine Civil Society movement based around the Centre for Alternative Development Initiatives (CADI) and the analysis of CADI activist Nicanor Perlas. This case is significant for the way in which a local struggle against aspects of the GATT/WTO global trade regime led to the articulation of an alternative notion of the global.

Perlas' engagement with globalization began with a campaign against GATT/WTO free-trade rules which was felt to allow excessive pesticide residues in Philippine fruit production leading to adverse health effects. Perlas' (1998) initial analysis led to a critique of elite-dominated economic globalization whose materialist preoccupations had led to the construction of this trading regime with unacceptable high social risks. His counter to this is an alternative based on ideals of civil society at both the national and the global levels. Such ideals are rooted in cultural institutions such as religious groups, voluntary organizations, and professional groups (Perlas 2000). The making of a global civil society is posited as a means of rectifying imbalances in the global order dominated by business and government.

Perlas describes what is required as three-folding, that is the integration of civil society with business and government. In practical terms this involves programmes such as tri-sector partnerships, multi-stakeholderships, and global social inclusion. Perlas' analysis picks up a familiar argument in social theory about social differentiation and attendant problems of integration. While differentiation of economy and society may sometimes be responsible for higher levels of economic growth and productivity, it may be said to create integration problems; wherever economic values and priorities become so predominant, they cease to connect with issues such as social cohesion and social justice. Much of the pressure for an increased presence for civil society in the re-making of globalization may therefore be analyzed as a move towards de-differentiation of global arrangements.

Glocalization

The five modes of articulation of the global with the local that have been considered so far typically distinguish global and local institutions and levels of activity. While relations between the two may, in some circumstances, be seen as antipathetical, they may also be treated as complementary. A *sixth* possibility, developed by Roland Robertson, is that the two may become so intertwined and interpenetrated that a new hybrid, the glocal, has emerged, together with processes of glocalization.

Examples we have already noted include niche marketing and religious syncretism. The concepts of glocal and glocalization have also been used outside a business or religious context in analyzing the functioning of institutions such as the nation-state and the city within a globalizing environment (Swyngedouw 1992, Brenner 1998). Many other examples are more cultural in focus.

Ahmed Gurnah (1997), writing on 'Elvis in Zanzibar', invokes the world of musical syncretism in the Zanzibar of the 1950s and 1960s in which he grew up, as a kind of inter-cultural fusion. In this cosmopolitan East African seaport with historic links to the Middle East, Asia, and Europe, young people's musical experience drew on Arabic love songs from Radio Cairo, records of Latin bands in Hollywood such as Xavier Cugat, as well as Elvis and later the Beatles. A similarly diverse cultural repertoire was available in the print media and cuisine. Rather than seeing these phenomena as the impact of cultural imperialism on passive audiences, Gurnah detects 'a sophisticated selection process' (120) in Zanzibari audiences. Local world-views were built on such an array of borrowed elements that it is impossible to neatly separate these into authentic indigenous traditions and imported foreign influences. Glocal audiences of this kind, arising in mobile and fluid settings with a long history of cultural borrowing, speak to 'more active, critical, complex, and responsive' forms of human agency than are perceived by theorists who assert global dominance over the local.

Another dimension of this issue involves the cultural invention of trans-national images to suit local purposes. Beck (2000) takes the example of consumption of 'African' cultural products such as dance and costume outside Africa, to demonstrate that Africa is as much an idea or imagined community, as a geographical entity. For diasporic communities in North America, the Caribbean, or Northern Europe, the seeking of African roots or of a Black aesthetic means appropriating and re-inventing elements selected from an 'African' repertoire that may not match in any direct way the reality of contemporary Africa. 'Africa' in this imagined sense is relocated to London or New York. Glocal fusions of this kind may not be a majority experience, but they are a significant presence wherever global migration has taken place.

These examples give some indication of the range of contexts in which this *sixth* approach to global–local articulations may be used. Without achieving any kind of dominant status either within academic literature or more generally within social life, ideas of the glocal do not go away. There are, nonetheless, some difficulties with the term, which suggest limits to its analytical utility. Most important is the nature of glocalization as some kind of relatively stable inter-penetration of elements. What mechanisms does fusion or inter-penetration comprise? Is the process typically complete or do the elements retain some kind of separate function and identity? And, can such fusions split apart in some kind of de-glocalization? In any case, why is it that societies and social groups indigenize what they borrow, such that localism can be so highly and earnestly praised as an authentic basis for identity and moral judgement in spite of its typically syncretic origins? Another way of putting this is to ask what explains the power of localist thinking among 'globally generated localizing strategies' (Friedman 1994, 1995).

One way of characterizing the functions associated with the global and the local is to think in terms of means–ends relationships. Although the global and the local may be co-present in a range of institutions and social practices, they may nonetheless be differentiated, as in the use of global means to reach local ends, or vice versa. In the slogan 'think globally, act locally', do we have a glocal inter-penetration or rather the use of local means to reach global ends such as the sustainability of life on the planet? Alternatively, where local states aim at global competitiveness to maximize national wealth and cohesion, are they functioning glocally or simply using global means to reach local ends? If localism in some form becomes more rather than less dominant in such cases, for example, where the integrity of local species is seen to require the culling of introduced species or where states wish to introduce economic protectionism, this would presumably amount to de-glocalization. To the extent that such pressures are resisted, does this mean the triumph of the glocal, or the dominance of embedded globalism within the glocal?

Questions of this kind raise the problem of hierarchies of power or influence within global–local fusions. Here again a large empirical research agenda remains outstanding. Robertson's location of the glocal within the sociology of religion and economic culture tended to neglect power differentials and other tensions between the global and the local. These are encapsulated by Zygmunt Baumann's decoding of glocal rhetoric as 'globalization for some, localization for others' (1998). Put in other words, the global is for mobile elite cosmopolitans, the local is for the immobile masses.

Summing up, we may locate limits to the analytical purchase of ideas of the glocal and glocalization wherever global and local relations fail to inter-penetrate, and instead remain only loosely coupled.

The *final* mechanism, named by Petrella, involves inter-local connections. Here the local sets free the local. Bearing in mind the broad sense given here to the local – embracing the regional, national, and sub-national, discursively as well as institutionally – this mechanism logically involves two types of situation. The first is where the local sets itself free. The second is where diffusion of social practices takes place from one local to another.

The idea of local self-liberation is typically associated with liberation struggles of local subjects to be free from imperial domination, and has a long historical pedigree. This ranges from historic struggles of the Jewish peoples to be free from Roman or Babylonian domination, to 20th-century struggles for national freedom from Austro-Hungarian, British, French, Portuguese, Soviet, Yugoslav, and Indonesian Empires and Federations. This category shades into another, that is the struggle of minorities for liberation from dominant nation-states, such as Basques from Spain or Kurds from Iraq. There are also movements among indigenous peoples, in Australia and Canada, for example, for some kind of national recognition or even secession.

One of the more difficult issues facing the idea of national or local self-liberation is the extent to which such struggles are purely local. This problem arises because such struggles are decreasingly autonomous and independent. Put another way, the local may achieve liberation in part through the intervention or influence of some other local. This might involve the diffusion of inspiration and more specific innovations from one context to another, or the competitive emulation of one local by another. In the former case it is noteworthy how national struggles for independence influenced and inspired each other, previous successes encouraging and informing later struggles. Thus 19th-century Italian independence influenced the Irish movement whose success in the 1920s further encouraged Indian nationalism whose success in turn in the 1940s encouraged African independence movements. This is not to say that such exogenous influences were all-important or decisive. But it is to say that such inter-local influences are of some significance in local liberation processes.

Inter-local influences may also involve the strategic intervention of a more powerful local. This typically occurs when a powerful nation-state sees it in its interests to give support to a national liberation struggle against a nation-state with whom the powerful nation is at war or in dispute. Celebrated examples include German agreement to the passage of Lenin through its territory back to Russia during the First World War. The effect of this was predicted to sow further dissension within Czarist Russia thereby weakening its war effort against Germany.

Conclusion

Using Petrella's *seven* mechanisms of global–local articulation allow development of a more complex account of globalization than that offered by first- and second-wave theories. In the first place they dispose of two simple propositions. The first is that the global is swallowing up or hollowing out the local. The second is that the local, while under pressure from the global, cannot be regarded as a resilient form of resistance, authentically located in autonomous non-global modes of existence. The reason why these ways of thinking are defective is partly that they tell a story that is very simplistic, ignoring contrary trends and complexities. Additionally, however, and beyond that, such approaches are founded on a false dualism between the global and the local – a dualism which is unsustainable in the light of global inter-connections and the inter-penetration of both global and local institutions and cultural practices.

This applies whether we consider the re-scaling of institutions such as states and modes of governance. But it also applies to more metaphorical or symbolic understandings of cultural practices and identities.

An even stronger statement of the inter-penetration thesis is provided by Robertson who claims that any sense of the local is now an aspect of globalization (1995: 33). This process is not the same thing as saying that globalization creates the homogenization of various locals into one pattern, but rather that inter-connection has reached the point where the government and governance and both the material and the symbolic culture of any locality have become effectively hybridized through global impacts. While the term 'glocal' is a useful way of signifying this, its main limitation is that it suggests total fusion rather than different degrees of inter-penetration. It is also unable to explain why so many glocal processes become re-indigenized by local populations.

Robertson's argument is probably better characterized as methodo-logical glocalism rather than methodological globalism. Another route to the same kind of conclusion, albeit one that by-passes the idea of the glocal, is provided in Scholte's (2000) discussion of methodological territorialism. This is defined as 'the practice of understanding the social world...in terms of territorial geography'. This practice may no longer be appropriate as a general methodology of research, given the extent of global inter-connection. However, this does not mean that territory is no longer important, whether in an institutional or metaphorical sense. For Scholte, we live in a globalizing not a thor-oughly globalized world. The task, then, is not to replace methodological nationalism or methodological territorialism with methodological globalism. Emphasis should rather be placed on the complex and dynamic ways in which territory is articulated and re-articulated with political institutions and cultural practices in a globalizing world.

In the following chapter we return to the question of globalization and human agency through an exploration of ideas of global civil society. These might perhaps be re-termed 'glocal civil society', in the light of the analysis developed in this chapter, but this has not been the way in which protagonists and analysts have proceeded.

6

Global Civil Society

In the last ten years or so, a great deal of interest and attention has been given to the emergence of global civil society (Keane 2003). If there is one idea that has captured a sense of human involvement in the making of global society, this is it. While the term itself has rightly been seen as a fuzzy mixture of moral, descriptive, and analytical meanings (Anheier *et al.* 2001: 11), this has not in any way restricted its ever-widening use in commentaries on globalization. Amongst the meanings attached to it are the idea of an autonomous social sphere beyond states and markets, the development of trans-national social movement activism from below, and the normative ideal of a virtuous cosmopolitan world free from local conflicts and national jealousies.

Proponents of global civil society are also very much a product of third-wave thinking about globalization (see Chapter 1). First, they challenge the fatalistic determinism of many first-wave accounts that see globalization as an unstoppable Juggernaut beyond human control. Such challenges to determinism are closely associated with the view that 'alternative global worlds are possible'. Some even go so far as to claim 'global civil society' as a progressive social force capable of radical social change, that is a new emancipatory force designed for a post-Socialist post-colonial world.

Equally, however, global civil society thinking is critical of second-wave commentaries that downplayed the significance and extent of trans-national developments. Whereas the idea of civil society developed historically as a characteristic of cities, city-states, and nations, third-wave thinking is strongly committed to the outmoded nature of this urban and national focus. Rather than exaggerated features of superficial global hype, global civil society, it is claimed, represents a new social reality. This is presented as either an alternative kind of 'globalization from below' or a communitarian alternative to 'globalization', defined in terms of neo-liberal capitalism.

In typical third-wave fashion, debates over global civil society have in the process moved beyond theoretical speculation and moral assertion, generating new evidence about a range of trans-national social activities and organizations. Two of the foremost projects of this kind are the London School of Economics grouping that produces the annual *Global Civil Society Yearbook* (Anheier *et al*. 2001, Glasius *et al*. 2002), and the Stanford University study of INGOs (Boli and Thomas 1999).

Within this chapter, we look first at an appropriate working definition of global civil society, and then turn to an analysis of the evolution of social activities and organizational forms that fall within it. We ask how new global civil society is, and explore further the complex ways in which such trans-national developments have been articulated with local and national institutions and identities.

'Civil society' is a term with a long historical pedigree. In classical and early modern times it was typically used to describe political communities whose self-governing purposefulness was contrasted with states of nature characterized by violence and lack of civility. From the mid-18th to the latter part of the 20th century it became identified with a distinct social sphere, differentiated from government, family, and sometimes from markets as well (Keane 2003).

Civil society in this sense was, however, seen in national terms, increasingly as that substratum of civil attachments and institutions upon which any stable democratic polity rests. Civil society became to be seen as a vital ingredient in democratic state-building in late 20th-century Latin America (Weffort 1989) and Eastern Europe (Havel 1985), just as it had earlier been in 19th-century Western Europe and North America. The utility of the term in this more recent context was that it served as an idea for opponents to authoritarian states, linking churches, trade unions, and intellectuals.

Evolution in the meaning of civil society has left its mark on the transposition of the concept beyond nation-states to the global arena. Analytical usages of the term typically focus on one or more of the following:

(a) the identification of a social sphere, differentiated from the state, the private world of the family, and the operation of the market, which is trans-national in its scope (Anheier *et al*. 2001);
(b) the expansion throughout the 1990s of trans-national social activism and cultural innovation from below (Perlas 2000, Pianta 2001);
(c) autonomous self-directed trans-national social action from non-governmental sources (Keane 2001, 2003).

This set of working definitions has a strongly contemporary resonance. The phenomena that have given rise to debates over civil society include the increasing influence of cross-border social movements such as Amnesty International or Friends of the Earth, and the impact of mass mobilizations of opinion on issues such as the free-trade regime of the WTO, or global warming and environmental protection. For those who seek alternatives to global capitalism and elite globalization, global civil society serves as a mobilizing resource to promote alternative values to those of economic liberalism.

Beyond these egregious headline phenomena, however, there lies a broader set of phenomena which constitute and comprise what might, in Durkheimian language, be called 'the material and moral milieux' of global inter-connection. Durkheim used this language as a way of understanding changes in patterns of social solidarity between traditional and modern societies, linked with an advancing division of labour, and expressed in local and national arrangements (Durkheim 1964 [1893]). Extending this vocabulary into a globalizing world assists in drawing attention to a far wider set of activities and actors. They include modes of inter-personal cross-border communication through a range of media of which the Internet is the most recent, global exchanges of scientific, technical, religious, moral, and artistic ideas, and transactions across borders through communities of language, economic co-operation, organizational solidarity, diasporic identification, and personal friendship.

To take this wider perspective is to frame global civil society as something more than an emergent trans-national discourse of moral and political protest against global economic arrangements – important though such movements from below clearly are. The reason for taking this wider view is that it enables us to retain a stronger analytical purchase on the diversity and complexity of trans-national ideas and activities that have developed from social spaces that have a significant autonomy from states.

The strongest statement in favour of this approach is provided by John Keane (2001). He sees global civil society as 'a vast interconnected and multi-layered social space that comprises many hundreds and thousands of self-directing and non-governmental institutions and ways of life.... This complex...looks and feels expansive and poly-archic.... Precisely because it comprises a bewildering variety of intersecting habitats and species; organizations, civic and business initiatives, coalitions, social movements, linguistic communities and cultural identities' (ibid.: 23). This approach contrasts with moral-political conceptions of global civil society that typically exclude markets because they are seen as elite activities that often damage civil life (Perlas 2000, Yoshikazu 2000). To neglect the civil aspects of markets is for Keane tantamount to saying that global civil society could exist without money or monetary exchange, held together simply by love, hard work, and mutuality.

One potential difficulty with this argument is that a similar case could be made for including state-centred politics within conceptions of civil society. Just as civil society is unthinkable without money and economic activity, so it might be thought equally unthinkable without constitutional and legal rights guaranteed by state power. Why, therefore, include markets but exclude the state? The reason for excluding the state is primarily to draw attention to centres of social activity and innovation outside states, and upon which states rely for their effective functioning. Within a national setting, the attempt to create stable post-Communist states in Eastern Europe has proven incredibly difficult in situations where a functioning civil society is lacking. Within a global setting, the demonstrable importance of non-state activities that operate beyond nation-states requires conceptual recognition. It is because global arrangements are not simply contained within inter-state arrangements that the concept of global civil society has risen to prominence as a robust and powerful concept.

Keane further elaborates his poly-archic notion of global civil society by specifying typical participants (ibid.: 27) and institutions (ibid.: 31). In the former category we may find athletes, campaigners, musicians, religious believers, managers, aid-workers, medics, scientists, journalists, and academics, while in the latter we may find households, community organizations, and linguistically shared norms such as friendship, trust, and non-violent co-operation. One advantage of this broad focus is that it directs our attention beyond the focus on social movements and activists that has received most attention in many previous studies (Ghils 1992). Global civil society in this sense is far broader than global NGO activism.

Anheier and Themudo (2002) have produced a threefold approach to global civil society, focusing on individual values, activities (e.g. research, relief), and organizations. The breadth of this perspective enables a balance to be struck between formal organizations at one end of the spectrum, through social movements and the more diffuse networks identified in Chapter 5, to individual level phenomena at the other. Clearly the three are not mutually exclusive in the sense that individuals with values constitute networks, movements, and organizations, while informal networks operate both inside and beyond formally constituted bodies.

Some historical pathways in the making of global civil society

The historical and spatial development of global civil society, defined
broadly, poses questions to which only very general answers may currently
be given. If we consider cross-border activities involving individuals,
networks, and organizations, then the origins of global civil society go
far back in time. As discussed in Chapter 2, long-run processes of
Imperial development, population movement, trade, and religious
expansion created archaic and proto-modern types of global civil trans-
action. Trading of products and technological diffusion, together with
the sharing of religious and scientific ideas, created forms of interaction
that pre-date contemporary phases of global civil society. These were
manifest within trading and mercantile cities, places of learning and
religious pilgrimage, and manifest through the spoken word or letter.
They are to be seen in St Paul's epistles to scattered Christian communities in the 1st century AD, to the extensive cross-border correspondence
of Erasmus, the 16th-century humanist. Organizations like the Benedictine
Cistercian order have been as medieval versions of trans-national
organization (Moulin 1980). Such activities pre-date the more recent
modes of long-distance 'civil' communication through the mass-produced
book, the newspaper, personal travel, and the World Wide Web.

Having said this, it is equally clear that such activities were never
completely autonomous from activities of state. Political patronage and
protection mattered a great deal in cross-border activities, including
trade, exploration, and rights to safe movement just as it did within given
territories. The 13th-century example of long-distance travel and cultural
diffusion of the Venetian Marco Polo and his family are instructive.
Here the celebrated visits to China and Western Asia depended on
patronage and safe passage, whether from the Papacy in Europe or the
various Khanates in the East (Larner 2001).

Global civil society, it has been said, has been largely a Western
affair. The universalizing civil legacies of the classical world, re-invigorated
during the Renaissance, paved the way for the globalizing liberal and
humanistic ideas of the modern world. The old adage that 'urban air
makes free' was first associated with the autonomous cities of late
medieval and early modern Europe (for a critical discussion of this
argument see Holton 1986). Their 'freedom' represented a break from
both aristocratic control and various types of centralized despotic
control associated with 'Eastern' patterns of political culture. Such
developmental contrasts between the West and the East are, however,
highly misleading, tending to obscure dynamic features of the world

beyond Europe, which had its own trading cities, centres of learning, and patterns of long-distance pilgrimage. One effect of this has been lack of awareness of non-Western patterns of cross-border exchange and interaction, for example within the Islamic world (for insights into this see Robinson 1993, Lapidus 2001).

There are, nonetheless, certain contrasts to be drawn when examining different pathways towards global civil society. One of the most important of these concerns is the relationship between the printed word, cross-border communication, and social change.

The development of mechanized printing in 15th-century Europe is rightly seen as an important historical moment. Its effects over the next centuries extend not simply to the technological possibility of mass communication, but also to the ways literate publics imagined themselves and their relationship with the world as a whole. Benedict Anderson (1983) has famously noted the importance of revolutions in printing to the development of national consciousness. Printing technologies, allied with vernacular languages, enabled individuals to imagine each other as co-members of a common national community. For Anderson, these effects apply equally to the nationalisms of Western Europe, Latin America, and, more recently, Indonesia.

Other scholars have, however, noted a historical contrast in readiness to use the printed word between Western and Islamic worlds. The contrast is between mediated and face-to-face communication. Whereas communication mediated through books and newspapers became a crucial feature of Western and Westernized civil societies in between the 17th and 19th centuries, the Islamic word was slower to take up print culture. The contrast here is not, however, between outward-looking and introverted social worlds. The Islamic preference, according to Robinson (1993), was rather for the authenticity of the spoken word of particular persons, whose interpretations of holy books and religious law could be traced back through a series of inter-personal linkages from particular teachers to students who in turn became teachers of the next generation. In a world of religious teachers and pan-Islamic cultural solidarities, an alternative pattern of global civil development to print-centred Western developments was evident well into the 19th century. While secularization and a greater convergence to Western models is evident in the contemporary world of Arabic newspapers (Hamm 2003) and television, it is striking how important the spoken word of individuals such as the late Ayatollah Khomeini or Osama bin Laden remains.

While contrasts of this kind may be drawn between different types of cross-border civil engagement, it is also important not to treat different global worlds as entirely separate and distinct civilizational spheres. Interaction, whether in the form of conflict, co-operation, or diffusion of ideas and technologies is an enduring feature of global history well before the present. A 'global moment' from the 19th century, which captures the complexity and inter-weaving of Western and non-Western cross-border exchange, is recounted by the pan-African writer Edward Wilmot Blyden (the following section is based on Blyden *et al.* 1871: 1–73).

Born of African descent in the free (i.e. non-slave), Caribbean port of St Thomas, Virgin Islands in 1832, Blyden was repatriated to West Africa at age 19 under the patronage of a Christian Missionary. After further education, he was himself ordained as well as rising to the position of Professor of Greek and Latin at Liberia College. There he pursued enquiries into African history prior to the slave trades, and as part of this gained an awareness of an Islamic presence south of the Sahara but inland from the African coast among groups such as Arabic-speaking Mandingoes. When Arabic literature was sent by a fellow Protestant minister based in Beirut, Blyden noted the inclusion of a number of questions pertaining to these West African Islamic groups. These he was finally able to answer when meeting an Arabic-speaking priest from the trans-Saharan trading town of Kankan in the interior.

It is easy to read the general history of cross-cultural encounters during the epoch of Imperialism as a racially informed confrontation between the West, in the shape of explorers, traders, soldiers, and missionaries. Within West Africa, the idea of Darkest Africa symbolized for many Westerners a sense of the unknown and uncivilized, on behalf of whom it was the white man's burden to intercede in the development of commerce, enlightenment, and spiritual conversion. But where exactly does Blyden fit into the dichotomy of West and non-West? While a Western-educated Christian, his interest in African history and its accomplishments was atypical of Europeans. Yet he cannot be said to have emerged from an African context in any unmediated sense. His position may thus be seen as an example of one of the 'third spaces' identified by post-colonial theorists.

A further example may be drawn from Bengal and global moments in the life of the academic and writer Brajendranath Seal, professor of Mental and Moral Sciences at Calcutta University between 1914 and 1920 (Lago 1972: 57 n). A member of the Bengali intelligentsia and associate of the poet Tagore, Seal had been invited in 1911 to be the first speaker at the Universal Races Congress, an important East–West conference of activists, intellectuals, and NGOs held in London (see especially Holton 2002). Seal, a polymath of extraordinary proportions, had come under the influence of Hegel through the instruction of Dr Hastie, the Scottish theologian and missionary. Hastie saw Hegel as part of the superior and more progressive Western idealist legacy to backward India, a legacy destined to overcome the backward idolatrous superstition he took to be central to Hindu religious practice (Hastie 1882).

Seal, by contrast, sought to integrate Hegel into a synthesis which valorized elements of Hindu thought and Bengali Romantic literature. This synthesis retained a Hegelian philosophy of history built around an unfolding universalism linking form and spirit. But it departed from Hegel in its positive re-evaluation of Oriental achievements in art, philosophy, and religion. The Orient, in other words, was as capable of progressive and universalistic contributions to world history as the Occident (Seal 1994 [1903]). Seal placed India within world-building processes that linked science, commerce, and inter-national law with a longer-term history embracing 'the ghosts of universal empires and universal churches' in the construction of a 'spiritual civilisation' (URC 1911: 23–24). Hegel's philosophy of history, including the idea of history as the working out of the dialectics of master–slave relations, has also been identified in the historical imagination of the leading African-American intellectual William du Bois (Lewis 1993: 139–140), also present at the 1911 Congress.

As with Blyden, the question arises as to whether Seal be seen as a Westernized Indian, an authentic exemplar of Bengali culture, or, as the evidence here suggests, the product of a syncretic inter-cultural milieu, blending a range of influences. Here distinctions between the West and the East have become so blurred that their continued usage as dichotomous contrasts misleads as much as they inform.

The line of argument sketched here with some detailed examples is that there are multiple globalized civil societies or spaces. The idea of a cultural dividing line between civil society and its 'others' is not that between a modern differentiated West and a traditional undifferenti-ated non-West. Rather the evidence from studies conducted across time and space suggests multiple overlapping and intersecting civil society networks may sometimes come into conflict rather than being inherent elements of a common overarching process. The argument here is similar to recent discussions of cosmopolitanism, where Holton (2002) and van der Veer (2002), following a series of papers in Cheah and Robbins (1998), speak of cosmopolitanisms rather than a singular paradigmatic Western liberal-democratic cosmopolitanism.

Given the overemphasis on organizational themes in much literature on global civil society, it is worthwhile giving further attention to some of the individual level aspects of the topic. There are a number of ways of doing this. Initially we focus on the text-letter which appears as a common feature in both historical and contemporary aspects of global civil interaction. Attention then moves on to examine recent changes in communications technology, associated with ideas of a cyberspatial civil society (Urry 2000: 74). Finally we examine individual attachments to globalism, embodying identitities and value commitments to trans-national entities, often grouped under notions of cosmopolitanism.

Communication and global civil society

There is, of course, no intrinsic connection between letter writing and globalization, the letter being an entirely flexible form of communication for local as much as global purposes. Up until the very recent epoch of low-cost telecommunications, it is nonetheless the case that the letter was the pre-eminent mode of both individual and organizational communication across boundaries. For such a system to be operated effectively across all borders, however, it was necessary to establish an effective cross-border letter mail service. The beginnings of such a system designed to overcome the maze of conflicting national services were laid with the establishment of the Universal Postal Union in 1874.

The sociologist, Ferdinand Toennies, in a 1911 review of recent world development, thought of science, the press, and the arts as arena in which important cross-cultural and cross-national exchanges had taken place (Toennies 1911). Taken together, they might be seen as key elements in the emergence of global civil society. What is striking is the relevance of the letter as a model of print-based communication in each sphere. Bazerman (2000), in particular, has pointed to the ways that letters have influenced a large range of modern print-based genres such as the scientific article, the newspaper, the novel, and the financial instrument. In the newspaper, for example, letters from correspondents as well as letters to the editor form crucial elements of both news and comment. One source of the novel is the epistolary tradition, whereby a series of letters are the form within which the narrative is set (Kenyon 1992). The scientific article, for its part, originated in the 17th century out of the correspondence of Henry Oldenburg, summarized in what was to become the Philosophical Transactions of the Royal Society (Bazerman 2000: 15–25). Although the age of the Internet has been associated with the eclipse of the conventional letter, it is again striking how the form of the email reproduces the letter format, blended with the format of the memorandum.

The significance of the letter as a mode of communication within global civil society is its capacity to convey person-to-person meaning with emotional immediacy, moral force, and reflexivity (Barton and Hall 2000). The inter-personal characteristics of the genre do not, of course, exclude family or some other group composition and reading of text, as may often be found in communication between migrants, the homeland, and the wider diaspora. Chain letters of this kind follow chain migration. Letters, in this sense, link worlds that are spatially separated. Here they may play cognitive, expressive, moral, and political roles, involving information, emotion, commitment, and political protest. In this way both public and private worlds as well as the intersection between them are engaged. Across spatially separated global spaces, letters, together with their recent offspring the email, are both indicators of the existence of a global civil society and carriers of civility.

Books, newspapers, and pamphlets may also be collectively read and discussed in both partially literate and more fully literate civil societies. With the rise of mechanized printing, books could be produced in many different publishing centres, often in different languages, creating a world of publishing houses and translating. The translator in this respect represents a key human actor in the development of global civil society, as the medium 'by which texts from one culture and language are transmitted to another' (Cronin 2003: 124). This role is a complex one, nonetheless, in the sense that translators, through engagement with cultural difference, are somehow 'at a distance' from their own social context, leaving them, in Cronin's view, as 'nomads-by-obligation...multiculturalists *ante verbum*' (ibid.: 126).

The civil world of letter writing, book publishing, and newspaper reading may have bridged space, but the speed of global civil interaction was circumscribed by the transport technologies of horse, camel, or sailing ship until the 19th century. While the advent of railways, as we have seen in Chapter 4, speeded up personal travel within particular land masses, it was a series of innovations associated with the telegraph, telephone, radio, air transport, and latterly digitalization and the Internet which speeded up transmission of information, and enhanced direct person-to-person communication of text and voice messages. The spread of the telegraph in the 1850s and 1860s was crucial to the capacity of communications media to relay news, and was linked with the development of wire services such as Reuters founded in 1851 (Read 1999). With subsequent enhancements made possible by telephone and radio, the speed of public and private civil transactions increased, creating the technical infrastructure for the construction of 'world news', and somewhat more nebulous ideas such as 'world opinion' and 'the international community'.

New technical possibilities are of course only a necessary not a sufficient cause of this kind of development. For much of the last 150 years, the development of the mass media and much mass media content had been designed to build nations (see Mac Laughlin 2001 on Ireland) and to build exclusive national if not nationalist walls around territories rather than cosmopolitan bridges to others. While the telegraph increased the speed of news transmission, the geographical extent of print media markets was limited to the speed of rail, and audiences were national at best and sub-national in the larger countries such as the US and Australia.

Nor has technology been all-determining in creating a national focus, since the nationalist policy preoccupations of most proprietors clearly have a political effect. And political factors remain important even in an age of global communications, in the manufacture, selection, and interpretation of news around national and sometimes xenophobic as much as tolerant global audiences. The Internet itself, while the most contemporary of communications technologies, is equally able to carry messages of racial hatred and nazi world-views as much as cosmopolitan tolerance. Two important conclusions follow. One is that global 'means' are perfectly compatible with local 'ends'. The other is that civil society contains a wide spectrum of views including racism as well as cosmopolitanism. Hate and loathing as much as love and comradeship are both, it seems, features of global civil society.

Another very different interpretation of the development of the Internet sees the emergence of virtual communities across cyberspace, communities which transcend national societies and forms of identification. Rheingold (1993), in particular, sees virtual interaction as a key element in global inter-personal interaction. A good deal of this argument stemmed from the intimate excitement generated among pioneering developers of computer-mediated communication around bodies such as WELL (Whole Earth Lectronic Link), many of them based in the San Francisco Bay area. The folksy feel of this world that extended rapidly outwards was reflected in the sub-title of early versions of Rheingold's book, 'Homesteading on the Electronic Highway'. By 2000, in a retrospective and revised edition, Rheingold has a more muted appreciation of the significance of Internet-based communication, emphasizing more of the dark side of the genre. Absence of corporeality, for example, can be a limitation as much as a source of freedom, allowing the inauthentic expression of personal views, and of course deception and potential abuse of confidences (Rheingold 2000: 330–331). The WELL itself degenerated into a world of rebellions, splits, feuds, and character assassination. This is consistent with the findings of Kollock and Smith (1999: 13), who argue that the Internet groups are likely to be anarchic if unmediated, and authoritarian if mediated.

Other analysts have also been wary of the line of argument that links the Internet with social emancipation. Some have queried how far the Internet has political consequences for the development of a new kind of electronic or e-democracy. Putnam (2000: 170–171) reports that several studies in the US, including his own, have found that Internet users are no more likely to have strong civic engagements than non-users. Others have disputed how far virtual communities are 'real' communities (Jones 1995) with some kind of binding effect outside the episodic sphere of virtual communication. One of the methodological difficulties is that the meaning of computer-mediated communication is not so much created by the networks as within them (ibid.: 12). Text-based cyber-electronic exchanges are relatively easy to capture and analyse as conversations. What is far harder to determine is the symbolic signifi-cance of virtual interactions for patterns of social solidarity and community. For Urry (2000: 173), virtual interaction may be more significant in developing 'new cognitive and interpretive faculties' among individuals linked to new forms of visual design than for any new form of community or civil society.

Taken overall, then, it is by no means clear that virtual communities are an increasingly significant element in global civil society. We turn now to questions of attitude and world-views.

Global civil society and global world-views

How far have world-views changed in the direction of some kind of global, trans-national or cosmopolitan direction, and how far is this either constitutive of or at least a supportive element in various milieux that comprise global civil society? It is supposed that a set of social changes ranging from increased personal travel, widespread use of the Internet, global satellite TV consumption, and increased flows of immigrants have shifted views in this direction. However, it is not clear that the purported change has taken place. This would not be the first occasion in which there are more explanations of a phenomenon thought to exist than there are data supporting the actual existence of the phenomenon itself. One major difficulty with social scientific discussions of cosmo-politanism, then, is the lack of empirical evidence. In what follows, the search for an answer to questions about the scale and modalities of cosmopolitanism takes a rather complex form.

Some reservations need to be made about the question under investigation. To refer to 'global' or 'cosmopolitan' world-views is a rather bland and generalized way of identifying a set of orientations and attitudes that vary significantly amongst themselves. It is helpful to begin with a simple model of a global–local spectrum. At one end of this are what is typically referred to as cosmopolitan views. Following Hannerz (1990, 1992) these refer to supra-national orientations that engage sympathetically with others. They may be contrasted with trans-national orientations that are more extensive than a territorially bound national or local affiliation but, nonetheless, contained within an enlarged but bounded sense of community. This category may include diasporic groups of migrants and global tourists. At the other end of the spectrum are locals with affiliations that are territorially bounded, and which rely on sharp distinctions between us and them.

This model is of some value in distinguishing between more open and more restricted modes of supra-national orientation. It has, none-theless, been criticized for drawing the line of distinction between them in an arbitrary Eurocentric manner, which among other things underplays class dimensions to cosmopolitanism (Werbner 1999). The gist of the criticism is that Hannerz places working-class migrant-settlers into the more bounded trans-national category, seeing them as content with creating a surrogate home outside the place of origin. Meanwhile, middle class professionals and elite members such as diplomats and managers are somehow regarded as cosmopolitan. The latter assumption has found powerful expression in recent speculative discourse on globalization. Here cosmopolitans are typically presented as elite-based or middle class (Castells 1996, Bauman 1998), sharply contrasted with working-class and marginalized populations condemned either to localism or to parochial and marginalized forms of movement.

One of the main problems with the elite-focused approach is that it neglects historic and contemporary evidence of working-class cosmo-politanism or cosmopolitanism from below. Historically this evidence is marshalled by Gilroy (1993), who locates forms of inter-cultural engagement with others within the mobile worlds of seamen and African-American slaves. The itinerant workers from many countries who played a key role in the establishment of bodies such as the militant Industrial Workers of the World or subsequent Communist Parties drew in significant measure on those who had worked or travelled across a range of milieux (Holton 1976, Burgmann 1996).

In the contemporary world, Werbner (1999) has spoken of 'working-class Pakistani cosmopolitans', whose labour migrations in Europe, the Middle East, and North America create 'global pathways'. These are claimed as cosmopolitans not trans-nationals in the sense that these pathways comprise not simply diasporic interactions but embrace engagement with non-diasporic worlds. These include the learning of other languages, incorporation into multi-national workplaces, and the learning of expertise in the material culture of the West. If we add working class, and non-Western sources of cosmopolitanism to the more familiar Western emphasis on liberal-democratic outward-looking virtue, we are clearly talking about somewhat different cosmopolitanisms with differing modalities.

The most extensive data on the distribution of territorial identities has been collected through the World Values survey data. Norris (2000: 162), reporting evidence of this kind drawn from 70 countries, finds that a primary orientation to the world as a whole, consistently averages around 15 per cent of respondents. This is significant but comes nowhere near the 50 per cent level typical for a local or regional affiliation, and the large minority of those who identify with nation.

The discussion so far has proceeded with a simple cosmopolitan-local spectrum. There is, however, a very real methodological difficulty with the spectrum model itself and that is the mutually exclusive assumptions that differentiate positions on the spectrum. Put another way, one cannot be classified as both cosmopolitan and local. This dualistic assumption has already been challenged in previous chapters, and remains valid here. The possibility is thereby raised of individuals in which the cosmopolitan (or global) and the local are somehow combined, fused, or in some kind of harmony or tension.

The critique becomes very relevant if we ask what are the limits to cosmopolitan thinking? Are these simply set by those whose affilation is to a less extensive entity trans-nationals and various kinds of national, regional, and local identity?

In the case of trans-nationalism as defined above, there is clearly evidence of combinations of orientations. Permanent or long-term settlers, for example, may develop dual or hyphenated identities, embracing both the homeland and the country of settlement. This creates Greek-Australians or Chinese-Americans. These hyphenated identities balance public integration within the new country of origin, with private maintenance of ethnic affiliation. This position is distinct from what has been called long-distance nationalism (Anderson 1992). Here, diasporic populations, some of them thousands of kilometres from the country of origin, maintain close ties with the politics and culture of the homeland, engendered or re-awakened in some cases by dramatic events such as civil war and bids for independence in what is regarded as the homeland. Skrbis' (1999) study of Croatian and Slovenian migrants in Australia in the period of recent Balkan conflict charts this kind of re-awakening.

Whereas in the case of long-distance nationalism we are talking of a globalized localism, instances of hyphenated identity point more to a kind of trans-nationalism. Neither represents cosmopolitanism in any thoroughgoing sense.

The robustness of nationalism and national identity is perhaps the major line of objection to the idea that there has been a shift towards greater cosmopolitanism. Smith (1990) has argued very powerfully that globalized identities are unlikely to ever carry the cultural resonances of the common historical lineage and sense of place available within nationalism. A globalized culture is either impossible to create or likely to be shallow in its effects. This, it might be thought, is why nationalism is a resurgent force in the world even in an epoch of globalization. The evidence for this lies both in continuing movements for national freedom among those who do not possess a state (e.g. Palestinians or Kurds), and in nationalist objections to supra-national regionalism found among EU countries unwilling to accept the euro, independent countries who fear domination by powerful neighbours, and even powerful countries like the US facing global terrorist attack.

And yet certain ideas of nationhood are by no means impervious to outward-looking engagement. There is, most importantly, a distinction between ethnic and civil or civic nationalism, that is between nationalism that is based on some notion of an ethnic community of blood ties (ethno-nationalism) and nationalism that takes a more civic conception of the collective rights and obligations of a given group of citizens (Brubaker 1992). Civic nationalists, as developed in the French Revolution, saw la France as outward-looking republican force that might facilitate the freedom of others from the tyranny that the ancien régime repre-sented. Contemporary civic nationalists may welcome immigrants and may not feel threatened by free trade.

The idea of an outward-looking civic nationalism is an important example of a more general point, namely that both trans-national and cosmopolitan orientations emerge from a specific context in time and space, and may draw upon such particularities to articulate elements of their cosmopolitan viewpoint. The scale and dimensions of these kinds of phenomena are, however, obscured when analysts simply seek to identify nationalists of cosmopolitans as singular identities.

One way of exploring this further is to ask about the range of affiliations individuals may hold – global, regional, national and local – how these elements are ranked, and how they articulate with each other. This method may be used not simply for migrant sub-sets of populations, but for populations in general. Phillips (2002) uses this approach in a study of the imagined communities to which Australians feel attached. The 1995 world values study asked about identities held simultaneously and how these were ranked. It is interesting that respondents felt no difficulty answering this question, indicating that the idea of combining differentially ranked orientations is a salient one.

Nation was the single most important orientation ranked first (43.3%), compared with locality, coming a close second at 32.3 per cent, with 'the world as a whole' being of comparatively minor significance at 9.9 per cent. The broad ranking did not change much when respondents were asked about the two most important orientations, with those combining nation and locality numbering a majority (58.4%). However, the proportion of those mentioning both nation and world (15.6%) is not insignificant, to which may be added those mentioning the world and the locality (6.4%), giving a total of one-fifth of the sample who had some kind of global orientation. Meanwhile, localists, identifying with locality and sub-national region numbered 19.5 per cent. This distribution of orientations is consistent with Smith's scepticism about the possibility of a global culture. Yet it also suggests that cosmopolitanism may be usefully pursued in combination with other orientations rather than as a free-standing de-contextualized philosophical commitment. The limited data currently available, however, make it hard to relate looking outward to specific experiences of globalization.

By beginning with individual level phenomena we have tried to determine whether some kind of sea change in values is evident as a cultural milieu from which global organizations might emerge. This has not, however, proven possible. What does seem more likely is that outward-looking orientations of a trans-national or cosmopolitan kind, emerge within national and local settings. How far value-change comes first and organization builds upon it, or the reverse causation applies – organizational activity changing values – is unclear.

Global civil society is not simply the collective construct of organizations and public activists. And yet such organizational aspects, both formal and informal are of immense significance, in linking the aspirations, activities, and discontents of the world's populations.

The organizational face of global civil society

We have already drawn attention in Chapter 3 to the importance of networks alongside more formal organizations in the development of globalization. Anheier and Themudo (2002: 191) make the point that the organizational forms of global civil society are extremely varied, comprising 'organizations, associations, networks, movements and groups, whose contours and the forces that shape them we are just beginning to fathom'. In Figure 4 we list a set of examples, including entities that are large and small in terms of membership or budgets, spatially centred or diffuse, carrying on quite different functions.

What these varied organizational forms have in common, according to Anheier and Themudo, is that they are less settled and in more flux than established politics (e.g. party systems), economic organizations (e.g. industries), and social policy regimes (e.g. welfare systems). The argument here assumes that more stable organizations unconstrained by centralized hierarchies are better able to seize opportunities arising from a new global conjuncture. New political opportunities have grown up with the end of the Cold War, while continuing reductions in the costs of communication make trans-national linkages more viable for movements and networks with limited resources. They also argue that value changes linked with ideas of individual opportunity and responsibility also play a part in underwriting global civil society initiatives from below.

This approach is useful but has a number of difficulties. First, many of the core organizations of global civil society are founded on very formal centralized bureaucratic principles, and have proven as robust, sometimes even more so, than political parties or welfare regimes. They include both large-scale charities like the International Committee of the Red Cross (founded 1863), and Save the Children Fund (founded 1920), as noted by Anheier and Themudo, but also many examples which they

Large-scale charities with hundreds of staff
Non-profit corporations with franchises in numerous countries
Transnational volunteer networks with no real expenditures
Virtual associations with no identifiable location
Single issue campaign groups
Philanthropic foundations with multi-billion dollar endowments
Savings clubs among migrant communities spread across different countries

Figure 4   Organizational forms of global civil society

Source: Anheier and Themudo (2002: 191).

neglect. These include long-enduring religious organizations like the Catholic and Anglican Churches, and trade unions many of which were founded in the 19th century. While there has, therefore, been a growing diversity of organizational types, it is important not to overstate its significance. Which of the newer forms, we might ask, will prove robust and which will run up against problems, such as the resource limitations of informal organizations facing long campaigns against powerful interests (see Yearley and Forrester 2000 on resource problems facing environmental movements campaigning against Shell).

The other main problem, which we have already noted, is the arbitrary exclusion of profit-making corporations from the analysis. To include them is, of course, to define global civil society in a way that excludes any necessary connection with radical politics from below. But it does have the merit of including the worlds of work, management and many forms of related professional, scientific, and technical organizations. Such activities and the flows of income, skills formation, and knowledge that arise from their activities not only effect civil society, defined as 'autonomous self-directed trans-national social action from non-governmental sources', but also help to constitute it.

To exclude trans-national corporations and the activities they represent on the basis of corporate power, low-wage practices in some locations, and poor environmental practice makes bad sociological sense. This is because the millions of human actors involved in corporate activities are part of society, implicating the livelihoods, world-views, and daily lives of those involved. To present the matter as a dichotomy between a small elite outside civil society and a mass of exploited victims within it, between the system and the life-world, is to deny corporations enable as well as constrain, and are learning and information environments as much as institutions of control. Gross inequalities of power, income, and responsibility are evident in many settings. Yet this, in a paradoxical sense noted originally by Marx, helps to stimulate, often through mechanisms of conflict, what might be referred to as forms of working-class civil society, alongside the civil worlds stimulated by the managerial and professional requirements of corporations. Trade union and campaign organization, membership of professional organizations, and global migration of both skilled and unskilled labour are all crucial to global civil society and are better understood if corporations are placed within rather than outside civil society.

If corporations are included, then their activities do fit at least part of the theory of evolving organizational types under consideration. While there is much diversity here, it is the case that the 19th-century bureaucratic model has given way to both multi-divisional structures and significant elements of decentralization (Chandler 1962, Castells 1996, 2001). Managing the trans-national corporation has seen not only shifts from industrial to geographical organization, but also a greater involvement in networking connections with suppliers, producers and distributors. In a minority of firms, such connections have also extended to NGO critics in areas like the environmental impact.

The most systematic evidence on the organizational face of global civil society has been provided by Boli and Thomas (1999). While they follow the convention of excluding corporations, their survey of 5983 inter-national 'not for profit non-state organizations' founded between 1875 and 1988 reveals a number of trends. Least surprising is the rapid expansion in INGOs from around 200 in 1900 and 800 in 1930 to 2000 in 1960, doubling to 4000 in 1980. The periodicity of this growth pattern also bears some resemblance to other major cycles of globalization, for example, as measured by levels of world trade as a proportion of world GDP. Similar periods of organizational expansion are evident in the period leading up to the First World War, and in the post-war period. Interesting divergencies are also evident, nonetheless, such as organizational growth in the inter-war period, where world trade never recovered its pre-war levels, and again in the late 1940s, when a period of organization-building associated with the establishment of the UN was not as yet accompanied by world trade revival. Indeed world trade did not recover to pre-1914 levels until the 1980s. These data are at first sight a reminder that economic globalization does not move in step with all other indicators, let alone drive forward all manifestations of organizational development.

The sectoral distribution of INGO formation, as measured in this study, is also instructive as a means of establishing a typology of types of INGO. Here, Boli and Thomas report that the largest single category of organizations (around one-third) was made up of scientific and technical bodies, including those dealing with technical standards, infrastructure, and communications as well as professional bodies. In addition another quarter of the total number of organizations were concerned with business activity, including industry and trade associations. These two categories together, representing over half the organizations identified, contain the core of INGOs, at least in terms of separately organized entities, but typically remain invisible. They include human actors such a 'physicists, radiologists, electronic engineers, bridge designers, and manufacturers', who 'set standards, discuss problems, disseminate information, argue points of law etc' (ibid.).

Boli and Thomas' discussion of this core, while it identifies a neglected area of human agency, is, nonetheless, somewhat skewed to the ostensibly neutral and technical claims of many component occupations within this group. It might equally be pointed out that such groups are typically engaged in forms of global regulation of all the entities that cross borders, whether goods, services, people, or technology. They are therefore key elements in governance structures. They are equally very broad and diverse in the forms of expertise that they promote, and the judgements that they take in leading debates in and around globalization. Some are in the direct service of multi-national corporations, and may qualify as part of Sklair's emergent global capitalist ruling class (2001). Others either seek an independent stance or are orientated towards critical social movements. This is clearly a diversity of viewpoint and input from experts such as lawyers or scientists into regulation and governance. Braithwaite and Drahos (2000), nonetheless, find that science and the law may supply discourses that unify in common projects among interests divided on other matters across almost every regulatory domain they studied (502–503).

Beyond this core come two categories each of which account for roughly 7–8 per cent of INGOs. One is involved with sport and leisure bodies that preside over events such as The Olympics and World Cup of various kinds, and which are regarded as providing global rituals for world populations. The other are groups involved with welfare and rights, which include bodies like charities and human rights organizations.

These data are useful in giving some sense of expansion patterns and typology to the discussion of INGOs typically pursued via case studies. However, two methodological cautions need to be noted in interpreting these data. One is that they cannot be used as measures of the scale of different activities within global civil society in terms of numbers of individuals involved. The data in this respect measure organizations not people. While a measure of per capita involvement in each organization would be ideal, it is impracticable beyond a certain point because some organizations have no individual members.

The second caution is that the data have been assembled to deal with inter-national organizational trends in what the authors regard as 'world culture'. There is no direct transferability here with ideas of global civil society. Indeed Boli and Thomas see close connections between INGOs and nation-states. Levels of national development, as measured by economic or educational indices, correlate with INGO growth patterns. This approach is nonetheless compatible with the third-wave approach to globalization as outlined here, and with the idea, discussed in Chapter 5, that the global and the national are often inter-linked as well as being inter-dependent.

Global civil society as an innovative radical force?

While global civil society can be interpreted in a far broader manner than is often evident, it is important to recognize the significance of NGOs both for their critical contribution to global debate, and as activists seeking to stimulate, implement, and monitor global change. Compared with the realist 'international relations' image of a world of nation-states and a global polity founded on nation-to-nation interactions, we now live in a rather different state of affairs. Rosenau (1990), for example, argues that the *state-centric* world of territorial sovereignty and security policed by states has now been joined by a second intersecting *multi-centric* world of autonomous non-government organizations. These actively seek normative trans-national outcomes to policy problems rather than pursuit of the sovereign interests of nation-states.

The proliferation of organizations means there are at least two worlds within the global polity. While the relationship between the two is seen as 'sometimes co-operative, sometimes competitive, and at all times inter-active', neither is reducible to the other. One of the most striking indicators of this is the development of what has been called parallel summits (Anheier *et al*. 2001: 4). Here meetings of the state-centred world are paralleled by meetings of the multi-centric world. One of the first of these occurred over 100 years ago, at the Hague Peace Congress of 1899. Here the official diplomatic sessions were shadowed by a 'parallel salon' (ibid.: 5) organized through non-government channels, where citizens met, petitions were organized, and a conference newspaper produced.

Such parallel submits have only become widespread in the last 20 years. Rosenau (1995) points to the environmental area as an example of a very recent shift from exclusively state-centric to a broader multi-centric summits. The contrast here is between the first inter-national conference in the environment held at Stockholm in 1972, and the Rio Earth Summit held 20 years later. The former was attended only by states. The latter embraced both formal sessions at which 118 heads of state were present, and a parallel set of Global Forum sessions with no formal agenda but responsive to the concerns of over seven thousand groups and individuals. The latter group passed a number of 'Treaties' of their own including a Framework Treaty on NGO Global Decision Making.

Meanwhile pressure was exerted on individual nation-states to take a clearer and more radical stance on environmental questions and to counter the influence of business lobbies seeking very limited forms of environmental regulation. Another prominent example of a parallel summit occurred at the 1995 Fourth World Conference on Women in Beijing, where official and unofficial events occurred more or less side-by-side. These episodes reflect not only the development of a multi-centric global polity, but also the importance of coalitions of NGO activity.

The diversity of organizational forms in global civil society is evident not simply in the distinction between individual and group activity, or between the formal and the informal, but also in the distinction between single-organization and multi-organization activity. The latter typically occurs where a set of organizations collaborate to achieve a particular aim, such as the Coalition to stop the use of Child Soldiers of the Campaign against Landmines. But it also emerges on a less continuous, more episodic basis where coalitions of organizations plan a more co-ordinated involvement with each other at Summits.

There is lastly the more spontaneous coming together of individuals and groupings excluded from particular summits such as the Seattle WTO meeting in 1999, or the annual meetings of the World Economic Forum. Such forms of spontaneity sometimes gel, as in street protests at the 1998 G8 meeting in Birmingham, England. Here 'a ring of 70,000 people mainly from church development agencies, formed a human circle around the summit' (Green and Griffith 2002: 50), forcing the issue of Third World debt onto the agenda. At the G8 meeting in Genoa the following year, organized protesters from 'Drop the Debt' coalition of NGOs pulled out of the protest March, which ended in police intervention and violence.

It remains true that issue-based coalitions and the unity felt among those largely excluded from state-centred or elite global events have bred a degree of commonality. This is reflected in the emergence of the World Social Forum (WSF), conceived as an alternative to the Davos-based World Economic Forum, around the slogan 'Another World is Possible'. Coalitions of the enraged, however, typically bring together those with rather different grievances and attitudes, and are not therefore necessarily to be seen as indicators of a more permanent and enduring solidarity. Opposition to 'neo-liberalism' may be an unifying factor, but the nature of the other worlds that might be possible is not clear (Andersen 2003). Nor has the WSF organization itself managed to satisfy the ultra-democratic aspirations for transparency and accountability of its support base (Albert 2002). The WSF meetings lack a central focus, and typically involve sets of panel meetings, workshops, and mass meetings to hear key speakers. While the World Economic Forum has been uncharitably written off as 'a cocktail party on steroids for elite business and political leaders' (cited Bruno 2002: 1), the WSF appears to provide an experience which has been not unfairly described as 'an Ideal Home Exhibition of Social Movements'.

A further difficult issue, discussed above historically, arises from the question 'How global is global civil society'? Data on internationally active non-government organisations (INGOs) (Anheier *et al.* 2001: 7) certainly suggest that 'global civil society is heavily concentrated in north-western Europe'. Over 60 per cent of the headquarters of INGOs are based in the EU. They argue that this relates to the heavily globalized character of the region, whether measured economically in terms of technological connectedness or in terms of support for global human rights regimes. These create both the wealth and the infrastructural capacity to organize bodies with a significant global reach, features which also apply to North America which is also the home of INGO headquarters.

Interestingly, however, if we move from INGO headquarters locations to INGO Membership, this has grown significantly both inside and outside the Northern hemisphere, where both Latin America and sub-Saharan Africa feature significantly (ibid.: 6). Porto Allegre, Brazil, was of course the location of the third WSF in 2003, and it was Brazilians that made up the majority of the 100,000 participants, and for whom the initial incomplete programme in Portuguese was intended (Andersen 2003: 198). There were, however, very few Africans, a situation reversed when the ISTR (International Society for Third Sector Research) Africa Network on Civil society met in Benin, West Africa, in May 2004 to discuss civil society development by Africans in Africa. This draws attention to the possible importance of regionalism as a more accessible and meaningful basis of civil society attachment. This is partially reflected in the development of Social Forums in Europe and Asia.

Among the larger INGOs like Amnesty International or Oxfam, a range of North–South connections are evident, again indicating a global civil society presence in many regions and nations. Oxfam International is a confederation of 12 organizations in more than 100 countries, with several thousand partner organizations in the South (Oxfam International 2003). It is not an individual membership-based organization, but functions rather as a co-ordinating centre for a range of activities with partners, activity that ranges from delivery of aid to policy advocacy. Its partners vary accordingly. On the service delivery side, partners organizations are often local or national, ranging from Legal-Aid Organizations in Cambodia to local community centres in Armenia delivering care to the elderly and the people with disability. On the policy side, Oxfam works in coalitions with other organizations to lobby bodies like the WB or the G8 nations.

Amnesty, for its part, has more than 1.5 million members in 150 countries, and an Urgent Action network of 85,000 volunteers able to respond rapidly to the need for rapid action over human rights abuses (Amnesty International 2003a,b). During 2002, Amnesty International initiated 468 such actions in 83 countries. They involved action on behalf of people who were at risk of or had suffered human rights violations including torture, 'disappearances', the death penalty, death in custody, or forcible return to countries where they would be in danger of human rights violations.

Another category of global civil society organization involves movements from outside the Northern hemisphere that have a significant degree of autonomy. Such organizations include COICA, established in 1984 as Co-ordinating Body for the Indigenous Peoples Organizations of the Amazon Basin (including Brazil, Bolivia, Columbia, Ecuador, Peru, Venezuela, Surinam, and Guyana). Mato (1991) argues that global inter-connections have clearly made the search for localized 'others' in the tradition of colonial anthropology outmoded. He quotes Felipe Tsenkush leader of the Federation of Shuar and Achuar peoples from Ecuador, to the effect that 'Most people don't know it takes a lot of work to be an indigenous leader these days. One has to send and receive a lot of faxes, attend numerous inter-national meetings and now one also has to learn to handle email' (ibid.: 196).

The analytical task when faced with such complexities is to explore the global–local connections at work in each case. Here the indigenous Amazonian civil society organizations, developed with support and funding from sources that included inter-national inter-governmental organization (the Organization of American States), the WB, national governments (e.g. US), and both national (the Smithsonian Institute) and INGOs (e.g. Green and ecological activists from Germany, Austria, and Holland, and the World Rainforest Movement). This is an example not only of North–South co-operation within global civil society, but also of the intertwined nature of grass roots and elite, non-government and governmental activity, a point we shall return to at a more general level further in this chapter.

What then of the impact of the radical global civil society movements? How much have they succeeded in re-making globalization in different or alternative ways. Answers to this question suggest both the strengths and the weaknesses of this kind of activity. Two kinds of general verdict have been suggested here.

One is that global civil society movements, NGOs, and social movements have changed the agenda of the global polity, bringing issues of global inequality, human rights, injustices of gender and ethnicity, and the environment sustainability into far greater focus than hitherto. Beyond this their influence has been limited. The second, more positive evaluation, is that such movements created what might well be referred to as a legitimation crisis for prevailing liberal approaches to globalization, which came to a head at Seattle. This has not only changed the agenda for discussion, but also brought some significant changes in the global environment, including real measures of Third World debt relief and an accelerating reform agenda within key institutions such as the WB.

Before accepting either of these assessments at face value it is important to set any evaluation in a broader context. A question of immense importance here is whether such change, as has been seen, emanates primarily from below, or whether re-shaping of agenda and policy has, in large part at least, emerged from elite initiatives.

From a cognitive viewpoint, the knowledge-base upon which radical civil society mobilization has taken place has emerged and been consolidated; has emerged from multiple sources, from the work of INGOs themselves, from the scientific community – itself a multi-centred entity – as well as more elite think tanks and major elite-sponsored 'independent world commissions'.

The 'independent world commissions' may be less significant in knowledge-generation than in its consolidation and diffusion. Important examples have included the 2 Brandt Commissions on North–South issues, the Palme Commission on Security, the Brundtland Commission on the Environment, the Nyerere Commission on the South's Perspectives, the Carlsen/Ramphal Commission on Global Governance, and the MacBride Commission on New Information Order. Richard Falk (1999) argues that the series of commissions represent a 'new vehicle of trans-national elite expression', based on self-selected eminent persons (8–9). They typically meet over 2–3 years, take evidence from a range of sources, but their reports are typically drafted 'by an invisible secretariat that relies on consultants for substantive inputs and is subject to revision and final approval by the Commission members especially the chair' (ibid.).

These commissions cannot be said to have directly engaged with and changed the policies of states. But they have had an educative effect in a number of areas. Brundtland, for example, focused on the idea of sustainable development as a way of bridging North–South tensions, linking the possibility of anti-poverty programmes with environmental protection. Palme, for its part, re-visited the concept of security hitherto set within geo-political realpolitik away from the everyday lives of the world's population. The broader idea of 'common security' emerged as a way of setting security issues with the shared interests of humanity.

The point here is not to play off elite and popular sources of changed thinking and policy against each other. This is partly because they often feed off each other, and partly because there are multiple sources of knowledge-based change. In some cases, especially where detailed knowledge of local human rights practices, environmental abuses, or humanitarian crises are involved, INGO networks are sometimes key holders of information in a better position to brief states than any other entity. Arts (2000) gives as examples the deliberations that led to the ban on the ivory trade and the 1990s moratorium on commercial whaling. Nonetheless, in many other cases, elites and UN- or state-funded research and enquiry 'from above' is equally crucial. There is thus a cautionary note to be struck in weighing up the specific role of radical civil society organizations. Neither they are the monopoly supplier of knowledge-related change, nor does change necessarily come from below. For Falk it is a romantic illusion to suggest it does.

Conclusion

The idea of global civil society can be explored for its sociological coherence as an aspect of living, for its institutional significance as a form of cross-border organization, and for its political impact as a form of popular mobilization. These three perspectives are analytically distinct though empirically linked. It is nonetheless important that one is not collapsed into the others. It is as yet unproven how far changes in the micro-milieux of everyday life under global conditions (perspective 1) create some form of mass mobilization (perspective 2), and in consequence how far civil society movements represent the populations within which they operate. Similarly it is difficult to assess whether the quieter less conspicuous worlds of INGO development (perspective 3) have had more or less impact on global arrangements than civil society organizations (perspective 2). What is clear is that global civil society is poorly researched, especially at the individual micro-level, and this inhibits more confident judgements about levels of cosmopolitan and outward-looking trans-national engagement.

At all levels and within all three perspectives, human agency matters. What differs is the types of actors involved and the range of settings in which they operate. The globally orientated activists of civil society appear alongside technical standard-setters, and alongside computer-users and letter writers. The net effect is a complex and sometimes cacophonous assemblage of voices, but one that is patterned according to the challenges that individuals and groups identify within local and national as well as global settings. How the agency of global civil society plays out in debates over globalization is the main theme of the next chapter.

7

Globalization and its Discontents

The most controversial aspects of globalization relate to issues of human welfare and social justice. There are at least two major questions here. The first concerns the patterns and distribution of global inequality and injustice. Is inequality falling or rising, and are concerns over injustice getting greater or lesser? The second involves explaining the trends found. Insofar as inequality is lessening or getting worse, is this because of globalization, some other set of factors, or a combination of the two? Put another way, does globalization enhance the human condition, including the capacity of human actors to participate in shaping their world, or does it undermine welfare and social inclusion?

Whatever answers are given to such questions, it is axiomatic to the argument of this book that patterns of welfare, inequality, and injustice are shaped by human agency of various kinds. The forms of globalization that may be identified are not therefore accidents or the blind products of fate. Rather they arise out of social activities and choices, even if the outcomes are not those expressly intended or expected. All this serves to reinforce the crucial importance of grounding any evaluation of global policy choices in research and analysis.

Questions of global welfare and justice are simultaneously and inescapably normative, relying on moral as well as analytical evaluation. This is one reason why debates over globalization have produced much popular indignation, episodes of mass street protest, and rhetorical conflict. At times it has looked as if such controversies were fated to produce irreconcilable polarization, with globalization cast either as moral villain or as a benevolent source of social progress. Global actors have appeared unambiguously either as sinners responsible for famine, poverty, and despair, or as benefactors bringing help capable of transforming tragedy into progress.

The polemical tone of such engagement has not, however, succeeded in monopolizing public discussion or intellectual analysis. One of the shakiest assumptions upon which polarized thinking depended was the idea of globalization as a singular and unitary phenomenon. This singularity usually rested on the simplistic chain of reasoning in which globalization meant economic globalization, and economic globalization meant free trade, deregulated markets, multi-national companies, and neo-liberal ideology. It was some such notion of globalization that generated critical or supportive hyperbole. Once the singularity of globalization is rejected, for reasons outlined at length in this book, the coherence of the moral confrontation between advocates and critics of 'globalization', so defined, becomes weakened if not fatally undermined. But if we take the alternative view that globalization involves multiple processes, and that the inter-action between, and the outcome of, these processes is uncertain, then the greater the need to unravel the different issues at stake in a manner that is analytically informed and grounded in evidence.

Beyond this questions of inequality and especially of injustice raise moral as well as analytical issues. Many aspects of inequality such as income levels and health status can be measured, though others such as the experience of poverty and abjection cannot. Wherever poverty lines are drawn – at US$1 or $2 per day – it is hard to separate the presentation of data from some sense of what the basic elements of a humane life consist of. Discussion of injustice, meanwhile, is inseparable from evaluative yardsticks. Changes in how different social groups or global actors make evaluations can themselves be charted empirically. One important development in the last 50 years is the growing influence of notions of human rights regarded as rights that *should be* accessible to all of human-kind, and implemented via UN declarations and conventions in relation to standards and targets.

The sense that injustice may be ubiquitous or on the rise is not simply a response to facts about the world. It is, in addition, the outcome of prevailing and contested standards of justice. Injustice may rise because moral standards change even while empirical trends remain the same. To study global injustice is, then, to study both the social processes and the changing moral climate. Social science cannot adjudicate between the moral validity of different yardsticks, though it may illuminate why individuals and groups develop the moral codes that they do. In the absence of an agreed global ethics, this becomes a complex task.

One immediate sign of the multi-dimensional complexity of the debate is the possibility of being 'for' some aspects of globalization, and 'against' others. There are, for example, those who support greater free trade, but who resist attempts at global regulation of environmental activities of corporations and national Governments. There are equally those who oppose free trade but who support the development of global human rights regimes. In other cases, as we have seen in Chapter 3, the global and the local intertwine, with global *means* (e.g. Internet campaigns) being used for *local* ends (e.g. Mexican Zapatista political mobilization) or global *thinking* being linked with *local* action, as in the popular slogan 'Think globally, act locally.' Proponents of economic nationalism and cultural autarky are still to be found, but it becomes harder to reject all manifestations of globalization, except at the cost of denying the multiple syncretic roots of much that is taken to be local. Small boutique wine producers may indeed celebrate the 'terroir' of particular patches of land, but the chemistry and technologies of viticulture and wine-making, and access to markets are increasingly dependent on the world beyond.

In the present chapter we shall explore further the multi-dimensional character of globalization, drawing attention to the complexity involved in assessing its impact on human welfare. A good deal of the evidence to be reviewed has been developed within academic debates, a number of which have picked up the title 'globalization and its discontents' (Sassen 1998, Green and Griffith 2002, Stiglitz 2002). Whereas Sigmund Freud (1975 [1930]) in 'Civilization and its Discontents' suggested that the rationalizing disciplines of civilization threatened the creative irrational force of the libido with pathological consequences for individuals, so the material and moral discontents associated with globalization pose fundamental questions about the future of human society; its sustainability, capacity for ethical behaviour, and readiness to distribute the fruits of economic growth in a fair and just manner.

This chapter is in two parts. In part one, we review evidence of global economic growth and its problematic relationship with human progress. We explore the impact of economic globalization for patterns of inequality and economic development. The aim here is to examine both positive and negative evidence linking globalization with an enhancement of human welfare. Consideration will be given to recent attempts to reform the ways in which the global economy operates with respect to questions of inequality. In part two, attention turns to the global polity and its relationship with national states and sets of citizens. Here the focus is on the evolving architecture of global institutions and problems associated with their remoteness from the world's citizens. The idea of a 'democratic deficit' has developed in large part as an indicator of the lack of any formal political involvement of the global population as such in global decision-making. This represents a second major global discontent alongside global inequality and poverty. It is also an area where attempts at reform are currently underway. Attention will be given here to what might be called *de facto* as well as *de jure* aspects of global decision-making, to governance as well as government, and to the need for radical overhaul of existing conceptions of democracy.

Globalization and human welfare

Images of starving populations in sub-Saharan Africa and parts of Asia stand as an indictment of the world's incapacity to make serious inroads into material poverty. The headline evidence reviewed in the 2003 Human Development Report of the United Nations Development Programme provides statistical grounding for the relevance of such images to debates over cause and consequence (UNDP 2003). During the 1990s, for example, 54 countries became poorer than they were in 1990, with life expectancy shrinking to 34, and an increased 'hunger rate' to 21 (ibid.: 2). Others, meanwhile, were too poor to collect relevant data (ibid.: 35). In Africa alone, about half the population live in extreme poverty, and about one-sixth of children die before age five, compared to respective rates of one-third and one-tenth for South Asians (ibid.: 34–38). The United Nations Children's Fund (UNICEF) in a recent report indicates that 11 million children die each year before their fifth birthday from malnutrition and preventable threats to health like diarrhoea (UNICEF 2003: 9).

These data begin to tell a tragic story, but there are other significant stories to be told. One is detectable improvements in aggregate human welfare, especially in Asia, and concentrated in urban areas of China and parts of the Indian sub-continent. During the 1990s, for example, the number of people in East Asia and the Pacific living on $1 per day was halved (UNDP 2003: 2), while under-five mortality was significantly reduced in Bangladesh, Bhutan, and Nepal. In selected African countries like Ghana and Mozambique, some striking global reductions in hunger were achieved (37). Meanwhile, UNICEF reports three out of four children receive some form of immunization before their first birthday compared with fewer than 10 per cent 30 years ago (UNICEF 2003: 12), saving an estimated 2.5 million lives each year.

Behind these more positive figures lie a mixture of improved economic growth rates, and some more effective global, state, and local development programmes.

The general approach of the Human Development Report supports the argument made in Chapter 3 that the concept of a Third World, uniformly trapped within poverty, starvation, and moral distress is outmoded. Over the last 30 years, life expectancy in the developing world has increased by 8 years, while illiteracy rates have been cut in half to 25 per cent (ibid.: 2). Yet, there is no doubt that very significant numbers of the world's population live in abject poverty. The poorest tend to remain the poorest, even if economic growth and development is transforming many parts of Latin America and Asia. This is both because economic growth is not uniform across the developing world and because even where it is, it does not necessarily translate to increased income for the poorest populations. There is, in other words, a great unevenness in the contemporary position of populations outside the economic triad of North America, Europe, and Japan. Why is this and what has it got to do with globalization?

Many current discontents are founded precisely on the view that globalization is responsible for this state of affairs. This view is visually sustained by images of low-wage sweatshops producing goods for multi-national corporations, by perceptions of powerful global regulatory bodies like the IMF dictating draconian terms for assistance to poor countries to meet financial crises, and from an overriding moral repugnance at the stark contrast between global 'winners' and 'losers'.

An intellectual assumption underlying such sentiments is that the dominant forces affecting economic well-being are exogenous, that is external to the countries involved. This seems reasonable in a globalized world of cross-border economic penetration and inter-connectedness. It is certainly preferable, as a starting point, to purely endogenous explanations which emphasize the decisive role of internal developments in determining whether national welfare advances or falls back. It is not, however, clear that exogenous explanations should entirely replace endogenous ones because factors such as geographical location, resource endowment, and presence or absence of a stable political order remain significant issues for the developmental prospects. This means that global poverty cannot simply be explained as a consequence of globalization. During the 1990s more than half of the world's poorest countries were involved in civil conflict destroying lives, hope, and any previous developmental gains (WB 2003: Ch. 1). It is arguable that for some countries, including a good deal of sub-Saharan Africa, the problem may in one sense be seen as too little involvement by external global actors in the form of capital, technology, education, and human rights rather than too much.

Exogenous influences remain very important in all settings, stable or otherwise, especially in an epoch of de-regulation of barriers to free trade and free movement of capital. Between the immediate post-war period and the 1980s, for example, global tariffs fell from about 20 per cent of the value of imports to around 5 per cent (Mandle 2003: 11). The trend has continued in subsequent rounds of the GATT/WTO regime. Rates of both global FDI in factories and equipment as well as portfolio investment in financial instruments have also increased rapidly. It is therefore a fair test of the efficacy of economic globalization that we ask how far patterns of economic growth and development over this period have reduced historic levels of inequality, and projected the world's regions and societies onto an upward trajectory. In pursuing these questions we leave aside for the moment methodological problems to do with the limitations of quantitative measures to encapsulate human welfare, merely pointing out that it is possible for quantitative indices and human experience to move in different directions (Thompson 1963).

At the aggregate level, the global economy has, as Sen (2001) and many others have indicated, produced a world whose wealth and material resources are greater than at any previous stage in human history. The distribution of the benefits of this process is, however, extremely uneven. As the WB itself pointed out in 2003,

> The average income in the richest 20 countries is already 37 times greater than in the poorest 20 nations. Globally, 1.3 billion people live on fragile lands – arid zones, slopes, wetlands, and forests – that cannot sustain them. Both the gap between rich and poor countries and the number of people living on fragile lands have doubled in the past 40 years. (WB 2003)

Income and inequality

Since there are no recurrent annual data which measure changes in the world's income distribution, it is very hard to produce a precise picture of overall, regional, and national trends. Some of the more systematic data come from the WB which periodically reviews the proportion of populations in the world's nations that live on or below $1–2 per day. These data are adjusted to take account of differences in the costs of living in different nations.

As at the close of the 20th century, the proportions living on less than $2 were well in excess of 80 per cent in India and Ethiopia, nearly 60 per cent in China, Nigeria, and Indonesia, and over 40 per cent in

Mexico and Turkey (WB 1999–2000: Ch. 1, 4). Using the even lower measure of $1 per day, around 1.2 billion people lived in absolute poverty in 1998 (WB 2003, Ch. 1). This snapshot reveals extraordinary poverty, but what trends are evident over time?

On a short-run perspective, recent WB data suggests that there has been an absolute decline in the numbers of those living on less than $1 per day (adjusted for price changes and purchasing power differentials) between 1980 and 1998 from 1.4 billion to 1.2 billion (ibid.: Ch. 1). Much of this is due to economic development in China with its very large population, the effects of this outweighing at least on a numerical basis the worsening of the position in much of sub-Saharan Africa. Even allowing for the China effect, East and South Asia still comprise around two-thirds of the world's very poor people, emphasizing that extreme poverty is not a purely African problem.

Another dimension to issues of income distribution involves the development of a more differentiated and complex global class structure. This has at least two elements. The first is the development of a middle class in the more expansive regions of Latin America and Asia. Taking China as a leading case, it is estimated that the numbers of Chinese earning at least $5000 per annum will double from 60 million to 120 million between 2002 and 2010 (Asia Inc, July 2003). One effect of this kind of development is the growth of national and multi-national corporations with headquarters in developing countries such as Mexico, Brazil, South Korea, and India, partly serving consumer markets in industries like the media and brewing, as well as global manufacturing markets. Another effect is the growth of the global market in higher education, where the children of the global middle class come to institutions in North America, Europe, and Australia for degree certification. Rather than thinking of the global economy as a polarization between a small rich elite and a huge set of impoverished victims, some attempt has to be made to come to terms with people occupying positions in between these two poles.

The second element involves assessment of inter-national migration from poor to rich countries as an avenue of improved welfare and upward social mobility. This is methodologically difficult to chart with any precision because calculations would have to be made comparing pre-migration incomes and prospects, with the post-migration position. It is clear that much global migration is a consequence of global inequalities (Castles and Miller 1993), and arises as millions of individuals seek a better life. Migration has become more globalized in the sense that flows link all regions of the globe, with a recent disproportionate emphasis on flows

from poorer to richer countries and regions (ibid.: Ch. 6). It is conventional to speak of both push and pull factors here; pull factors include
better prospects abroad, or at least the perception of such benefits, while
push factors include both material deprivation and political and civil
conflict in countries of origin.

While the short-run experience of migration for those lacking skills is
often one of low-wage employment or unemployment, this tends to lessen
over time. Remittances from lower-skilled manufacturing and service
workers, both men and women, to countries of origin are a significant
indicator of this. Were immigration controls to be relaxed, there is
no doubt that very significant numbers of the world poor would seek
mobility elsewhere, even though any large-scale movement of this kind
would almost certainly be counter-productive. Global labour markets
also exist for high-skill and professional workers, mainly men, who often
do very much better in their country of destination, provided demand
for such labour is buoyant. The segmentation or stratification of migrant
employment patterns in richer countries is typified in service work within
global cities, where migrants working in financial and knowledge-based
services do far better than those working in retail, office-cleaning, and
hospitality services. Much of the latter workforce is also highly feminized,
reproducing an unequal gender division of labour (Sassen 1998).

We now turn to examine longer-term research into global inequality
patterns between and within nations. These have been analysed by
Bourguignon and Morrisson (1999), and O'Rourke (2002). These data
take into account the gross domestic product per head, and the population
levels of different countries. They show that world inequality has increased
since 1820 and the present day, with the more rapid increases being
evident between 1820 and 1910, and again between 1960 and the 1980s.
These were both periods of expanding free trade and global market
integration. Extreme caution is, however, required in interpreting
these data because they include both within-country inequality and
between-country inequality. Within-country inequality is likely to be
driven by internal political factors, such as the presence of welfare-state
redistribution, as well as external ones. Between-country inequality in
an increasingly inter-connected economic world is likely to be a stronger
measure of the effects of economic globalization.

Taking this distinction into account, the data show that between-
country inequality increased until around the 1980s while within-country
inequality decreased. At that point, there appears to have been a shift, with
between-country inequality lessening. This break of trend is supported
by other economic research (Schultz 1998, Boltho and Toniolo 1999,

Melchior *et al*. 2000), though not all (e.g. Milanovic 1999). These data seem to support critics of economic globalization for the period up to 1980, but are less supportive thereafter. There appears, on the face of it, to be a very striking discrepancy here between the recent data on absolute poverty and the data on between-country inequality. Yet on closer inspection, we may simply be dealing with the effect of 20-year growth in China, the world's most populous country, which on a per capita basis may account for a good deal of the recent between-country improvement.

Rehearsing data on world income levels and distributions is an import-ant exercise, but an even more significant matter is the linking of cause and effect. Does economic globalization, in some sense, cause material improvement, obstructed only by endogenous limits, or is its primary effect one of trapping many countries in a state of underdevelopment, in which some go backwards and others go forward at a slower rate than might otherwise be the case? Where improvement is measurable, can this be linked with particular mechanisms of globalization such as free trade and capital inflows or are the cause and effect patterns less uniform and more complex than such questions imply?

One form that capital inflows have taken is FDI in production and service activities. Much of this has arisen through the re-location of low-cost manufacturing to some, but not all, developing countries. This is reflected in the rapid expansion of FDI throughout the last four decades, and especially in the 1980s and 1990s. Data from the UNCTAD indicate that Global FDI flows increased by around 24 per cent in the second half of the 1980s, 20 per cent in the early 1990s and 25 per cent between 1996 and 1998 (United Nations 1999). While much FDI had previously been between richer countries, the proportion directed elsewhere was seven times greater between 1987 and 1997, and especially prominent in Latin America and East Asia (WB 1999, Table 6.1).

One result has been an expansion in the share of developing coun-tries in global manufacturing exports from around 3 per cent in 1970 to approximately 18 per cent in 1990 (Krueger 1995: 43). Manufacturing exports, ranging from textiles and footwear to computer assemblies have also risen as a proportion of total exports to between 40 and 70 per cent in countries like Brazil, Egypt, India, Mexico, Philippines, and Thailand (WB 1999: Table 4.5). This has generated export-led growth and devel-opment, widening the export base of many developing countries beyond primary production. This pattern is, however, very far from universal, and many developing countries still struggle to market primary prod-ucts such as foodstuffs or cotton in the highly protected markets of

Europe, North America, and Japan. In such cases, the problem is not free trade but rich country protectionism. Thompson Ayodele (2003), co-ordinator of the Institute for Public Policy Analysis, Lagos, Nigeria, calculates that the increased African trade that might result from reduced European subsidies to their own producers would allow Africa to pay 10 per cent of its US$ 30 billion foreign debt.

Mandle (2003) has analysed data on a range of developing countries with different levels of export performance, different per capita income, different rates of poverty (using the $2 per day measure), and different patterns of literacy. He finds a clear correlation between exports and economic growth. This is in turn linked with improvements in literacy rates, countries with the highest levels of exports per capita typically having the highest literacy rates (ibid.: 19). Increased literacy is not, however, a simple function of economic growth, with positive programmes sponsored by institutions such as UNICEF and the WB also being crucial in lifting literacy in general, as well as narrowing the literacy gap between males and females in recent years. In this sense, improved literacy may be seen as both a cause and an effect of economic growth. Successful development, for Mandle, is a matter of not simply capital or technology, but also human capital resources, and these depend heavily on non-economic processes.

Free trade and fair trade

There is a strong body of evidence connecting free trade and increased FDI with the export-led development of a number of developing countries. The advantage of this data is that it is reasonably comprehensive across space and time, and is thus superior to arguments based on episodic case study evidence over shorter periods. The disadvantage with the optimistic case is that it plays down negative consequences of free trade. These include rich world penetration into poor country markets, often displacing local producers of foodstuffs, creating greater food insecurity. More fundamentally the world trade regime that developed in the 1960s and 1970s was constructed very much in the interests of the richer countries in that certain economic sectors remained sequestered from its provisions. Free trade may have been an ideological mantra in the West, but some key food-producing sectors such as wheat (Friedman 1994) remained highly regulated while trade liberalization was pursued elsewhere. Rich country protectionism of farmers, as we noted above, obstructs the access of many of the poorest primary-product-dependent countries to North American and European markets. In the case of the world cotton market, for example, some of the poorest African countries like Burkina Faso and Benin are inhibited from competition with American producers who receive large Government subsidies enabling them to keep down prices (Ayodele 2003).

A further set of issues arise from the low-cost nature of much developing country production, where workers are typically unprotected by effective trade union and human rights. This is seen by many critics as a race-to-the-bottom in labour standards, and is often accompanied by similarly low standards of environmental regulation. Concerns of this kind came to a head during protests at the WTO meeting in Seattle. Criticisms of low wages may arise on moral grounds, unacceptable in a world of rapidly increasing wealth. They may also reflect concerns of low-skill workers employed in richer nations that their jobs will be vulnerable to low-wage industries overseas. From the viewpoint of workers in poorer countries, by contrast, low-wage factory work may be more attractive than even lower-wage subsistence agriculture. Moral abhorrence on the part of wealthier populations may cloud an appreciation of the modest but significant developmental advances and opportunities in poorer countries.

An associated issue is that of the use of very low cost child labour in a number of developing countries. Is this stimulated by globalization, or dependent on other factors? A study by UNICEF economists, Cigno *et al.* (2002), found that exposure to inter-national trade, if anything, reduces the use of child labour, though the effect was not a strong one. Their reasoning is that child labour is practised in areas with very low educational levels and where there is no material incentive for families to have children educated. This argument is consistent with Mandle's emphasis on the importance of literacy rates to labour productivity and economic advance.

A pertinent line of criticism which picks up ideas of normative regulation of trade is the move to replace 'free trade' with 'fair trade'. This is defined by Oxfam as 'about paying poor producers a fair price, and helping them gain the necessary skills and knowledge to develop their businesses and work their way out of poverty' (Oxfam 2003). This would appear to subordinate market-based price determination with a more ethically responsive approach. The radical civil society movements reviewed in Chapter 6 are strongly committed to this movement. This is expressed both at a global level in lobbying activity directed at the WTO and at the G8. It is also expressed in practical activity.

Fair trade practices within civil society organizations include direct purchase from small producers at 'fair' prices, the branding of products regarded as emanating from 'fair' trade practices including the payment of fair wages, and the retailing of fair trade products. The International Federation for Alternative Trade (IFAT) is a global network of over 160 Fair Trade organizations in more than 50 countries, which works to improve the livelihoods and well-being of disadvantaged people in developing countries.

While the scale of the fair trade sector appears very small and most unlikely to displace regular-market-based resource allocation and price determination, the broader ideal of market fairness has penetrated a good way into more mainstream discourses. It is somewhat paradoxical, however, that despite the alternative value-based commitments of the movement, it is the liberal idea of making markets work better by opening up to poorer countries products that has made the most impact.

Global trade, as has already been noted, is intimately connected with global mobility of capital and finance. These three aspects of economic globalization have each generated critical commentary as discrete issues, as well as receiving criticism as an integrated neo-liberal development package. FDI, for example, has been seen as excessively dependent on tax concessions and infrastructural supports from recipient Govern- ments, in a way that tends to undermine national sovereignty. This has not prevented almost all Governments seeking to attract FDI. But it has led to protest. Much of this has focused on attempts to create a harmon- ized Multilateral Agreement on Investment (MAI) in the late 1990s. This scheme would have restricted the rights of nations to discriminate between different investors, for example, giving preferences to national over trans-national investment. The collapse of talks over the matter has been as an unambiguous victory for anti-globalization critics, but it is equally significant that the more powerful nations did not agree amongst themselves on the case for strong levels of harmonization (Mandle, ibid.: Ch. 5).

Global debt

Further problems have arisen within global financial arrangements, where developing countries have found themselves afflicted with balance of payments problems and high levels of indebtedness. Governments have also accumulated large amounts of debt, some of it commercial, and some in the form of 'official credits'. Third World indebtedness grew alarmingly in the 1980s and became a major critical rallying point in the 1990s. While the developing countries commercial debt crisis of the 1980s was largely resolved through a mixture of cancellation, and payment in lieu of environmental policy change (Desai and Said 2001: 60), public debt has proven harder to resolve. This is partly because institutions like the WB and rich country Governments do not believe in writing off debt. In the poorest countries with the least trading opportunities, including debtors such as Uganda, Mozambique, and Niger, it has proven impossible to repay.

The idea of public debt cancellation gained ground at this time. A campaign on this issue begun in 1996 by Jubilee 2000, a mainly church-based coalition in the UK, and quickly spread (ibid.: 62–63). Opinion poll evidence in the UK suggested nearly 70 per cent of the population preferred that the Government celebrate the millennium by cancelling Third World debt rather than building the Millennium Dome. By the year 2000, Jubilee 2000 campaigns were running in 68 countries, including Angola, Togo, and Honduras, as well as Sweden, UK, and US. The effect was not only to get debt back on the agenda, but to create a climate in which a significant amount of debt cancellation was achieved. According to Ann Pettifer, one-time Director of Jubilee, UK, 'while poor debtor nations were [previously] often cowed by the financial power and clout of bureaucracies serving the G7 powers', the existence of a strong mass movement encouraged poor country leaders to 'appeal over the heads of bureaucracies like the IMF to the electorates in Western countries' (cited ibid.: 62 – authors parenthesis).

Just as much criticism of 'free trade' is more a critique of rich country protectionism than globalization *per se*, so much criticism of the 'Third World debt crisis' may be seen as directed at particular rich country Government lending schemes than the global economy. Desai and Said (ibid.: 64) argue that this is because countries that are abysmally poor cannot get commercial loans and are therefore forced into unequally designed deals with national Governments and the multi-lateral agencies. This point has some force, since it is the *capitalist* nature of the global economy rather than its *trans-national* character that rules out non-commercial transactions. This situation contrasts with the Asian financial crisis of the late 1990s, where more successful developing countries, able to attract commercial loans, faced dramatic withdrawals of trans-national capital.

The global movement of finance ranges from short-run movement of funds to take advantage of momentary or short-term movements in interest rates and foreign exchange process, to portfolio investment in shares. This highly mobile finance is distinct from the more settled medium- to long-term movements involved in direct investment. With new communications technology, the world money markets are open on a 24-hour basis, and it is estimated that several trillion dollars of funds are moved around the globe every day. Developing countries have both benefited from the liquidity provided by these funds, and been left vulnerable to the adverse effects of their mobility in moments of crisis. There has in fact been chronic financial instability over the last few decades, simultaneous with expanding free trade and FDI. Beginning with the Mexican default on debts in 1982, and further crisis in 1994–5, this then extended to Asia in 1997, Russia in 1998, and Brazil in 1999.

Challenges to the making of globalization through the Washington Consensus

Since 1980, the financial problems of developing countries have typically been handled via the so-called 'Washington Consensus' (a term that originated from the economist John Williamson), enshrined in the twin global regulatory bodies of the IMF, and WB. The favoured remedy for most of this period was to provide financial support to meet crises and stimulate development, but only in return for acceptance of terms ('conditionality') which committed recipients to particular kinds of liberal political economy. These have typically sought to create functioning markets by reducing inflation and deregulating economic activity. High interest rates and cuts in Government expenditure ensued, the latter often meaning cutbacks to education and health spending, as well as an ending of price subsidies on staple goods. Increased unemployment, poorer public services, and a higher cost of living generated protest and instability, privations that were rarely relieved by perceptible short-term improvements in economic growth.

Critics of such global regulatory arrangements are legion. Sub-Saharan Africa was a recipient of 29 IMF/WB packages during the 1980s. While per capita incomes declined by 30 per cent over the same period (Hoogvelt 1997: 170–171), very little appears to have been achieved. Rather, as Kevin Watkins, writing in 1995 for the charity Oxfam, points out:

> market deregulation has often reduced the opportunities for poor people ... [served] ... to exclude vulnerable communities ... [and] ... has made employment more insecure (Watkins, 1995: 107).

Meanwhile, IMF and WB policies at this time failed in most cases to produce either economic growth or social protection. While a greater flexibility is evident in the implementation of IMF/WB packages over time, the overall thrust of such criticisms remains.

By the end of the 20th century the Washington Consensus was crumbling. There were a number of reasons for this. First, the pace of global development in many of the poorer countries remained slow or non-existent. Second, the continuing instability of the global financial system made it clear to many that an urgent re-structuring of the entire architecture of current institutional arrangements was required. Third, pressure from below – in the form of critical ideas as well as street protest – had helped to transform the agenda of debate on the global economy previously dominated by rather narrowly conceived neo-liberal nostrums. Fourth, significant sections of global elites ranging from the financial speculator, George Soros (2002), to the economist, Joseph Stiglitz (2002), began to publicly challenge Washington Consensus precepts. Global discontents, it seemed, had surfaced within the core institutions and networks of the global economy.

A number of attempts have been made to distinguish various positions in contemporary debates on economic globalization. Drawing on a number of sources, these include (a) isolationists, (b) statists, (c) supporters, (d) reformists, and (e) alternative globalists. Each focuses on particular ways of opposing, regulating or re-shaping, un-making or re-making globalization. These positions may be separated for analytical purposes, but in practice individuals and groups may combine or shift around between two or more of them.

Isolationists tend to treat globalization and global capitalism as synonymous. Their ranks include some environmentalists – notably within Friends of the Earth, supporters of local autonomy, and local protest movements such as the Landless Peasants Movements in Brazil (MST). *Statists*, on the other hand, seek to rebuild the nation-state or blocs of nation-states as a counter to trans-nationalism. This category includes both conservative defenders of national sovereignty against global economic penetration and regulation (e.g. much of the US legislature), and sections of the Left who associate the nation-state with progressive institutional support for welfare redistribution and economic planning. A number of those who criticize the American contribution to economic globalization are to a significant degree criticizing American statism, as projected through inter-national organization.

Supporters include libertarian and liberal institutions and individuals, embracing both promoters of market-centred economic liberalism, and those who promote civil society as a source of cultural creativity and as a counterweight to centralized states. They include influential media such as *The Wall Street Journal* and *The Economist*, as well as organizations like the American Enterprise Institute and the Indian Society for Civil Society (Desai and Said 2001: 66). Some cosmopolitans and global multi-culturalists might be included, but they might also fit within the following two categories.

Reformers typically subscribe to liberal or cosmopolitan world-views, but argue for serious institutional change. They are typically critical of forms of neo-liberalism that exclude explicit consideration of social, communal, and ethical issues. Soros and Stiglitz are two elite examples, but many segments of trans-national non-government organization fit here also. *Alternative globalists*, meanwhile, are more critical of liberalism. This can take a radical approach to institutional re-shaping around different values. But it may equally try to infuse global orientations with spiritual, environmental, and ethical considerations. They may sometimes be as utopian as isolationists, but in a period of rapid social change and global uncertainty it is by no means clear which of today's utopia will turn out to be fertile sources of social action, and which will be destined for marginality. Both Esperanto and Environmentalism appeared promising sources of cultural innovation around one hundred years ago, but it is only the latter that has blossomed.

This framework may have analytical advantages, but it requires sensitivity in application due to cross-category linkages and overlaps. It is perhaps unwise to apply it to individuals since the subtleties of their arguments may defy attempts to classify them into boxes. Walden Bello, the Phillipine-born writer based in Bangkok, who appears as an 'isolationist' in one such classification (ibid.: 65) re-appears as an intellectual influence on 'reformists' in another (Green and Griffith 2002: 56). Bearing these reservations in mind, one particular area of creative overlap involves statists, reformists, and alternative globalists.

Many statist currents, from Dr Mahathir's interventionist Malaysian Government strategy during the Asian financial crisis to the Clinton Administration's NAFTA, are clearly not forms of national or regional isolationism. Rather they seek selective engagement with the global economy, strongly mediated through state or state-like structures. This may be seen as a kind of alternative globalism, but without any necessarily strong value-commitment to cosmopolitanism or spiritual one-worldism. It may also lead to attempts to re-form global regulatory arrangements, though typically in support of declared national interests.

Alternative globalists currents, for their part, may seek to replace or strongly limit market forces and the sway of economic institutions, or may wish to reform the global economy, as part of a more far-reaching cultural renewal agenda (e.g. the Philippine activist Nicanor Perlas 2000). The major difficulty for those who wish to debate economic policy reform issues, however, is the lack of a strong and distinctive alternative economic strategy to that of free trade and FDI. As has often been pointed out, the collapse of the Soviet system and the movement of China towards greater global economic integration has meant that centralized state-centred development strategies have far less credibility than they once had.

The most widely discussed alternative discourses have hitherto been around some notion of economic nationalism or neo-mercantilism. These are in a sense statist, and of course relevant to both developed and developing countries and regions. One possible scenario, advanced by second-wave sceptics of the hyper-globalization hypothesis (see Chapter 1), is that processes of trans-national integration will be arrested by sets of nations regionally organized into competitive blocs. For Hirst and Thompson (1996), this has produced a kind of triadization based on Europe, the Americas, and the Asia-Pacific. Instead of a globally inte-grated world economy, the picture is rather one of regionalization, around spatially limited zones, regional corporate investment strategies, and neo-merantilist state structures (Thompson 1998, Rugman 2001). The overriding policy aim then becomes national and regional competi-tiveness rather than economic openness *per se*.

This option draws on very real limits to the idea of globalization as an all-powerful force, corrosive of all borders and state policies and footloose in its mobility. The difficulties with the argument are twofold. First, the dynamics of globalization have continued to spread beyond the zones originally encapsulated in the triadization argument, encompassing much of the East and Southeast Asia and parts of Latin America. Second, the regional option requires some effective national power base, able to stand up to the de-regulationist thrust of the global regulatory organ-izations, and the Big Powers in the world political order. This option is not really an effective one for smaller weaker states.

Globalization's discontents have not gone away, and may in a sense always be with us. There are several reasons for this. First, improve-ment in real patterns of inequality and injustice is or is not evident over the short or long term, the sense that more could always be achieved is now deeply embedded in human consciousness. This is partly due to the enormous impact made by critical social movements, knowledge and advocacy networks, and individuals within both civil society and states, and often through creative interaction between the two. Pressure from below has been effective in changing agenda and in certain areas of reform, such as debt reduction, though its impact has been exaggerated in other spheres, such as the collapse of the MAI. Scientific knowledge, elite opinion, and shifts in multi-national company policy are also crucial elements in the picture, and have made their own contribution to change in areas of environmental policy shift (e.g. action over the hole in the ozone layer, Rowlands 1995), or the erosion of the Washington Consensus. All this interestingly suggests that human agency matters, that the global order is, to an extent, plastic, and that it can be changed. This applies even though there is every immediate reason to be pessimistic about the impact of current poverty-reduction strategies.

The problem, nonetheless, remains that political globalization lags behind economic and globalization, and that notions of democracy and the political process have not yet come to terms with the far-reaching implications of global inter-connectedness and inter-dependence. While economic globalization is increasingly trans-national, most global political organizations from the UN to the WTO are rather inter-national, dependent on the support and co-operation of nation-states to a large degree. A second reason for the ubiquity of global discontent lies in the seeming disjuncture between the way politics has conventionally been understood in terms of national sovereignty, and the trans-national way in which the global order appears to operate. One way of referring to this problem is to speak of a 'democratic deficit'.

Global discontents, knowledge, and the global political order

Much discontent with the global political order is best understood through the following two lines of thought. In the first line, the global order has been mismanaged in such a way that global development has been inhibited, institutions have failed to deliver what might reasonably be expected of them and the global economic order has been rendered more unstable. This line of argument has produced contemporary calls for institutional reform.

In the second line of thought an all-powerful global economy dominates global politics and global culture creating and reproducing inequality and injustice. This assumption is a major feature of world-system theory. It is also a widely held view among activists. The implication is that while markets and global corporations retain current levels of power and influence, neither national Governments, citizens, nor global regulatory institutions have the autonomy or freedom to curb global power imbalances. The net effect is to exclude or severely diminish the access of those lacking power to the management of the global economy.

Two different types of responses have been made to this state of affairs, which may loosely be labelled *cognitive* and *political*. The cognitive response claims that the contours of globalization and the causes of inequality can be better understood, and that this understanding could lead to a re-shaping of global institutions on the basis of better knowledge. This approach places a good deal of emphasis on epistemic communities and experts and their more effective involvement in processes of global government. The political response emphasizes a democratic deficit in current institutional arrangements, and the need for a more representative and inclusive approach to global democracy. For some, the cognitive problem arises from the political one. A more inclusive and a more democratic order would be better at finding out and representing problems than an elitist one. For many, the two lines of argument are intertwined (e.g. Khor 2001, Stiglitz 2002).

In the first part of this chapter we have reviewed a range of analysis and evidence about patterns of inequality and their causes. The major cognitive difficulty identified in this discussion has been the ideological pursuit of economic liberalism in global policy-making and institutional management. The beneficial effects of trade, investment, and currency de-regulation were asserted almost as a mantra, far in advance of evidence that they really worked in any straightforward way. With the benefit of hindsight, this argument has been most vigorously pursued by George Stiglitz, former Chief Economist at the WB and defector from the Washington Consensus regime (Stiglitz 2002).

Stiglitz' argument is that the institutions of the Washington pursued economic de-regulation so mechanistically and with such little regard for the real impact made that they created chronic global instability, inhibited global development, and failed in very large measure to make significant inroads into poverty and inequality. His critique is not so much whether such policies created economic growth, here the picture is mixed, but rather whether they created the kind of growth that helps poor people (Stiglitz 2003). Ideology rather than knowledge drove policy, and the policy was largely responsible for driving economic globalization.

The effects of this approach are evident in the areas of finance, trade, and investment, all subject to an ideologically driven agenda. In finance, the IMF 'made mistakes in all the areas it had been involved in: development, crisis management, and in countries managing the transition from communism to capitalism' (Stiglitz 2002: 18). Structural adjustment programmes were pursued without adequate awareness of the underlying institutional context in which they were launched, any cognizance of problems with the excessively rapid pace of their introduction, or any effective evaluation of their social consequences. The failure of the IMF regime came to a climax in the 1990s when IMF measures made the Asian economic crisis worse (ibid.: 98–132) and wasted billions of dollars of loans trying to manufacture capitalism in Russia without any suitable or sustainable institutional framework capable of regulating markets (ibid.: 133–165).

Stiglitz' critique is directed more at the IMF, described as 'learning-impaired', rather than the WB seen as a 'learning' institution. While the former is wedded to narrow forms of macro-economic analysis, the latter has, despite its strong historic connection with the IMF and Structural Adjustment, come to realize that the sociology and politics of development offer broader insights relevant to policy-makers. While the IMF may not be impervious to criticism (Eichengreen 2002), internal debate appears more robust within the Bank, and this, together with external pressure, has led in the last ten years to a more open, inclusive, and innovative outreach to policies and sources of opinion previously marginalized. This has seen the WB take up 'social capital' initiatives as ways in which non-market institutions and networks can facilitate development through increased knowledge transfers upward as well as downward, and increased capacity-building (Stone 2000b: 168). The development of micro-credit schemes, the initiatives on gender and development, and the formation of the GDN (Stone 2000a) are three examples of this trend.

But is knowledge really the problem, or is it politics? To put the matter this starkly is, of course, to invite the riposte that both are inter-related and equally relevant. Eichengreen (2002) in his review of Stiglitz argues that much of the problem with the IMF was that it became too political and too closely linked with US foreign policy preoccupations. He recommends giving Bank officials greater autonomy, job security, and the status of an independent Central Bank able to resist politically motivated instructions from home Governments. For more radical critics, such measures would still leave defective forms of economic thinking in place, and would be no more democratic than before.

The political response that calls for greater inclusion and democracy has much appeal among both 'anti-globalization' protesters, and government and non-government movements in developing countries. Martin Khor, Director of the Third World Network, a think tank based in Malaysia, sees, like Stiglitz, the need to combine better knowledge with a re-shaping of institutions of global governance. Drawing on the work of developing country economists (Akyüz 1995, Bhaduri and Nayyar 1996, Ghazali 1996), alongside Western analysts, he argues that developing countries are faced with a dilemma. Either they open up in the hope of gaining benefits but at the risk of social dislocation without discernible benefit, or they take a more cautious risk-averse approach with the potential that benefits are foregone. This dilemma is faced in a context of great external pressure even for the stronger developing countries, as evident in the recent Asian financial crisis.

A cautious strategy that attempts a way through this dilemma is to adopt forms of selective rather than wholesale liberalization, forms that balance State and market over time frames that are sustainable. In the financial sector this may mean balancing controls over short-term capital movements with a more medium-term financial de-regulation within a context in which local knowledge and institutional capacity is in place (Khor 2001: 74–75). Similarly in the area of trade he argues that

> liberalization should not be pursued automatically in a Big Bang manner. Rather what is important is the quality, timing, sequencing, and scope of liberalization ... and how the process is accompanied by.... Other factors such as the strengthening of local enterprises and farms, human resource and technological development, as well as the build-up of export-capacity and markets. (ibid.: 36)

Many of these sentiments are echoed in Stiglitz' recent contribution to the UNDP Human Development Report (Stiglitz 2003). Here the point is made that China and other reasonably successful East and Southeast Asian countries did not follow the Washington Consensus, were slow to remove tariffs, and in China's case have not fully liberalized their capital account. Industry and trade policies were used in many such countries to promote exports and technology transfer against Western advice. Export-led strategies may not, however, be entirely effective where rich country markets are protected, and global capital markets expensive to access.

Overall, then, the issue is one of re-shaping the architecture of the global economic order, rather than letting the market spontaneously re-allocate resources in ways that prove de-stabilizing and often inimical to poverty-reduction and fairness. Against the oft-quoted argument that Africa has suffered by not being sufficiently included in economic globalization, Stiglitz retorts that it is equally the case that Africa has suffered from the way the globalization has been managed (ibid.).

But what difference would greater global democracy make and how would it be institutionally expressed? One initial challenge here is, of course, to determine who represents or speaks for the world populations. This question is raised by the apparent regulatory capture of many of the key global organizations by Western interests, creating what might be called 'global governance without global government' (Stiglitz 2002: 21). If finance ministers and central bankers attend the IMF and trade ministers the WTO, they are no doubt able to represent the views and interests of their respective finance and business communities. But Stiglitz was by no means the first to ask who exactly speaks for the peasant working to pay off their countries IMF debts or local businessmen faced with IMF value-added tax regimes?

The idea of democratic deficit, which has been applied to national political systems and organizations, applies with perhaps even greater force to the global polity. Here power differentials between rich and poor, men and women, organizations and individuals, corporations and elected representatives, elites and grass-roots organizations have been seen as massive, enduring, and yet de-stabilizing and pathological in their effects. The image of global elites resident within gated communities protected by high-tech security against discontented and deprived populations outside (Castells 1996) is a very powerful one. It feeds into a sense of the 'global cosmocracy' who manage, or as critics would say, mismanage the world (see the discussion in Held and McGrew 2002, Chapter 5). But is it accurate or sufficient as a depiction of the global political order?

Following Coleman and Porter (2000: 388), this may be disaggregated into six inter-related issues. These are lack of transparency in decision-making, few opportunities for direct participation in the democratic process, insufficient attention to the quality of deliberative processes, lack of representation of a wide body of interests, problems of effectiveness in the institutions of representative democracy, and a lack of fairness in global political outcomes.

The tension between representative and participatory democracy lies behind much discord. A good deal of global discontent is a plea for greater popular participation in shaping the world. The difficulty with implementing greater participation is, however, that of how to apply ideals developed in ancient city-states where small bodies of citizens could meet and debate in common to modern mass society. This is hard enough to apply in nation-states and much more difficult in a global context. A number of responses to this are possible. Some critics retreat into localist isolation, for example, while pragmatic critics 'act locally' even while they 'think globally'. Elite supporters retain more faith in representative bodies, and elite networks, into which some reforming critics may be co-opted.

Paradoxically, democracy, in its representative sense, is also a value used by a number of economic globalization's supporters against their critics. On the one hand, critics argue that multi-national corporations, the IMF or WTO are not democratically accountable for their actions. Supporters of economic globalization, on the one hand, counter by claiming that activists and NGOs are not elected or accountable either. The problem here is partly one of *representation*, that is who best represents the view of the people, and partly one of *legitimacy*, namely who is properly empowered to take decisions. Critics of globalization often claim they are closer to the people while supporters point out both that activists are un-elected and that elected national legislatures must approve the funding of global regulatory bodies.

The idea of deliberative democracy is perhaps a way of bridging such disputes, focusing on the importance of deliberation according to both cognitive and ethical issues in discussion. Truth matters alongside battles of values, and this introduces issues about the important role of scientific and professional expertise in modern society (Giddens 1994), alongside lay opinion. Much deliberation takes place outside parliamentary chambers and Government policy documents. Some is public and some is not. Conflict abounds over issues of process (e.g. lack of transparency) and issues of substance (e.g. how can poverty be lessened). These are hard to resolve though conflicts over single issues may be easier to resolve than those over the overarching rules of global order, such as global trading arrangements or codes of practice for multi-national companies. Governance networks may, then, only form where a degree of processual and sometimes substantive agreement exists.

Much of this emergent pattern of global governance around networks, outlined in Chapter 3, may then be viewed as an emergent shift to deliberative governance. Such arrangements do not dispose of the idea of power differentials but they do focus our attention less on notions of the global political order as interaction between sovereign bodies, and more on the *de facto* world of trans-national and inter-national debate, conflict, and negotiation. Here national sovereignty and state sovereignty remain relevant as reference points, even if they comprise only part of the terrain occupied by global political processes.

Government, then, continues both inside and outside governance arrangements. Inter-governmental arrangements offer at best conditional sovereignty for nation-states and, unless a hegemonic political force appears, are likely to continue to do so. This conditionality is becoming institutionalized within emerging regional blocs, the most elaborate of which is the EU. Here recent accession arrangements are organized in such a way that new candidates for entry must comply and converge with existing models of conditional or 'pooled' sovereignty previously negotiated between national partners.

Within the global arena as a whole, Green and Griffith (2002: 66) detect a changing dynamic interplay between 'globalization, the global governance institutions and social movements'. Debate has shifted from entrenched positions of the early 1990s (co-terminous with early phases of thinking on globalization), as global institutions responded to public discontent, becoming, they claim, 'more inclusive and democratic' (ibid.). Evidence for this, they claim, includes the growing self-confidence and unity of countries from Africa in the 2001 Doha meetings of the WTO. Other supporting evidence, noted above, includes the opening up of the WB to wider interests and policy options. These data may seem a little thin to support the idea of a sea change of view. Certainly the refusal of the 2003 Cancun meeting of the WTO to tackle rich country protectionism indicates the continuing capacity of developed countries to brush aside issues affecting the poorest countries in Africa and elsewhere (Ayodele 2003). Other evidence points to continuing obstacles in including women as knowledgable actors with global development reform processes (e.g. Whitehead and Lockwood 1998). Cornwall (2003), in a review of different types of attempt at gender-inclusion and participation, is more impressed with limits than achievement.

How far the global regulatory system is open to reform is unclear, with resistance from richer countries compounding vulnerabilities and limitations affecting those who seek change. First, there are divisions on a number of issues between state and non-state actors. These include a split between the states of developing countries and NGOs on the inclusion of environmental and labour issues in WTO agreements. Where the former see these as potential excuses for back-door protectionism, the latter see them as making considerable inroads into the domination of liberal economic principles in the global arena. Second, there are splits between reformers and more radical critics. The politics of the street and the politics of institutional reform are not mutually exclusive but it sometimes appears that they are. The difficulty with any such polarization is that both poles are in danger of different kinds of denial. For radical critics, there may be denial of the agency of reformers and elements of success in re-shaping institutional priorities, programmes, and their consequences. For reformers, on the other hand, it is the moral urgency of immediate action that appears to be denied.

One sociological commentary on the relationship between reformers and radical critics is that it reproduces one of the fundamental dilemmas of contemporary modernity. On the one side, there is the modernist assumption that problems have solutions and that a combination of individual reason and institutional design – balancing efficiency, democracy, and social cohesion – should be capable of resolving any challenge. On the other side, the rapid development of individual, technological, and institutional mobility and fluidity has cast us adrift from the legacy of 19th-century institutions, undermined a sense that reason and science can deliver the goods that people seek, and yet raised heightened expectations of universal personal well-being. In radical form this might be paraphrased as 'What do we want? Global justice! When do we want it? Now!' How far and how speedily these sentiments might become reality is deeply uncertain. But the moral force behind them shows no sign of dissipating.

Conclusion

This chapter has reviewed both evidence of global inequality and progress towards enhanced human welfare. I have also outlined some of the main positions taken on debates over what should be done. The broad conclusions that emerge can be summarized as follow.

First, economic globalization has enhanced many aspects of human welfare, including living standards and increased opportunity for communication, at least for many. Yet it has so far proven incapable of addressing the most intractable features of global inequality and injustice. Since there is much to gain from engagement with economic globalization, *isolationism* is scarcely a credible policy position.

Second, a number of the causes of global inequality are less to do with economic globalization, and more to do with either rich country protectionism, or with local rather than global causes of inequality, injustice, and corruption. This again suggests that *isolationism* is a dubious policy option. Yet there are equally strong arguments as thoroughgoing *supporters* of economic globalization.

A third, equally emphatic point is, then, that global markets themselves, as institutionalized through Washington Consensus policies and operated via global corporations, have neither made decisive inroads into current inequality nor produced forms of global governance that are simultaneously effective, fair, and legitimate. This is reflected both in splits among elite globalizers and in critical pressure from below. If isolationism and supportive neo-liberalism are unsatisfactory that leaves the three remaining positions of statists, alternative globalists, and reformers.

A fourth conclusion, consolidated in Chapter 5 and also consistent with the discussion of trans-national networks in this chapter, is that *statism* is inadequate for the effective development, regulation, and re-making of the global order that we now have. This is partly because many current problems such as environmental protection or human security are global in scope and require co-ordinated global action. It is also because inter-national co-operation between states is vulnerable to the self-interest and concentrated power of the more powerful states. Norms capable of regulating self-interested states in areas such as human rights or environmental sustainability typically emerge less from the wisdom of states, but in large measure from multiple sources of knowledge and moral suasion within civil society. States remain players, and typically possess organizational capacities that many organizations and social movements lack. National affiliations and identity also still loom large. Nation-states cannot, therefore, be ignored by any global policy position.

We are left, in this argument by elimination, with *alternative globalists* and *reformers*. Much of the action in debates over the re-making of globalization is centred on a dialectic between these two, the former elaborating ideals of political and cultural globalization and the latter seeking to address deficiencies by re-making institutions according to new or reformulated agenda emphasizing governance rather than government. This dialectic is by no means free of conflict, with alternative globalizers seen by reformers as utopian, and reformers vulnerable to co-option by un-reconstructed economic globalizers, according to their more radical critics. In the processes, alternative globalizing activists and reformers of global institutions represent two major forms of human agency in the global scene.

A final sociological observation, here, is that these two positions are characteristic of third-wave understandings of globalization. They stand on the wreckage of first-wave isolationists and supporters. And while drawing on second-wave statist skepticism, they more adequately reflect current complexities in the understanding of globalization. Both recognize that there are different forms of globalization, and both are committed to the proposition that human action matters and can make a difference. They are united, at least in the sense of being against fatalism.

In the final concluding chapter we return to some of the main themes of the book and identify some questions that require further exploration.

8

The Making of Globalization: Puzzles and Prospects

Discussion of globalization often proceeds as if its meaning and main features were clear and that having been identified, the sole remaining task is to determine whether it is a force for good or bad. In this study I have tried to show that it is a far more challenging task to determine the realities that lie behind the many phenomena associated with globalization. This in turn makes attitudes towards globalization an equally difficult matter to unravel. If globalization means different things to different people, then the meaning of attitudes for and against it cannot be taken at face value. What exactly people are for and against needs to be unravelled, just as much as the many realities of social change often assembled under the umbrella of globalization.

This book is intended as a contribution to the understanding of globalization and to the clarification of issues at stake in the assessment and evaluation of global trends. While difficult to define, I take globalization to refer to a range of cross-border phenomena of such significance that they warrant a distinct label and a specific kind of analysis. Much social activity is no longer centred on the world of nation-states and national affiliation, but is located far more on patterns of inter-connection, inter-dependence, and communication that permeate states, regions, and localities.

Two of the major propositions underlying the study reflect the third-wave approach to globalization identified in Chapter 1. The first argues that globalization is many distinct processes, rather than one single overarching process. The second sees globalization both as the outcome of human activity and as a set of processes that have profound consequences for human activity. We shape or try to shape our lives and destinies, as well as being shaped by each other and by processes that may be beyond our capacity to fully perceive or comprehend. To say this is to retrieve both analysis of and moral judgement about globalization from two unfortunate positions. One is fatalism, in which globalization is a malevolent force either out of control or in the hands of powerful elites in the grip of ideological fervour about free trade or world government. The other is that kind of ultra-scepticism which claims that either globalization does not exist or if it does, its significance has been hyped up in an exaggerated fashion.

The argument that globalization is very far from being a single unified master process or system has two components: a historical argument and a contemporary one. The historical argument, elaborated in Chapter 2, indicated that many trends associated with globalization, such as cross-border connectivity, inter-dependence, and the idea of the world as a single place, have multiple long-term origins. Globalization is not a one-master process, but a set of inter-locking, though sometimes conflicting, trends. Some of these can be directly connected with explicit human intention while others seem to emerge from activities designed for another purpose. Warriors and merchants, migrants and pilgrims may sometimes have set out to create empires of power, promote republics of commerce, locate havens of safety, or realize earthly kingdoms of divine will. But this does not apply in all cases, nor do global outcomes necessarily emerge from globalizing intentions.

Meanwhile in Chapter 3 attention moves to consider contemporary developments. The argument that globalization may best be seen as a system with a single unified logic was rejected neither because systemic elements cannot be found, nor because the power of the global capitalist economy was disputed. The argument is rather that emphasis on a single overriding system-logic is inconsistent with evidence of the complexity and multi-dimensional character of global processes.

Economic globalization is certainly a major structural influence on patterns of global income, wealth, and a major and perhaps the single most important concentration of power. However, political, social, and cultural developments are not simply to be understood as derivatives of global capitalism. Business, states, and supra-national institutions are, of course, closely inter-connected across many policy domains including trade, finance, investment, market-supporting infrastructural development, and many others. But beyond these connections there are other globalizing cross-currents and processes not dominated by profit-seeking and its institutional consolidation. These include individuals and families migrating and communicating across boundaries in search of better lives, the diffusion of cultural repertoires and identities across borders, and a range of organizations, networks, and activists seeking alternative world orders to that offered by global capitalism, operating from below and from above. These involve issues such as an effective global security built on co-operation rather than a military balance of power, as well as the construction of environmentally sustainable social development for the globe and, equally importantly, a global human rights regime. Here attitudes, organizational objectives, and sometimes policy outcomes too are very far from uniformly dominated by capitalist interests across time and space.

Put simply, there is too much else going on to warrant reducing globalization to a singular entity. Simply assembling further evidence of capitalist power does not undermine this counter-argument. What would undermine it would be the evidence that alternative forms of globalization are reducing in significance, and that such forms can be explained in terms of a single overriding cause. Debates over globalization are not, in general, moving in this direction, rather the reverse. Globalization, in short, is many things rather than one single order of things.

This being said, there remain many challenges to an understanding of its complexity. In Chapter 3 we noted the range of explanatory approaches and organizing metaphors drawn upon in pursuit of an understanding of things global. These stretch from systems and structures through fields, networks, and webs, to forms of rapid movement and fluidity. There is no consensus among scholars as to which, if any, of these is the single most useful approach and, failing any such agreement, it remains preferable to approach globalization through a proliferation of approaches, as suited to the particular questions under consideration.

If globalization is too mobile and changeable to be easily encompassed by any existing conception of system and structure, while retaining enduring features alongside fluidity, mid-range options within this spectrum of positions may perhaps offer the most fruitful way forward. Examples include the idea of a global field composed of differing structures and forms of communication as proposed by Roland Robertson, or the broad-ranging work on global networks which, in their emphasis on multi-centred relationships stretched across borders, help to provide insights into patterns of governance, business activity, knowledge exchange, and resistance to globalization.

Other dimensions of global complexity in relation to time and space were outlined in Chapters 4 and 5. Major emphases here included the multiplicity of times and spaces opened up and imagined in globalizing processes. In rejecting notions like the annihilation of space by time, or the idea that globalization means one single time frame, the discussion relies throughout on the centrality of human agency in the shaping and imagining of global arrangements.

Human agency

The theme of human agency in the making of globalization is reflected in the title of this book. The key argument here is that globalization is not an irresistible, uncheckable, and completely irreversible force transforming social arrangements in an unparalleled way. Human agency matters as do institutional attempts to incubate, shape, and regulate change. The types of globalization that have emerged are, especially in contemporary times, largely products of human intention. This applies to the development of multi-national companies and global regulatory institutions, as well as the myriad networks of global civil society, or the micro-processes of global migration and inter-cultural engagement. Such processes may be shaped by actors from above and from below, and this applies to both in spite of vast global inequalities of power, and in some cases because of it. Moral outrage and anger, as much as the search for profits or global technical-problem-solving, motivate and mobilize actors on the global scene.

Intentions have, of course, been overtaken by unforeseen consequences as in popular uses of the Internet, intended originally as a communications system that would allow states and the military to survive in the case of nuclear war. Similarly much of the ideological fervour in support of free trade has failed to reduce global poverty on the scale many of its proponents had expected. Reform programmes have then emerged from failures to shape globalization according to socially acceptable norms and standards as much as from its successes.

Until recent times, global capitalism was never an explicit aim of producers, traders, or politicians, though expansiveness in search of markets, raw materials, capital, labour, and technology are clearly evident for a number of millennia. Nineteenth-century Imperialism and doctrines of worldwide free trade represent a more explicit form of outward projection, as do doctrines of a single religious cosmos or more secular forms of cosmopolitanism. The great world religions are perhaps the pioneering globalists, especially where connected with a monotheistic religion. But prior to the last 250 years or so, conceptions of globalism have generally been less explicit, whatever traces may be found anticipating later doctrines and world-views. Meanwhile the economic, political, and cultural processes which such world-views helped to create and within which they were embedded may have turned out different.

For those who seek a global meaning for social activity or to explore identity and modes of living across border, there are very sharp limits to global capitalist dominance. The globalizing world religions do not dance to the tune of any kind of economic world system. This applies both to Islamic resistance to 'Western' materialism and to very significant Christian and inter-faith campaigns which hold global capitalism (or simply greed) as largely to blame for continuing global inequality. Beyond this, large segments of global civil society, especially those connected with social movements, have taken very strong stands against both economic inequality and the global democracy deficit. Activists against global capitalism may not be elected, but they do represent significant bodies of dissenting opinion that regard global capitalism as illegitimate, and the existing political order as deficient in addressing such concerns.

Arguments about the importance of agency also link with arguments about limits to globalization, to the idea that the future of globalization can be shaped and re-shaped, and to suggestions that some or possibly all of the globalizing processes we have discussed in this book are reversible. Historical analysis certainly suggests that we should beware of too confident an approach to the direction of social change. Will we get more and more globalization or has globalization gone too far? Once again the answer is a complex one because globalization is itself complex and multi-dimensional. If Hopkins and his associates (Hopkins 2002a) are correct then globalization moves through a series of transitions, the latest being a shift from a modern to a post-colonial type. One aspect of this shift is a greater presence and involvement of the world beyond Europe and North America in the shaping of global futures, though as yet there is no profound shift in power away from what is conventionally described as the West. The idea of a Third World united only in the depths of its material misery should now be discarded even though material misery is still the current fate of large sections of the world's population.

Another aspect of the shift in forms of globalization, explored in Chapter 6, is the emergence of global civil society as a robust element within global political and moral debates and activities. This already marks a kind of globalization from below. Whether the movements for radical change that have eventuated produce radical social change, remain dominated by elite-based globalization, or become co-opted in reform strategies is not clear. What is noteworthy, nonetheless, is that there has recently been an enormous and growing effort at global institutional reform, some of which is charted by Braithwaite and Drahos (2000), and evident also in the websites of global non-government organizations, as well as the WB. The depth and ubiquity of reform processes, sketched in Chapter 7, speak both to the legitimation crisis that economic globalization currently finds itself in, and to the mobilizing power of global civil society movements and the expansion of globally oriented knowledge among epistemic communities.

Rather different scenarios emerge, however, if we take heed of the work of James (2001), who suggests that previous phases of globalization have been succeeded by phases of de-globalization. The mechanisms at work here suggest that globalizing upswings create excessive problems of differentiation. A typical example of this is where global economic processes gain too much freedom from social and political regulation. This may take the form of highly mobile flows of finance, goods, or labour, moving in or out of nations in ways that de-stabilize nation-states. The three leading examples would be short-term financial outflows that, if left unchecked, lead to currency devaluation and credit contraction, increased imports from low-wage countries that threaten employment, and real or perceived inflows of immigrant labour that are believed to threaten domestic labour markets and social cohesion. The counter-tendency towards de-globalization has, then, often been to place restrictions upon these forms of mobility, a process that may be seen as de-differentiation through re-assertion of nationally based political regulation. These scenarios indicate among other things that the nation-state is not dead neither as a state nor as a source of popular identification and affiliation.

At the time of writing, the US-led global alliance pursuing the 'war on terror' represented, if anything, an attempted re-assertion of military-based state power. This has been dubbed 'regressive globalization', in part as a contrast to the normatively positive connotations many observers have given to globalizing trends such as the advance of global civil society and moves towards the construction of a human rights regime more responsive to popular concerns. The assertion of military power of this kind cannot, however, be read simply as a response to excessive differentiation. Its rationale is connected far more to the evolving shape of the global order, and to the struggle of interests within that order. There is some ambiguity, however, as to whether such developments constitute another form of de-globalization around a resurgent national realpolitik, and how far they amount to a new kind of unilateral global authoritarianism or G1. Such questions also raise speculation about the fiscal sustainability of a new quasi-imperial world order.

One major theoretical question about globalization remains very difficult to resolve with any degree of precision. This involves understanding of the relationships between global, regional, national, and local arrangements, and patterns of experience. This question lies at the heart of the evolution of the three waves of thinking about globalization. Whereas the first wave tended to see the global dominating and eroding the national and local, the second reversed the argument, seeing the global being limited and in many senses dependent on the national or regional. Third-wave approaches recognize the co-existence and inter-relations between these various layers of social life. Such connections are not necessarily corrosive or mutually incompatible, and we may say that the global and the national or local may under certain circumstances depend on each other.

It is perhaps useful, however, to take all of this one step further through the general approaches we take to social analysis in an epoch of globalization. This may be done by considering methodological issues, especially those that define the unit of analysis from which we start. The approach referred to as *methodological nationalism* took this to be the nation-state, where we analyse various national societies and their inter-national relations with each other. To the extent that this is now outmoded, should we switch to *methodological globalism*, where the globe is the unit of analysis within which nations are contained as only one of many elements? Or, in the light of third-wave theory, is it more appropriate to think in terms of *methodological glocalism*, the defining characteristic of which approach is a world of phenomena that are simultaneously global and national. Rather than sort phenomena into those that are global and those that are not – a characteristic of both the other approaches – the procedure here, as demonstrated by Robertson, is to observe the inter-penetration of the two, in so many contexts from niche-markets for businesses, to hybrid cultural forms such as world music, to cosmopolitan identities that draw on particular traditions in developing cosmopolitan perspectives. To achieve this, however, would require that the awkward hybrid word 'glocal' would itself cross over into mainstream speech and discourse.

Normative issues and the making of a better world

What then finally of the burgeoning disatisfaction and anger with gross global inequalities of power and life-chances. What, in short, are the prospects for a globally just and fairer world order?

Much of the evidence reviewed in Chapter 7 suggests that hopes that serious inroads may be made into global poverty, and progress made in achieving improvements in human rights are slow at best, and ineffective or counter-productive at worst. Many continue to seek reform or more radical change to the major features of economic globalization and the Bretton Woods regulatory framework that has prevailed up to the present. And many critics from below suggest that something like a momentum for change is underway, symbolized by the Seattle demonstrations, limited successes in debt reduction for the poorest countries, and an evident split within global elites over the continuing value of Washington Consensus doctrines.

For those who think this way, there is a tendency to invoke new social movements from below or global civil society as means whereby global arrangements might become fairer, more just, and more democratic. While sympathetic to this scenario, the sceptic might equally point to the enormous difficulties that lie in the way of this vision, including the extremely fragile sense of inter-cultural trust and cosmopolitan solidarity in the contemporary world. It might seem reasonable to assume that the emergence of global conditions of existence for individuals and groups, reflected variously in migration, travel, and the Internet, would create the basis for a revived cosmopolitanism in world culture, and there is some evidence in support of this view, especially if we include consideration of glocal fusions of global and local identity. The difficulty is that such evidence does not take the robust form of a dominant social trend. Other evidence as in current conflicts in and over the Middle East point in different directions including polarized 'culture wars' or 'wars of civilizations'. Borders may be porous to varying degrees, but they remain in place for a number of purposes from immigration control to membership of national communities.

Globalization is certainly a matter about which moral and political choices can and are being made rather than an inevitable and irreversible fate. Choice always takes place in a context of constraint, but it is important not to underestimate the myriad choices, public and private that go into the making, reversing, and re-making of globalization. The global patterns of relationship traced in this study are social products, and as such amenable to moral engagement and re-evaluation, public policy re-design, and individual and collective choice. There is nothing especially natural or necessary about the prevailing architecture of global markets or about the kinds of global civil society that radical critics of globalization wish to bring about. Nor can history be read as moving inexorably towards any particular kind of global outcome. Visions of the future like accounts of the present remain profoundly contested. Which global utopia, if any, prove fertile and which prove barren seems impossible to determine. This is less a matter of the failure of social scientific analysis than a recognition of global complexity and uncertainty.

A key part of this complexity is reflected in the enormous dilemmas in somehow creating post-national institutions that are global in reach but local in relevance and sensitivity. Inequalities of market access and unaccountable concentrations of corporate, regulatory, and military power are major problems, but they do not exhaust the agenda of institutional challenges that globalization creates. Further challenges are associated with the current lack of practical models of global politics or global culture that appear attractive to world populations. It is true that politics is always a matter of conflict between interests and that the possibility of cultural conformity is a dangerous illusion that can only ultimately be achieved by force even if unsustainable in the long term. We should neither expect the birth of new global arrangements to be painless nor that sustainable globalization would be conflict-free. Even so, suspicion and enmity, and insecurity and mistrust populate the globe as much as hope and creativity. Between the two stand morally engaged reformers, types of global actors edged out of the public dramas of moral confrontation between saints and sinners, but significant players nonetheless. This book is dedicated to them.

Bibliography

Abaza, M. and G. Stauth (1990), 'Occidental Reason, Orientalism and Islamic Fundamentalism: A Critique', in M. Albrow and E. King (eds), *Globalization, Knowledge, and Society*, London: Sage, 209–230.

Abdullah, A. (1996), *Going Glocal: Cultural Dimensions in Malaysian Management*, Kuala Lumpur: Malaysian Institute of Management.

Abu-Lughod, J. (1989), *Before European Hegemony: The World System AD 1250–1350*, Oxford: Oxford University Press.

——(1993), 'Discontinuities and Persistence: One World System or a Succession of Systems', in A.G. Frank and B. Gills, *The World System: Five Hundred Years or Five Thousand?* London: Routledge, 278–291.

Agbebi, M. (1911), 'The West African Problem', in G. Spiller (ed.), *Papers on Inter-racial Problems*, London: King, 341–348.

Ahmed, A.A. (1992), *Postmodernism and Islam*, London: Routledge.

Akami, T. (2002), 'Between the State and Global Civil Society: Non-official Experts and Their Network in the Asia-Pacific, 1925–45', *Global Networks*, 2(1), 65–81.

Akyüz, Y. (1995), 'Taming International Finance', in J. Michie and J. Grieve-Smith (eds), *Managing the Global Economy*, Oxford: Oxford University Press, 55–90.

Albert, M. (2002), 'WSF: Where to Now?', http://www.zmag.org/wsf220.htm.

Albrow, M. (1990), 'Introduction', in M. Albrow and E. King (eds), *Globalization: Knowledge and Society*, London: Sage, 3–13.

Alexander, J. (1984), *Theoretical Logic in Sociology, The Modern Reconstruction of Classical Thought: Talcott Parsons*, vol. 4, London: Routledge.

Amnesty International (2003a), 'About the Urgent Action Network', http://web.amnesty.org/pages/ua-index-eng.

——(2003b), 'Facts and Figures: The Work of Amnesty International', http://web.amnesty.org/pages/aboutai_facts.

Andersen, B. (2003), 'Porto Allegre: A Worm's Eye View', *Global Networks*, 3(2), 197–200.

Anderson, B. (1983), *Imagined Communities*, London: Verso.

——(1992), 'Long-Distance Nationalism', *Wertheim Lecture*, CASA, University of Amsterdam.

Anesaki, M. (1923), *The Religious and Social Problems of the Orient*, New York: MacMillan.

Anheier, H., M. Glasius, and M. Kaldor (eds) (2001), 'Introducing Global Civil Society', *Global Civil Society*, Oxford: Oxford University Press, 3–22.

Anheier, H. and N. Themudo (2002), 'Organisational Forms of Global Civil Society: Implications for Going Global', in M. Glasius, M. Kaldor and H. Anheier (eds), *Global Civil Society Yearbook*, Oxford: Oxford University Press, 191–216.

Appadurai, A. (1998), *Modernity at Large*, Minneapolis: Minnesota University Press.

Appiah, K.A. (1998), 'Cosmopolitan Patriots', in P. Cheah and B. Robbins (eds), *Cosmopolitics: Thinking and Feeling Beyond the Nation*, Minnesota: University of Minnesota Press, 91–114.
——(2003), 'Citizens of the World', in M.J. Gibney (ed.), *Globalizing Rights*, Oxford: Oxford University Press, 189–232.
Arts, B. (2000), 'Political Influence of NGO's on International Environmental Issues', in H. Goverde, P. Cerny, M. Haugaard, and H.-H. Lentner (eds), *Power in Contemporary Politics: Theories, Practices, Globalizations*, London: Sage, 132–147.
Asia Inc. (2003), 'Rise of the Bourgeosie', *Asia Inc.*, July, 8.
Atan, G.B. (1996), *The Effects of DFI on Trade, Balance of Payments and Growth in Developing Countries, and Appropriate Policy Approaches to DFI*, Penang: Third World Network.
Augé, M. (1995), *Non-Places*, London: Verso.
Ayodele, T. (2003), 'Subsidies Underline WTO Hypocrisy', *Australian Financial Review*, 30 December, 47.
Ballantyne, T. (2002), 'Empire, Knowledge and Culture', in A.G. Hopkins (ed.), *Globalization in World History*, London: Pimlico, 115–140.
Barber, B. (1996), *Jihad versus McWorld*, New York: Ballantyne Books.
Barton, D. and N. Hall (eds) (2000), 'Introduction', in *Letter Writing as a Social Practice*, John Benjamins Amsterdam, 1–14.
Bauman, Z. (1998), 'On Glocalization: Or Globalization for Some, Localization for Others', *Thesis Eleven*, 54, 37–49.
Baxi, U. (2000), 'Human Rights: Suffering Between States and Markets', in R. Cohen and M.S. Rai (eds), *Global Social Movements*, London: Athlone Press, 33–45.
Bayly, C.A. (1996), *Empire and Information: Intelligence Gathering and Social Communication in India 1780–1870*, Cambridge: Cambridge University Press.
——(2002), '"Archaic" and "Modern" Globalization in the Eurasian and African Arena, c. 1750–1850', in A.G. Hopkins (ed.) (2002), *Globalization in World History*, London: Pimlico, 47–73.
Bazerman, C. (2000), 'Letters and the Social Grounding of Differentiated Genres', in D. Barton and N. Hall (eds), *Letter Writing as a Social Practice*, John Benjamins Amsterdam, 15–30.
Beck, U. (2000), *What is Globalization?* Cambridge: Polity.
Benko, G.B. (1990), 'Local versus Global in Social Analysis: Some Reflections', in A. Kulinski (ed.), *Globality versus Locality*, Warsaw: University of Warsaw, 63–66.
Bennison, A.K. (2002), 'Muslim Universalism and Western Globalization', in A.G. Hopkins (ed.), *Globalization in World History*, London: Pimlico, 74–97.
Berger, S. and R. Dore (eds) (1996), *National Diversity and Global Capitalism*, Ithaca, NY: Cornell University Press.
Bhaduri, A. and D. Nayyar (1996), *The Intelligent Person's Guide to Liberalization*, New Delhi: Penguin Books.
Billig, M. (1995), *Banal Nationalism*, London: Sage.
Blaise, C. (2000), *Time Lord: Sir Sandford Fleming and the Creation of Standard Time*, London: Weidenfeld and Nicholson.
Blyden, E.W., T. Lewis, and T. Dwight (1871), *The People of Africa*, New York: Randolph.

196   *Bibliography*

Boerzel, T.A. (1998), 'Organizing Babylon – On the Different Conceptions of Policy Networks', *Public Administration*, 76, 253–273.

Du Bois, W. (1993) [1903], *The Souls of Black Folk*, New York: Knopf.

——(1970) [1915], *The Negro*, London: Oxford University Press.

——(1939), *Black Folk: Then and Now*, New York: Octagon.

Boli, J. and G. Thomas (1999), *Constructing World Culture: International Nongovernmental Organizations Since 1875*, Stanford: Stanford University Press.

Boltho, A. and G. Toniolo (1999), 'The Assessment: The Twentieth Century – Achievements, Failures, Lessons', *Oxford Review of Economic Policy*, 15(4), 1–17.

Boulton, M. (1960), *Zamenhof: Creator of Esperanto*, London: Routledge.

Bourdieu, P. (1993), *The Field of Cultural Production*, New York: Columbia University Press.

——(1998), *Acts of Resistance*, Cambridge: Polity Press.

Bourguignon, F. and C. Morrisson (1999), *The Size Distribution of Income Among World Citizens, 1820–1990*, World Bank: Paris.

Boyne, R. (1990), 'Culture and the World System', in M. Featherstone (ed.), *Global Culture: Nationalism, Globalization, and Modernity*, London: Sage, 57–62.

Braithwaite, J. and P. Drahos (2000), *Global Business Regulation*, Cambridge: Cambridge University Press.

Braudel, F. (1972), 'History and the Social Sciences', in P. Burke (ed.), *Economy and Society in Early Modern Europe*, London: Routledge, 11–41.

Brenner, N. (1998), 'Global Cities, Glocal States: Global City Formation and State Territorial Restructuring in Contemporary Europe', *Review of International Political Economy*, 5(1), 1–37.

Brubaker, R. (1992), *Citizenship and Nationhood in France and Germany*, Cambridge, MA: Harvard University Press.

Bruno, K. (2002), 'World Economic Forum Protests Pose New Challenges for Anti-Globalization Movements', *Corpwatch* at http://corpwatch.radicaldesigns.org/article.php?id=1468.

Burawoy, M. (2000), 'Grounding Globalization', in M. Burawoy, J.A. Blum, S. George, Z. Gille, T. Gowan, L. Haney, M. Klawiter, S.H. Lopez, S. O'Riain (eds), *Global Ethnography*, Berkeley: University of California Press, 337–350.

Burgmann, V. (1996), *Revolutionary Industrial Unionism*, Cambridge: Cambridge University Press.

Cannadine, D. (2001), *Ornamentalism*, London: Allen Lane.

Carroll, W.K. and C. Carson (2003), 'The Network of Global Corporations and Elite Policy Groups', *Global Networks*, 3(1), 29–58.

Carroll, W.K. and M. Fennema (2002), 'Is There a Transnational Business Community?', *International Sociology*, 17(3), September, 393–420.

Castells, M. (1996), *The Rise of the Network Society*, Oxford: Blackwell.

——(2001), *The Internet Galaxy: Reflections on the Internet, Business, and Society*, Oxford: Oxford University Press.

Castles, S. and M. Miller (1993), *The Age of Migration*, Basingstoke: MacMillan.

Chakrabaty, D. (2000), *Provincializing Europe: Postcolonial Thought and Historical Thought*, Princeton, NJ: Princeton University Press.

Chandler, A. (1962), *Strategy and Structure: Chapters in the History of the Industrial Enterprise*, Cambridge, MA: MIT Press.

Chase-Dunn, C. (1989), *Global Formation: Structures of the World Economy*, Oxford: Blackwell.

Chase-Dunn, C. and T. Hall (1997), *Rise and Decline: Comparing World Systems*, Boulder: Westview.

Cheah, P. and B. Robbins (eds) (1998), *Cosmopolitics: Thinking and Feeling Beyond the Nation*, Minnesota: University of Minnesota.

Cigno, A., F. Rosat, and L. Guarcello (2002), 'Does Globalization Increase Child Labor', *World Development*, 30(9), 1579–1589.

Cohen, R. and S. Rai (eds) (2000), *Global Social Movements*, London: Athlone Press.

Coleman, W. and A. Perl (1999), 'International Policy Environments and Policy Network Analysis', *Political Studies*, 47, 691–709.

Coleman, W. and T. Porter (2000), 'International Institutions, Globalisation and Democracy: Assessing the Challenges', *Global Society*, 14(3), 377–398.

Cornwall, A. (2003), 'Whose Voices? Whose Choices? Reflections on Gender and Participatory Development', *World Development*, 31(8), 1324–1342.

Connor, W. (1994), *Ethnonationalism: The Quest for Understanding*, Princeton, NJ: Princeton University Press.

Cox, R. (1981), 'Social Forces, States, and World Orders', *Millenium: Journal of Interdisciplinary Studies*, 10(2), 126–155.

——(1987), *Production, Power and World Order*, New York: Columbia University.

——(1992), 'Multilateralism and World Order', *Review of International Studies*, 18, 161–180.

Cronin, M. (2003), *Translation and Globalization*, London: Routledge.

Curtin, P. (1984), *Cross-Cultural Trade in World History*, Cambridge: Cambridge University Press.

Davidson, B. (1998), *West Africa Before the Colonial Era: A History to 1850*, London: Longman.

Delanty, G. (1995), *Inventing Europe: Idea, Identity, Reality*, Basingstoke: MacMillan.

Desai, M. and Y. Said (2001), in H. Anheier, M. Glasius, and M. Kaldor (eds), *Global Civil Society*, Oxford: Oxford University Press, 51–78.

Diamond, L. and J. McDonald (1996), *Multi-Track Diplomacy*, West Hartford: Kumarian Press.

Dicken, P. (1998), *Global Shift: Transforming the World Economy*, London: Chapman.

Durkheim, E. (1964) [1893], *The Division of Labour in Society*, New York: Free Press.

Economist (2003), 'Years of Plenty?', 12th July.

Eichengreen, B. (2002), 'Mr Stiglitz went to Washington', reprinted from *Foreign Affairs*, in *Australian Financial Review*, 22nd July.

Esping-Anderson, G. (1990), *The Three Worlds of Welfare Capitalism*, Cambridge: Polity Press.

Falk, R. (1995), *On Humane Governance: Towards a New Global Politics*, Cambridge: Polity Press.

——(1999), 'Pursuing the Quest for Human Security', in M. Tehranian (ed.), *Worlds Apart: Human Security and Global Governance*, Tauris: London, 1–22.

Frank, A.G. (1990), 'A Theoretical Introduction to 5000 years of World-System History', *Review*, 13(2), 155–248.

Frank, A.G. and B. Gills (1993), *The World System: Five Hundred Years or Five Thousand?* London: Routledge.

Freud, S. (1975) [1930], *Civilization and Its Discontents*, London: Hogarth Press.

Friedman, J. (1994), *Cultural Identity and Global Process*, London: Sage.

——(1995), 'Global System, Globalization and the Parameters of Modernity', in M. Featherstone, S. Lash and R. Robertson (eds), *Global Modernities*, London: Sage, 69–90.

Friedmann, H. (1994), 'Distance and Durability: Shaky Foundations of the World Food Economy', in P. McMichael (ed.), *The Global Restructuring of Agro-Food Systems*, Ithaca: Cornell University Press, 258–276.

Friedmann, J. and W. Goetz (1982), 'World City Formation: And Agenda for Research and Action', *International Journal of Urban and Regional Research*, 6, 309–344.

Frith, S. (ed.) (1989), *World Music, Politics and Social Change*, Manchester: Manchester University Press.

Gans, H. (1979), 'Symbolic Ethnicity', *Ethnic and Racial Studies*, 2, 1–20.

Geiss, I. (1972), *The Pan-African Movement*, New York: Africana Publishing.

Geyer, M.H. and J. Paulmann (eds) (2001), 'Introduction: The Mechanics of Internationalism', *The Mechanics of Internationalism: Culture, Society, and Politics from the 1840's to the First World War*, Oxford: Oxford University Press, 1–25.

Ghils, P. (1992), 'International Civil Society: International Non-governmental Organizations in the International System', *Social Science Journal*, 133, 417–431.

Giddens, A. (1981), *A Contemporary Critique of Historical Materialism*, vol. 1: *Power, Property and the State*, London: MacMillan.

——(1991), *Modernity and Self Identity*, Cambridge: Polity.

——(1994), 'Living in a Post-Traditional Society', in U. Beck, A. Giddens, and S. Lash, *Reflexive Modernization*, Cambridge: Polity Press, 56–109.

——(1999), *Runaway World*, London: Profile.

Gill, S. (1990), *American Hegemony and the Trilateral Commission*, Cambridge: Cambridge University Press.

——(1992), 'Economic Globalization and the Internationalization of Authority', *Geoforum*, 23, 269–283.

Gilroy, P. (1993), *Black Atlantic: Modernity and Double Consciousness*, London: Verso.

Granovetter, M. (1985), 'Economic Action and Social Structure: The Problem of Embeddedness', *American Journal of Sociology*, 91(3), 481–510.

Green, D. and M. Griffith (2002), 'Globalization and Its Discontents', *International Affairs*, 78(1), 49–68.

Grove, R. (1995), *Green Imperialism: Colonial Expansion, Tropical Island Edens and the Origins of Environmentalism*, 1600–1860, Cambridge: Cambridge University Press.

Gurnah, A. (1997), 'Elvis in Zanzibar', in A. Scott (ed.), *The Limits of Globalization*, London: Routledge, 116–142.

Gurvitch, G. (1963), 'Social Structure and the Multiplicity of Times', in E.A. Tiryakian (ed.), *Sociological Theory, Values and Socio-Cultural Change*, London: Free Press, 171–184.

Haas, P.M. (1989), 'Do Regimes Matter? Epistemic Communities and Mediterranean Pollution Control', *International Organization*, 43, 377–403.

Hamm, B. (2003), 'Asian Culture and Newspapers', in S. Martin and D. Copeland (eds), *The Function of Newspapers in Society: A Global Perspective*, Westport, Conn: Praeger, 47–90.

Hammarskjold, D. (1962), 'The International Civil Servant in Law and in Fact', in W. Foote (ed.), *The Servant of Peace: A Selection of the Speeches of Dag Hammarskjold, 1953–61*, London: Bodley Head, 329–353.

Hammerton, J. (2004), 'The Quest for Family and the Mobility of Modernity in Narratives of Postwar British Migration', *Global Networks*, 4(3), 271–284.

Hancock, D. (1995), *Citizens of the World: London Merchants and the Integration of the British Atlantic Community, 1735–85*, Cambridge: Cambridge University Press.

Hannerz, U. (1990), 'Cosmopolitans and Locals in World Culture', in M. Featherstone (ed.), *Global Culture: Nationalism, Globalization and Modernity*, London: Sage, 237–252.

——(1992), *Global Complexity*, New York: Columbia University Press.

Harper, T.N. (2002), 'Empire, Diaspora, and the Languages of Globalisation', in A.G. Hopkins (ed.), *Globalization in World History*, Pimlico: London, 141–166.

Harvey, D. (1996), *Justice, Nature and the Geography of Difference*, Oxford: Blackwell.

Hastie, W. (1882), *Hindu Idolatry and English Enlightenment*, Calcutta: Thacker Spink.

Havel, V. (1985), *The Power of the Powerless: Citizens Against the State in Central-Eastern Europe*, London: Hutchinson.

Hay, C. and D. Marsh (eds) (2000), 'Introduction', *Demystifying Globalisation*, London: Palgrave, 1–17.

Hayford, C. (1903), *Gold Coast Native Institutions*, London: Sweet and Maxwell.

Held, D. (1995), *Democracy and the Global Order*, Cambridge: Polity.

Held, D. and A. McGrew (2002), *Globalization/Anti-Globalization*, Cambridge: Polity Press.

——(eds) (2003), 'The Great Globalization Debate', *The Global Transformations Reader*, Cambridge: Polity, 1–50.

Held, D., A. McGrew, D. Goldblatt, and J. Perraton (1999), *Global Transformations*, Cambridge: Polity Press.

Hirst, P. and G. Thompson (1992), 'The Problem of "Globalization": International Economic Relations, National Economic Management and the Formation of Trading Blocs', *Economy and Society*, 21, 357–396.

——(1996), *Globalization in Question*, Cambridge: Polity Press.

Hobsbawm, E. and T. Ranger (eds) (1983), *The Invention of Tradition*, Cambridge: Cambridge University Press.

Hodgson, M. (1974) [1958–9], *The Venture of Islam*, 3 vols, Chicago: Chicago University Press.

Holm, H.-H. and G. Sorensen (1995), *Whose World Order?* Boulder: Westview Press.

Holton, R. (1976), *British Syndicalism*, London: Pluto Press.

——(1985), *The Transition from Feudalism to Capitalism*, Basingstoke: MacMillan.

——(1986), *Cities, Capitalism, and Civilization*, London: Allen & Unwin.

——(1998), *Globalization and the Nation-State*, Basingstoke: MacMillan.

——(2000), 'Globalization's Cultural Consequences', *Annals of the American Academy of Political and Social Sciences*, 570, pp. 140–152.

——(2002), 'Cosmopolitanism or Cosmopolitanisms? The Universal Races Congress of 1911', *Global Networks*, 2(2), 153–170.

Holton, R. and B.S. Turner (1986), *Talcott Parsons on Economy and Society*, London: Routledge.

Holton, S. (2001), 'Segregation, Racism and White Women Reformers: A Transnational Analysis, 1840–1912', *Women's History Review*, 10(1), 5–25.

Hoogvelt, A. (1997), *Globalisation and the Postcolonial World*, Basingstoke: MacMillan.

Hopkins, A.G. (ed.) (2002a), *Globalization in World History*, London: Pimlico.

——(ed.) (2002b), 'The History of Globalization – and the Globalization of History', *Globalization in World History*, London: Pimlico, 11–46.

Hopkins, D.N. (ed.) (2001), *Religions/Globalizations: Theories and Cases*, Durham NC: Duke University Press.

Howe, S. (1998), *Afrocentrism*, London: Verso.

Hsiung, P.-C. and Y.-L. Wong (1998), 'Jie Giu Connecting the Tracks: Chinese Women's Activisim Surrounding the 1995 World Conference on Women in Beijing', *Gender & History*, 10(3), 470–497.

Huntington, S. (1996), *The Clash of Civilizations and the Remaking of the World Order*, New York: Simon and Schuster.

Hymer, S. (1979), *The Multi-National Corporation: A Radical Approach*, Cambridge: Cambridge University Press.

Jackson, R. (1991), *Quasi-States: Sovereignty, International Relations, and the Third World*, Cambridge: Cambridge University Press.

James, H.H. (2001), *The End of Globalization: Lessons from the Great Depression*, Cambridge, MA: Harvard University Press.

Johnson, E. and D. Stone (2000), 'The Genesis of GDN', in D. Stone (ed.) (2000), *Banking on Knowledge: The Genesis of the Global Development Network*, London: Routledge, 2–23.

Jones, S. (ed.) (1995), 'Understanding Community in the Information Age', *CyberSociety: Computer-Mediated Communication and Community*, London: Sage, 10–35.

Kalberg, S. (1994), *Max Weber's Comparative Historical Sociology*, Cambridge: Polity.

Kaldor, M., H. Anheier, and M. Glasius (eds) (2003), 'Global Civil Society in an Era of Regressive Globalization', *Global Civil Society*, Oxford: Oxford University Press, 3–34.

Kamrava, M. (1995), 'Political Culture and the Definition of the Third world', *Third World Quarterly*, 16(4), 691–711.

Keane, J. (2001), 'Global Civil Society?', in H. Anheier, M. Glasius, and M. Kaldor (eds), *Global Civil Society*, Oxford University Press, 23–47.

——(2003), *Global Civil Society*, Cambridge: Cambridge University Press.

Keck, M. and K. Sikkink (1998), *Activists Beyond Borders: Advocacy Networks in International Politics*, Ithaca, NY: Cornell University Press.

Keohane, R.O. (1986), *Neo-Realism and Its Critics*, New York: Columbia University Press.

Khor, M. (2001), *Rethinking Globalization*, London: Zed Books.

Kollock, P. and M. Smith (eds) (1999), 'Communities in Cyberspace', *Communities in Cyberspace*, New York: Routledge, 3–25.

Kraft, H.J. (2002), 'Track Three Diplomacy and Human Rights in South-East Asia', *Global Networks*, 2(1), 49–63.

Krueger, A.O. (1995), *Trade Policies and Developing Nations*, Washington, DC: Brookings Institution.

Lago, M. (1972), *Imperfect Encounter: Letters of William Rothenstein and Rabindranath Tagore, 1911–41*, Cambridge, MA: Harvard University Press.

Landes, D. (1983), *Revolution in Time*, Cambridge, MA: Harvard University Press.

Lapidus, I. (2001), 'Between Universalism and Particularism: The Historical Bases of Muslim Communal, National and Global Identities', *Global Networks*, 1(1), 37–55.

Larner, J. (2001), *Marco Polo and the Discovery of the World*, Newhaven, CT: Yale University Press.

Le Goff, J. (1980), *Time, Work and Culture in the Middle Ages*, Chicago: Chicago University Press.

Levitt, T. (1983), 'The Globalization of Markets', *Harvard Business Review*, May–June, 92–102.

Lewis, D.L. (1993), *W.E.B. du Bois; Biography of a Race, 1868–1993*, New York: Holt.

Lubeck, P. (2002), 'The Challenge of Islamic Networks and Citizenship Claims: Europe's Painful Adjustment to Globalization', in Nezar Al Sayyad and M. Castells (eds), *Muslim Europe or Euro-Islam*, Lanham, MA: Lexington Books, 69–90.

Lyons, T. (2001), 'The Clash of the Bold and the Beautiful', *Policy, Organisation and Society*, 20(2), 22–43.

McGrew, A. (1992), 'Conceptualizing Global Politics', in A. McGrew and P.G. Lewis (eds), *Global Politics*, Cambridge: Polity, 1–28.

Mac Laughlin, J. (2001), *Re-imagining the Nation-State: The Contested Terrains of Nation-Building*, London: Pluto Press.

McNeill, W. (1964), *The Rise of the West: A History of the Human Community*, Chicago: Chicago University Press.

——(1990), 'The Rise of the West after Twenty-Five Years', *Journal of World History*, 1, 1–22.

McMichael, P. (2000), 'A Global Interpretation of the Rise of the East Asia Food Complex', *World Development*, 28(3), 409–424.

Magyar, K. (1995), 'Classifing the International Political Economy: A Third World Proto-Theory', *Third World Quarterly*, 16(4), 703–716.

Makimoto, T. and D. Manners (1997), *Digital Nomad*, Chichester: Wiley.

Mandle, J.R. (2003), *Globalization and the Poor*, Cambridge: Cambridge University Press.

Mann, M. (1993), 'Nation-States in Europe and Other Continents: Diversifying, Developing, not Dying', *Daedulus* (Summer), 115–140.

Mato, D. (1991), 'On Global and Local Agents and the Social Making of Representative and Indigenous Peoples' Identities in Latin-America', in G. Therborn and L.-L. Wallenius (eds), *Globalizations and Modernities – Experiences and Perspectives of Europe and Latin America*, Swedish Council for Planning and Co-ordination of Research, Stockholm, 194–209.

Mazrui, A. (1990), *Cultural Images in World Politics*, London: Currey.

Melchior, A., K. Telle, and H. Wiig (2000), 'Globalization and Inequality: World Income Distribution and Living Standards 1960–1998', *Studies on Foreign Policy Issues*, Report 6B. Royal Norwegian Ministry of Foreign Affairs, Oslo.

Mernissi, F. (1993), *Islam and Democracy*, London: Virago.

Milanovic, B. (1999), 'True World Income Distribution, 1988 and 1933: First Calculations Based on Household Survey Alone', Policy Research Working Paper 2244, World Bank, Development Research Group, Washington, DC.

Moulin, L. (1980), 'Les Origines Médiévales de la Transnationalité', in *Proceedings of the World Forum of Transnational Organizations*, Brussels: UAI.

Mowlana, H. (1996), *Global Communication in Transition: The End of Diversity?* London: Sage.

Munck, R. (2000), 'Labour in the Global', in R. Cohen and S. Rai (eds), *Global Social Movements*, London: Athlone Press, 83–100.

——(2003), 'Debating "Globalisation and its Discontents"', *Irish Journal of Sociology*, 12(1), 85–97.

Nayyar, D. (1997), *Globalization: The Past in Our Future*, Penang: Third World Network.

Norris, P. (2000), 'Global Governance and Cosmopolitan Citizens', in J. Nye and J. Donahue (eds), *Governance in a Globalizing World*, Washington, DC: Brookings Institute, 155–177.

Nustad, K. and O. Sending (2000), 'The Instrumentalisation of Development Knowledge', in D. Stone (ed.) (2000), *Banking on Knowledge: The Genesis of the Global Development Network*, London: Routledge, 44–62.

Ohmae, K. (1990), *The Borderless World*, London: Collins.

——(1996), *The End of the Nation State*, London: HarperCollins.

Olesen, T. (2004), 'The Trans-National Zapatista Solidarity Network', *Global Networks*, 4(1), 89–107.

O' Brien, R. (2003), 'The Global Knowledge Gap', *Global Networks*, 3(1), 1–6.

O'Riain, S. (2000), 'Networking for a Living: Irish Software Developers in the Global Workplace', in M. Burawoy, J.A. Blum, S. George, Z. Gille, T. Gowan, L. Haney, M. Klawiter, S.H. Lopez, S. O'Riain (eds), *Global Ethnography*, Berkeley: University of California Press, 175–202.

O'Rourke, K. (2002), 'Globalization and Inequality: Historical Trends', *Annual World Bank Conference on Development Economics*', 39–67.

O'Rourke, K. and J. Williamson (1999), *Globalization and History*, Cambridge, MA: MIT Press.

Osiander, A. (2001), 'Sovereignty, International Relations, and the Westphalian Myth', *International Organization*, 55(2), 251–287.

Overbeek, H. (2000), 'Transnational Historical Materialism: Theories of Transnational Class Formation and World Order', in R. Palan (ed.), *Global Political Economy: Contemporary Theories*, London: Routledge, 168–183.

Oxfam (2003), http://www.oxfam.org.uk/fair_trade.html.

Oxfam International (2003), 'Partners', http://www.oxfam.org/eng/campaigns_part.htm.

Parsons, T. (1951), *The Social System*, Chicago: Free Press.

Pauly, L. (1996), *The League of Nations and the Foreshadowing of the International Monetary Fund*, Essays in International Finance, 201, Princeton: Department of Economics.

Payne, A. (2000), 'Globalization and Modes of Regionalist Governance', in J. Pierre (ed.), *Debating Governance Authority, Steering and Democracy*, Oxford: Oxford University Press, 201–218.

Perlas, N. (1998), 'Globalization and Philippines 2000: A Betrayal of Philippine Society?', in N. Perlas, J. Sharman, and E. Navalt, *Proceedings of National*

Conference 'Civil Society: Creative Responses to the Challenge of Globalization, September 1996', Quezon City: Centre for Alternative Development Initiatives.

——(2000), *Shaping Globalization: Civil Society, Cultural Power and Threefolding*, Quezon City: CADI and Globe Net 3.

Petrella, R. (1995), Presentation to the conference 'Gestion locale et régionale des transformations économiques, technologiques at environmentales', Organised by the French Commission for UNESCO, Fondation Maison des Sciences de l'Homme, and the French Ministry for Higher education and Research, cited in J.-L. Racine (2001).

Phillips, T. (2002), 'Imagined Communities and Self-Identity: An Exploratory Quantitative Analysis', *Sociology*, 36(3), 597–617.

Pianta, M. (2001), 'Parallel Summits of Global Civil Society', in H. Anheier, M. Glasius, and M. Kaldor (eds), *Global Civil Society*, Oxford: Oxford University Press, 169–194.

Poggi, G. (1978), *The Development of the Modern State*, London: Hutchinson.

Polanyi, K. (1957) [1944], *The Great Transformation*, Boston: Beacon Press.

Putnam, R. (2000), *Bowling Alone*, New York: Simon and Schuster.

Racine, J.-L. (2001), 'On Globalisation: Beyond the Paradigm – States and Civil Societies in the Global and Local Context', in R.S. Melkote (ed.), *Meanings of Globalisation: Indian and French Perspectives*, New Delhi: Sterling Publishers, 1–40.

Raychaudhuri, T. (1994), 'Dominance, Hegemony and the Colonial State: The Indian and African Experiences', in D. Engels and S. Marks (eds), *Contesting Colonial Hegemony: State and Society in Africa and India*, London: British Academy Press, 267–281.

Read, D. (1999), *The Power of News: The History of Reuters*, Oxford: Oxford University Press.

Reich, R. (1992), *The Work of Nations*, New York: Vintage Books.

Renouliet, J.-J. (1999), *L'Unesco Oubliée: La Société des Nations et la Co-opération intellectuelle (1919–1946)*, Paris: Sorbonne.

Rheingold, H. (1993), *The Virtual Community*, Reading, Mass: Addison-Wesley.

——(2000), *The Virtual Community*, Cambridge, MA: Cambridge University Press.

Rhodes, R. (1997), *Understanding Governance: Policy Networks, Governance, Reflexivity, and Accountability*, Buckingham: Open University Press.

Rhodes, R. and D. Marsh (1992), 'New Directions in the Study of Policy Networks', *European Journal of Political Research*, 21, 181–205.

Rich, P. (1986), *Race and Empire in British Politics*, Cambridge: Cambridge University Press.

Rieger, E. and S. Liebfried (2003), *Limits to Globalization*, Cambridge: Polity.

Ritzer, G. (1995), *The McDonaldization of Society*, Thousand Oaks: Pine Forge Press.

Robertson, R. (1992), *Globalization: Social Theory and Global Culture*, London: Sage.

——(1995), 'Glocalization, Time-Space and Homogeneity-Homogeneity', in M. Featherstone, S. Lash and R. Robertson (eds), *Global Modernities*, London: Sage, 25–44.

Robinson, F. (1993), 'Technology and Religious Change: Islam and the Impact of Print', *Modern Asian Studies*, 27(1), 229–251.

Robinson, G. (1995), *The Dark Side of Paradise: Political Violence in Bali*, Ithaca: Cornell University Press.

Roddick, A. (2001), 'Anita Roddick on Globalisation', *[Ecobal] Sustainable Ireland Network Bulletin*, 2(5), http://csf.colorado.edu/archive/2001/balance/msg00386.html.

Rodrik, D. (1996), 'Why do more Open Economies have Bigger Governments?', NBER Working Paper 5537, Cambridge, MA, National Bureau of Economic Research.

——(1997), *Has Globalization gone Too Far?* Washington, DC: Institute for International Economics.

——(1999), *The New Global Economy and Developing Countries: Making Openness Work*, Washington, DC, Overseas Development Council.

Rosenau, J. (1990), *Turbulence in World Politics: A Theory of Change and Continuity*, Princeton, NJ: Princeton University Press.

——(1995), 'Organisational Proliferation in a Changing World', *Issues in Global Governance*, London: Kluwer Law, 371–403 (published by Commission on Global Governance).

——(1996), 'The Dynamics of Globalization: Toward an Operational Formulation', *Security Dialogue*, 27(3), 247–262.

——(2000), 'Governance in a New Global Order', in D. Held and A. McGrew (eds), *Governing Globalization*, Cambridge: Polity Press, 70–86.

Rosenzweig, R. (1998), 'Wizards, Bureaucrats, Warriors and Hackers', *American Historical Review*, 103(5), 1530–1552.

Rowlands, I. (1995), *The Politics of Atmospheric Change*, Manchester: Manchester University Press.

Rugh, W. (2003), 'Arab Cultures and Newspapers', in S.E. Martin and D.A. Copeland, *The Function of Newspapers in Society: A Global Perspective*, Westport: Praeger, 13–30.

Rugman, A. (2001), *The End of Globalization*, New York: Random House.

Said, E. (1991) [1978], *Orientalism*, Harmondsworth: Penguin.

Sakamoto, Y. (2000), 'An Alternative to Global Marketization', in J. Nederven Pieterse (ed.), *Global Futures: Shaping Globalization*, London: Zed Books, 98–116.

Sarbah, J. (1906), *Fanti National Constitution*, London: Clowes.

Sassen, S. (1994), *Cities in a World Economy*, Thousand Oaks: Pine Forge Press.

——(1996), *Losing Control? Sovereignty in an Age of Globalization*, New York: Columbia University Press.

——(1998), *Globalization and its Discontents*, New York: New Press.

——(1999), 'Digital Networks and Power', in M. Featherstone and S. Lash (eds), *Spaces of Culture: City, Nation, World*, London: Sage, 49–63.

Savir, U. (2003), 'Glocalization: A New Balance of Power', *Development Outreach*, November, http://www1.worldbank.org/devoutreach/article.asp? id=226.

Scholte, J.A. (2000), *Globalization – A Critical Introduction*, Basingstoke: Palgrave MacMillan.

Schon, D. (1971), *Beyond the Stable State*, New York: Norton.

Schultz, T.P. (1998), 'Inequality in the Distribution of Personal Income in the World: How is it Changing and Why? *Journal of Population Economics*, 11(3), 307–344.

Scott, A. (ed.) (1997), *The Limits of Globalization*, London: Routledge.

Seal, B. (1994) [1903], *New Essays in Social Criticism*, Calcutta: Papyrus.

Sen, A. (2001), 'Global Doubts as Global Solutions', Alfred Deakin Lecture, May 15, Melbourne, Australia, http://www.abcnet/rn/deakin/stories/s2969/8.htm.

Shaw, M. (2003), 'The Global Transformations of the Social Sciences', in M. Kaldor, H. Anheier, and M. Glasius (eds), *Global Civil Society*, Oxford: Oxford University Press, 35–44.

Sklair, L. (1991), *Sociology of the Global System*, New York: Wheatsheaf Harvester.

——(2001), *The Transnational Capitalist Class*, Oxford: Blackwell.

Skrbis, Z. (1999), *Long-Distance Nationalism: Diasporas, Homelands and Identities*, Aldershot: Ashgate.

Smith, A.D. (1983), 'Nationalism and Social Theory', *British Journal of Sociology*, 34, 19–38.

——(1986), *The Ethnic Origins of Nations*, Oxford: Blackwell.

——(1990), 'Towards a Global Culture?', in M. Featherstone (ed.), *Global Culture*, London: Sage, 171–192.

Smith, V. (2003), 'Nobel Prize Winner: Globalization is Good', *Anchorage Daily News*, 6 September, http://globalization.about.com/b/a/024249.htm.

Soros, G. (2002), *Open Society: Reforming Global Capitalism*, London: Little Brown.

Stiglitz, J. (2000), 'Scan Globally, Reinvent Locally: Knowledge Infrastructure and the Localization of Knowledge', in D. Stone (ed.), *Banking on Knowledge*, London: Routledge, 24–43.

——(2002), *Globalisation and its Discontents*, New York: Norton.

——(2003), 'Poverty, Globalization and Growth Perspectives on Some of the Statistical Links', in UNDP, *Human Development Report*, 80.

Stone, D. (ed.) (2000a), *Banking on Knowledge: The Genesis of the Global Development Network*, London: Routledge.

——(2000b), 'Think Tank Transnationalism and Non-Profit Analysis, Advice and Advocacy', *Global Society*, 14(2), 153–173.

——(2002), 'Global Knowledge and Advocacy Networks', *Global Networks*, 2(1), 1–12.

Street, J. (1997), 'Across the Universe: The Limits of Global Popular Culture', in A. Scott (ed.), *The Limits of Globalization*, London: Routledge, 75–89.

Street, P. (2003), 'Stabilising Flows in the Global Field: Illusions of Permanence, Intellectual Property Rights and the Transnationalization of Law', *Global Networks*, 3(1) January, 7–28.

Struyk, R. (2002), 'Transnational Think-Tank Networks: Purpose, Membership and Cohesion', *Global Networks*, 2(1), 83–90.

Sutton, C.R. (2004), 'Celebrating Ourselves: the Family Reunion Rituals of African Caribbean Transnational Families', *Global Networks*, 4(3), 243–258.

Swank, D. (2002), *Global Capital, Political Institutions and Policy Change in Developed Welfare States*, Cambridge: Cambridge University Press.

Swyngedouw, E. (1992), 'The Mammon Quest: "Glocalisation", Inter-spatial Competition and the Monetary Order; The Construction of New Scales', in

M. Dunford and G. Kafkalas (eds), *Cities and Regions in the New Europe: The Global–Local Interplay and Spatial Development Strategies*, London: Bellhaven Press, 39–68.

Therborn, G. (1999a), 'Introduction: The Atlantic Diagonal in the Labyrinths of Modernities and Globalizations', in G. Therborn and L.-L. Wallenius (eds), *Globalizations and Modernities – Experiences and Perspectives of Europe and Latin America*, Stockholm: Swedish Council for Planning and Co-ordination of Research, 11–40.

——(1999b), 'The Global Future of the European Welfare State', in G. Therborn and L.-L. Wallenius (eds), *Globalizations and Modernities – Experiences and Perspectives of Europe and Latin America*, Stockholm: Swedish Council for Planning and Co-ordination of Research, 242–262.

Thompson, E.P. (1963), *The Making of the English Working Class*, London: Gollancz.

Thompson, G. (1998), 'Globalization and Regionalization', *Journal of North African Studies*, 3(2), 59–74.

Tilly, C. (1984), *Big Structures, Large Processes, Huge Comparisons*, New York: Russell Sage Foundation.

Tiryakian, E. (1984), 'The Global Crisis as an Interregnum of Modernity', *International Journal of Comparative Sociology*, 25(1–2), 123–130.

Toennies, F. (1911), 'Science, Art, Literature and the Press', in G. Spiller (ed.), *Papers on Inter-Racial Problems*, London: King, 233–243.

Toynbee, A. (1934–61), *A Study of History*, 12 vols, Oxford: Oxford University Press.

UNICEF (2003), *Annual Report*, http://www.unicef.org/publications/pub_ar03_en.pdf.

United Nations (1999), *World Investment Report*, New York: United Nations.

United Nations Development Programme (UNDP) (2003), *Human Development Report*, New York: Oxford University Press.

Universal Races Congress (URC) (1911), *Record of the Proceedings of the First Universal Races Congress*, London: King.

Urry, J. (2000), *Sociology Beyond Societies: Mobilities for the Twenty-First Century*, London: Routledge.

——(2003), *Global Complexity*, Cambridge: Polity Press.

van de Ven, H. (2002), 'The Onrush of Modern Globalization in China', A.G. Hopkins (ed.), *Globalization in World History*, London: Pimlico, 167–193.

van der Veer (2002), 'Transnational Religion: Hindu and Muslim Movements', *Global Networks*, 2(2), 95–110.

Vietnam Labor Watch (1997), *Boycott Nike*, http://www.saigon.com/~nike/report.html.

Virilio, P. (2000), *The Information Bomb*, London: Verso.

Wallerstein, I. (1974), *The Modern World System*, New York: Academic Press.

——(1976), 'A World System Perspective on the Social Sciences', *British Journal of Sociology*, 27(2), 343–352.

——(1979), *The Capitalist World Economy*, Cambridge: Cambridge University Press.

——(1984), *The Politics of the World Economy: The States, The Movements and the Civilizations*, Cambridge: Cambridge University Press.

——(1990a), 'Culture as the Ideological Battle Ground of the World System', in M. Featherstone (ed.), *Global Culture: Nationalism, Globalization, and Modernity*, London: Sage, 31–56.

——(1990b), 'Culture is the World System: A Reply to Boyne', in M. Featherstone (ed.), *Global Culture: Nationalism, Globalization, and Modernity*, London: Sage, 63–66.

——(1991), *Geopolitics and Geoculture*, Cambridge: Cambridge University Press.

Waltz, K. (1979), *Theory of International Politics*, New York: Addison-Wesley.

Watkins, K. (1995), *The Oxfam Poverty Report*, Oxford: Oxfam.

Weber, M. (1978) [1920], 'Author's Introduction', *The Protestant Ethic and the Spirit of Capitalism*, London: George Allen & Unwin.

Weffort, F. (1989), 'Why Democracy?', in A. Stepan (ed.), *Democratizing Brazil: Problems of Transition and Consolidation*, New York: Oxford University Press, 327–350.

Weiss, L. (1997), 'Globalisation and the Myth of the Powerless State', *New Left Review*, 225, 3–27.

Werbner, P. (1999), 'Global Pathways: Working Class Cosmopolitans and the Creation of Transnational Ethnic Worlds', *Social Anthropology*, 7(1), 17–35.

Whitehead, A. and M. Lockwood (1998), Gender in the World bank's Poverty Assessments: Six Case Studies from Sub-Saharan Africa, Mimeo, Geneva: RISD.

Wilkinson, D. (1987), 'Central Civilization', *Comparative Civilizations Review*, 7 (Fall), 31–59.

Wills, J.E. (2001), *1688: A Global History*, London: Granta Books.

World Bank (1999), *World Development Indicators*, Washington, DC: World Bank.

——(1999–2000), *World Development Report*, Washington, DC: World Bank.

——(2003), *World Development Report*, Washington, DC: World Bank, http://econ.worldbank.org/wdr/wdr2003.

Yearley, S. and J. Forrester (2000), 'Shell: A Sure Target for Global Environmental Campaigning', in R. Cohen and M.S. Rai (eds), *Global Social Movements*, London: Athlone Press, 134–145.

Yoshikazu, S. (2000), 'An Alternative to Global Marketization', in J.N. Pieterse (ed.), *Global Futures: Shaping Globalization*, London: Institute of Social Studies, 98–116.

Zapatistas Discussion Group (2004), http://www.zapatistas.org.

Index